EUROPEAN HEROES

HEROES

Myth, Identity, Sport

Edited by

Richard Holt, J.A. Mangan

and Pierre Lanfranchi

FRANK CASS
LONDON • PORTLAND, OR.

First published in Great Britain by
FRANK CASS & CO LTD
Newbury House, 900 Eastern Avenue
London IG2 7HH, England

and in the United States by
FRANK CASS
c/o ISBS
5804 N.E. Hassalo Street, Portland, Oregon 97213-3644

Library of Congress Cataloging-in-Publication Data
A catalog record of this book is available from the Library
of Congress.

British Library Cataloguing in Publication Data
A catalogue record of this book is available from the
British Library.

ISBN 0-7146-4578-8 (hb)
ISBN 0-7146-4125-1

This group of studies first appeared in a Special Issue on 'European Heroes:
Myth, Identity, Sport' in *The International Journal of the History of Sport*,
Vol.13, No.1, published by Frank Cass & Co. Ltd.

Printed in Great Britain by
Antony Rowe Ltd.

Contents

Acknowledgements

Very special thanks are extended to Doris Mangan for her sterling work as copy-editor, proof-reader and indexer. The many hours of patient and careful attention to these aspects of preparation for publication have ensured the appearance of this volume on schedule.

Prologue: Heroes of a European Past

RICHARD HOLT and J.A. MANGAN

Sport and Europeanisation have not gone hand in hand. An ever-increasing enthusiasm for sport as part of male popular culture has certainly been part and parcel of modern Europe for almost a century. The games of the nineteenth-century public schools of Britain steadily spread throughout Europe in the twentieth century. Soccer was played all over Europe by all classes by the mid-1920s. Indeed, soccer was one of the first sports to adopt a formalised European dimension with the setting up of the European Cup in 1955, coincidentally just as the original Six were finalising plans for a European Community! Nevertheless, while in mass modern European culture, at least among the male half of the population, sport (and soccer in particular) has been more important than art, music or literature, it has remained rooted in the nation-state.

An appreciation of this fact and an ambition to promote the idea of a 'People's Europe' prompted the Centre for European Culture at the European University Institute in Florence to offer a series of seminars in the early 1990s on the theme of 'Sport, Culture and Nationalism', one of which was devoted to the subject of 'the sporting hero in contemporary Europe'. The contributors to this collection of essays explore the symbolic meanings that have been attached to sport in Europe by considering some of the mythic heroes who have dominated the sporting landscapes of their own countries and to share the heroes, their achievements and their reputations with fellow Community members. The ambition is to understand what their icons stood for in the eyes of those who watched them or read about them; vessels into which were poured all manner of gender, class and patriotic expectation: for this reason 'national myth', as Raphael Samuel and Paul Thompson have noted, 'can weigh heavily on private tradition and experience'.[1]

In the ambiguous world of mythology the historian moves between the conscious roles of demystifier and demythologist, both passing on the mythical tales that have accrued around the heroic figure and, on occasion, seeking to set them in their cultural context, to explain their social purpose and to explore their communal significance.[2] This is the task the contributors have set themselves.

'In certain African religions,' says Michael Novak, 'a distinction is drawn between profane time, real time and the time of heroes.' Profane time is spent in utilitarian effort, real time encapsulates the insecure uncertainty of life, while the time of heroes represents a glorious 'dream-time', when the heroes of the past 'broke free from the daily mediocrity of human life and ascended to those peaks of existence which always beckon human beings'.[3] 'We simply must have heroes,' argues Marshall Fishwick. 'They give us blessed relief from our daily lives which are frequently one petty thing after another.'[4] But they do more. Marina Warner writes admiringly in *From the Beast to the Blonde: on fairy tales and their tellers,* of the French philosopher Felix Guattari and his brave dream of 'the possibility of a utopia' on earth and of a transformation of the planet – a living hell for too many – into 'a universe of creative enchantments' – a happy inspiration; and surely it is not too grand to assert that the great mythological heroes of sport take mankind some way – if perhaps only a little way – along the path of transformation.[5] Theirs is a world of creative enchantments. Perhaps in such circumstances athletes become more than mere entertainers. They become mythical icons representing mastery over mortality.[6] Certainly in Roland Barthes' *Mythologies* modern sports are presented as analogous to the theatre of antiquity – contemporary dramatic contests with epic heroes from whose exploits the sporting public derive concentrated vicarious excitement which compensates for drawn-out everyday monotony[7] These 'culture heroes'[8] allow the non-heroic access to catharsis in culturally consecrated ceremonies. Moreover these heroes epitomise the qualities their society esteems.

> Who'er excels in what we prize
> Appears a hero in our eyes.[9]

In his distinguished study of life in a New England community Lloyd Warner uncovered the views on its heroes and villains because, in his words,

> Each growing individual sees, feels, and hears beliefs and values not as abstract concepts and principles but as integral, personal parts of loved or disliked persons whom he experiences through social and personal interaction ... Abstract principles, precepts, and moral judgements are consequently more easily felt and understood and more highly valued, when met in a human being endowed with a symbolic form that expresses them. Obviously the 'hero' is ideally suited to this role.[10]

Furthermore, there is certainly something in Umphlett's assertion that spectators in identifying with their sport heroes are really spectators of themselves.[11]

In the New World, claims Michael Oriard, 'the hero-making impulse is strong ... because genuine folk heroes have not had centuries in which to

grow in the minds of the people'.[12] Consequently the American athlete-hero
is an especially prominent product of the hero- making impulse. Sports lend
themselves well, suggests Oriard, to the production and presentation of
heroes. They exist in an 'apolitical, asocial, amoral, even timeless, placeless
quality of the athletic contest itself enabling the heroes of the contests to
remain unchanged after decades'.[13] And in this context the triumph of the
athlete-hero is an apotheosis, but it is an apotheosis not simply of a personal
nature. The athlete-hero 'bestows boons on his friends', especially that
special joy of success.[14] The athlete-hero in modern America is the hero of
the 'land of opportunity' – the supreme role model. He joins a set of icons
– the ethical self-made man made successful on earth and in heaven by
espousing piety, frugality and diligence, the economic self-made man
dominant by means of aggression, competitiveness and forcefulness, the
developed man made mature through self-improvement, self-culture and
self-reliance. The athlete-hero, says Oriard, is now a pre-eminent cultural
manifestation – the most widely popular and most attractive self-made man
in America.[15] He sustains the rags-to-riches American Dream, personifies
the democratic ideal of open accessibility to privilege and allows all 'to
share in his glory' and to 'live' vicariously. Furthermore, the athlete-hero
represents the American belief in the possibility of perfection.[16] He is, in a
real sense, the ultimate realisation of Renaissance idealism, Enlightenment
ambition and New World optimism in a setting in which perfection rests in
America herself. He is the common man made uncommon man and in this
regard as relevant in his role in modern Europe as in modern America.

John MacKenzie, writing of the hero in yet another modern context,
requests that the hero myths of the British Empire be analysed within the
framework of the formation of cultural stereotypes of the hero *and* their
psychic power operating upon the development of the empire 'through the
collective consciousness of its citizens'.[17] Perhaps the same request should
be made of analyses of European sporting heroes. Heroes have served, and
serve, precisely the same collective ends in both national and supra-national
settings! They were, and are, a source of collective identity, status and pride.

G.M. Trevelyan, in eloquent and impassioned mythical phraseology,
once described William Wallace, recently 'factionalised' in the Hollywood
spectacular *Braveheart* and the fourteenth- century Scottish equivalent of
England's King Alfred, France's Joan of Arc and Switzerland's William
Tell, as an unknown Scottish knight who lit a fire which nothing has ever
since put out:

> a new idea was brought into the world. It had no name then but now
> we should call it democratic patriotism. It was not the outcome of
> theory – the unconscious qualities of a people had given it reality in a

sudden fit of rage. Theories of nationhood and theories of democracy would follow afterwards to justify or explain it. Meanwhile it stood up; a fact.[18]

Wallace, the democratic patriot, as several modern historians would attest, is a potent myth which for centuries has served a political end – Scottish Nationalism. And in a real sense his descendants refurbish the myth every two years at Murrayfield, headquarters of the Scottish Rugby Union, when 'Flower of Scotland', the recently adopted militant and militaristic anthem of many Scottish nationalists, reverberates around the ground with special intensity on the visit of the English.

What is true of the heroes of Oriard, Mackenzie and Trevelyan is equally true of European sporting heroes who become archetypes representing a set of personal qualities and heroic characteristics not only supremely valued by society but seen by contemporaries and succeeding generations as having major instrumental power.[19] Arguably Europe now needs such unifying heroes and it is perhaps preferable they come from future gamesfields rather than past battlefields!

In European, as in American, mythology sports heroes are relative newcomers. Thomas Carlyle had no need for them in *On Heroes, Hero-Worship and the Heroic in History* but in the Age of Sport the sporting hero has come centre-stage. Carlyle's heroes were divinities, prophets, poets, priests, men of letters and kings. It is scarcely to be doubted, however, that if he was alive today in Ecclefechan he would have added 'futballer' to his list. 'To say there is a case for heroes,' protests Arthur Schlesinger, 'is not to say that there is a case for hero worship'. The prostration of the average man before the great man is destructive of human dignity.[20] Carlyle would have had no truck with such hairsplitting. If he missed the Age of Sport he fully understood the potency of the hero, the need for heroes and the indestructibility of hero worship. He argued energetically that the faculty for myth and hero was universal.[21] 'It endures forever,' he wrote, 'while man endures.'[22] Elsewhere he stated: 'The Hero has always been worshipped. It will ever be so. We all ... love, venerate and bow down submissive before great men.'[23] And one passage in the concluding chapter of his famous work has a contemporary immediacy: 'It is a great subject, and a most grave and wide one, this which ... I have named *Hero-worship*. It enters deeply, as I think, into the secret of Mankind's ways and vitalest interests in this world *and is well worth explaining at present*'[emphasis added].[24]

It has been suggested that, 'In classical times heroes were god-men; in the Middle Ages they were God's men; in the Renaissance universal men; in the eighteenth century enlightened gentlemen; in the nineteenth century self-made men. In our own time we are seeing the common man become heroic'[25] (and it might be added more often than not as a sportsman or woman). However in the modern world of multifarious recreations, extensive leisure and technological complexity the sports hero or heroine comes in many guises. Mythological heroes of sport differ in their morphology and their functions.[26] Nevertheless a sport without a hero is like Hamlet without the Prince, and yet the varieties and purposes of sporting heroism are rarely examined. The sporting public is too busy worshipping to reflect on the objects of its fascination and those few whose business it is to take an analytical view have been absorbed in other things. The history of sport has been keen to establish its historical credentials by considering the social, cultural and political *context* of performance rather than the performers themselves. One reason for this is certainly that historians of sport, understandably, have sought to avoid breathless eulogy. Instead of praising famous men, which has been the sports writer's proper job, the historian's task has been to explore the social conditions that gave rise to modern sport, the ideological meanings it acquired and the cultural purposes it served. This new (and thriving) approach has mostly focused on types of sport, social classes and entire nations. The individual has been rather overlooked.

Different ages and cultures have their representative heroes – but 'all heroes are true to their age'.[27] Mythological heroism can, and does, assume every conceivable cultural form: 'Like Proteus, as described by Homer in the *Odyssey*, it takes all manner of shapes of things that creep upon the earth, of water likewise, and of fierce fire burning' but heroes are invariably the products of their period.[28] They mirror the place and times in which they live. 'Heroes represent a people, and by discovering the meaning of their character ... we discern the moral figure in the tapestry of a nation.'[29] They reflect its values, aspirations and ambitions – 'the rise and fall of heroes is tied in with a culture's ultimate purposes'.[30] Through them, for precious moments, the culture is united. If it is true that the Greeks depicted the heroic image in mythological metaphors, the Romans in biographical archetypes, the Middle Ages in hagiographical images[31] and the Industrial Age in entrepreneurial caricatures, what is the heroic image of our age? Perhaps the athlete entertainer, 'focused', bold, stylish but above all glamorous, wealthy, admired and envied, the personification of success in the Age of Materialism, Media Make-Believe and Beautiful People. 'Our age has produced a new kind of eminence ... as characteristic of our culture and our century as was the divinity of Greek gods of the sixth century B.C. or the chivalry of Knights ... in the middle ages .... This new kind of eminence is celebrity.'[32] The entertainer's pre-eminence has become such an established characteristic of our age that it is hard to appreciate that it was not always so. It has taken modern prosperity and new developments in electronics for the entertainer to flourish. To adapt slightly Georg Grella's depiction of James Bond as hero, the contemporary sports hero is the hero of the Consumer Culture: a conscious, hedonistic consumer *par excellence*, exploring with equal fervour the world of brand-name products and testing the subtle differences in food, clothes, perfume and women.[33] His fundamental attraction lies in the fact that 'with our unprecedented power to magnify the images and popularize the virtues of heroes, our machinery multiplies and enlarges the shadows of ourselves'.[34] The 'Graphic Revolution', to use Boorstin's phrase, has produced synthetic heroes, man-made by press secretaries, public relations and media experts – the Big Name is now the Big Man[35] – and fills the roles of emotional inspirationalist, spiritual integrationalist and vicarious escapist.

Past sportsmen fitted the requirements of this evolved heroic pattern reasonably well. They had grit and determination – the prerequisites of all heroes. Surviving setbacks to come back and attempt to win at the highest level has always been inherently heroic. To give all was all any man could do. The actions of such men spoke louder than their words. Bartali 'lost' a race but won public affection for the tenacious manner of his 'defeat' – if coming second in the Tour or the Giro can be considered as losing; Carpentier and Schmeling both lost but lost courageously and were not dishonoured. Failing can be a kind of success. Aesthetics were important too. Failing with style was almost preferable to a graceless victory. Most of the men whose lives are considered in this volume were stylists: the graceful Hobbs, the fluid Kopa, the elegant Borotra, Coppi, beautiful in harmony with his machine alone on a bare mountain. If this grace and vigour could defy the passage of time, so much the better. Those whom the Gods love either die young or successfully defy the advance of age – Bartali winning the Giro in his late thirties, Jack Hobbs opening for England in his forties. Heroes, of course, were not supposed to be too complex or clever. However, goodness, in the general sense of human decency, was important. To refuse to take unfair advantage was an ideal to which the European hero was expected to aspire even if he did not always succeed. In Europe supreme physical performance was not enough if the individual was perceived as egotistical, temperamental and arrogant, unlike in America where the egotism, brute force and brutishness of a Babe Ruth or a Jack Dempsey were more easily accepted in the harsher Darwinian cultural climate.

The twentieth century has produced an annual event which is indisputably heroic and in a sense has come to define the very idea of the hero in Europe; an event which requires almost superhuman powers of endurance from competitors who have come not only from France but also from Italy, Spain, Belgium, the Netherlands, Switzerland with a sprinkling of Germans and a few British: the Tour de France. In recent years, with the globalisation of sport through television, competitors from around the world have been drawn in but for most of the century it has been west and south European, beginning as a breeding ground for French heroes, gradually expanding into the Benelux and across the Alps and the Pyrenees, the ascent of which became focal points of this epic journey.

For the Tour is inherently heroic, a kind of mythic journey through ancient provinces, littered with sacred ruins, the bones of Saints, great mountain ranges and the scenes of former battles. No-one who rides or watches the Tour is allowed to forget the great men who went before and the great 'attacks'and 'escapes' around which their legends were built.[36] As Roland Barthes noted, the riders often had nicknames that recalled 'an earlier age when the nation reverberated to the image of a handful of ethnic heroes: Brankart le Franc, Bobet le Francien, Robic le Celte, Ruiz l'Ibère, Darrigade le Gascon'.[37] Time itself became enmeshed in the mythology of the Tour and its great riders; there were parcels of years when public and private chronologies converged; people spoke of 'les années Bobet' or 'the Coppi years' seeing the passage of their own lives in terms of the historic moment of their heroes. And as one rider reached his peak, so another younger one would emerge to challenge; there were Kings and Dauphins of the Tour, an endless struggle of youth and age, fought out day after day, shoulder to shoulder in the mountains; Christophe and Lambot in 1919, Bottechia and Henri Pelissier in 1923, Coppi and Bartali, Merckx and Ocana; Bernard Hinault denied a record-breaking sixth win in the Tour by the young American Greg Lemond. But this was also a tale with a twist that saw the 'young lion' come to the aid of the 'old soldier' from time to time as Vietto memorably did for Antonin Magne in 1934 winning the plaudits of the press for his selflessness; here was 'the kind of man the Tour needed, a young hero, brave and impulsive, both determined and refined, fierce and yet sensitive'.[38] Then there were those who gave everything but were destined never to win. The sight of Poulidor seconds behind Ancquetil battling in vain for the lead on the slopes of the Puy de Dôme was thrilling and heroic. The loser in this case was better loved than the winner – an aspect of European sport more conspicuous by its absence on the other side of the Atlantic.

The Tour was rooted in the nationalism and militarism of the turn of the century, a product of the anti-Dreyfusard Baron de Dion, who set up his own sporting newspaper, L'Auto, which in turn founded the Tour in 1903. L'Auto controlled not only the itinerary but the presentation of the performance, and constructed heroes in its own image. The tone was nationalistic from the start; this was to be a proving ground for the French hero, 'le petit soldat' who could stand his ground and retake the Rhine. This was an image that shifted somewhat between the wars to a more sleek and stylish stereotype without ever really shaking off the social Darwinist sense of the survival of the fittest. Although the Tour was conceived as a deliberate celebration of the grandeur of France, its appeal spread beyond the French. Other nations redefined themselves through the race: the 'Flandriens', for example, a string of fine Flemish cyclists of the pre- and post-First World War years, whose exploits in the Tour raised the national and linguistic consciousness of Flanders. The Swiss and the Italians also had their transcendent moments and personalities. Here the British stand apart. Just as the cricketer is a kind of English hero quite without meaning or resonance in Europe, so in Britain, at least until recently, the cyclist has been ignored. The only Briton to have worn the yellow jersey is not much known outside cycle-racing circles here. He was Tommy Simpson, who collapsed and died on the Mont Ventoux in terrible heat, and is remembered by the French as a martyr to the toughest event in the world. For the British, evidence of drug abuse diminished what little national interest they had in Simpson; for the French he was someone prepared to give his life for the race.[39]

Each nation, of course, interprets its sporting achievement according to its own intellectual traditions. This is particularly true of Europe where profoundly different states with sharply contrasting political cultures live side by side. Germany has been much taken up with *Turnen*, the distinctive form of gymnastics devised in the early nineteenth century which evolved along more militaristic and chauvinist lines than was first envisaged by its founder, Jahn, who is the subject of Eisenberg's essay here; the later Nazi manipulation of sport has naturally enough also attracted attention and forms a backdrop to Gehrmann's portrait of Max Schmeling. French academics have studied sport mainly in relation to education and religion, the twin themes of Republican history. They have paid scant academic attention to great men. This ideological conflict within French sport is personified in the life of Borotra, who became Minister of Sport in the early days of Vichy. The essay by Wahl and Lanfranchi turns to concerns more familiar in North America: the hero as immigrant. Given Italian history it is hardly surprising that the Catholic Church and Fascism considered by Pivato should play so big a part in the making of the Italian sporting hero. The British of course, have mainly considered sport in the context of class, contrasting the amateurism and imperialism of the elite with the evolution of professional sport for the large urban working class. In this class context the mythical role of the gentleman-sportsman in the guise of public school 'blood' as moral messenger depicting the desirability of a sacrificial militarism in the Age of the New Imperialism, discussed by Mangan, may come as something of a surprise to those who are ignorant of the bloodthirsty reputation of the English in European history. Nevertheless in recent years upper-middle class militarism in Britain in the late Victorian and Edwardian eras has been clearly established by various historians and the existence of the phenomenon can now be in little doubt. How the gentleman amateur as hero became the professional hero in cricket, a sport that sharply separated England from the rest of Europe, described by Holt, seems an appropriate topic to set alongside the more proletarian image of the professional footballer presented by Mason. And so on. Each nation has had its distinctive fascination with the qualities associated with the hero – not least in inter-war Vienna where intellectuals discussed the significance of Sindelar as the embodiment of a Viennese way of playing.

Such names have been the stuff of dreams. These dreams were mostly linked to the national values of the dreamer. Yet there have been some more subtle cross-cultural similarities as well. Heroes were often linked to the idea of collective rebirth: Jahn after the catastrophic Prussian defeat at Jena, Carpentier and Borotra after the pyrrhic victory of 1918; Schmeling the 'good' German or Bartali who stayed clear of Mussolini and gave the Italians – or the Catholic part of the nation at least – something to cheer about. Britain, where continuity prevailed, had no need for myths such as these. Its myths were concerned with producing players who 'played the game' on gamesfield and battlefield. The British also had myths of mobility, of players who became gentlemen, like Jack Hobbs. Modest material success, a suburban villa, cars and holidays were an increasingly important part of the image of success in the first half of the twentieth century but men like Kopa or even Schmeling, who savoured their relative affluence, were not as far removed from the realm of the ordinary man as the sporting 'superstars' who have succeeded them. European heroes, unlike their American counterparts, were not supposed 'to be in it for the money'. Modest wealth was quite acceptable but vast riches sat uneasily with the idea of the sporting hero as a common man with uncommon gifts. The hero had first and foremost to be driven by pride in performance and for the greater glory of the community he symbolised. Even in boxing, with its transatlantic riches, earning huge purses was not enough to win public esteem. No longer, of course. In the pursuit of the material little now divides the European from the American mythical hero or heroine of sport. Indeed, wealth enhances the mythical image.

The fame of sporting heroes spread like the ripples in a pond, seeping into the national psyche, touching the individual imagination and the collective sensibility. The study of psychological mechanisms that permit one individual to assume such power in the inner world of another is fascinating but it is not the point at issue here. It is rather the fruits of such processes of identification at the collective level that attract the historian; the change in the concepts of the sporting hero and of heroism in the context of various traditions and temporal and geographical circumstances is what in different ways these essays are about. From Italian cyclists to French and German boxers, English, French and Austrian footballers to cricketers and gymnasts, in sports the hero has been a symbol or emblem, linking the style of the performance with a sense of a wider community – a class, a city, a region, an ethnic group or religious denomination, a nation and, most strikingly, perhaps even an empire.

This process has been often described but rarely analysed. Sports biographies abound. We like to read about our heroes and such books sell well enough to persuade publishers to publish more. Until recently, however, hagiography has been the order of the day. Books about the great sportsmen of modern times have been like the Lives of the Saints, or The Book of Chronicles and Book of Numbers, recording outstanding achievements, shot by shot, race by race, match by match. All this was woven into a seamless story of success. This was the process by which heroes were made, for few could see the performance in person. They relied on a description of it. Yet sporting heroes were not just 'made' or 'constructed' by the media. Unlike film stars or recording artists they had to give a live performance. There was a supreme integrity in the great sporting performance – it was live, spontaneous and unrepeatable. Within the media until recently the press has been the crucial influence for most of the time; the journalist formed in words the image that would reflect to the public what was unique and compelling in the performance and from the beginning of the century there were photographers who embellished and dramatised great deeds, cameramen, not just great film makers like Riefenstahl, but the legions who put together Pathe News or Movietone, and those voices who spoke through radio to millions of fans following English Test matches or the Tour de France.

Sporting heroes were frequently 'born great' and 'achieved greatness', combining remarkable natural talent with careful discipline and training. But they also had 'greatness thrust upon them' by an emerging group of jobbing journalists, ex-players, entrepreneurs and enthusiasts whose love of sport led them to idolise its best practitioners. Worship of the performance naturally crossed over into worship of the performer. Great players became first local figures, then more public ones, graduating to national celebrity. But what turned a celebrity – a 'star' in the vocabulary of the cinematic age – into a hero? The answer, in a word, is 'character'. Heroes came to be known for their public virtues as well as their public performances. They were given a persona to suit the needs of the public which did not necessarily correspond to the private reality. What sports heroes were like off the field naturally seemed irrelevant to those who wrote, or ghosted, lives made famous by physical performance. Players as citizens, husbands, fathers, or voters or anything but performers were not within the remit of the writer, who was most frequently a sports journalist. Journalists have been the image-makers but journalists write for a market and to a deadline. Great moments made good copy. Where the historian wants to know about what was *usual*, the sports writer naturally – and in his own terms rightly – seeks to put a suitably favourable gloss on what was *exceptional*.

Distinguished writers like Montherlant occasionally wrote about sport but writing of the highest quality has been rare both on sports in general and heroes in particular. There are, of course, some good sporting lives, a few of cricketers in England or cyclists in France. Europe, however, lags behind North America not only in the 'warts and all' exposé but more surprisingly in serious historical biography. Where are the European counterparts of Bill Baker's critical life of Jesse Owens or Randy Roberts' candid study of Dempsey? All this, of course, will change as social history moves away from its roots in the Forward March of Labour. Narrative is now making a comeback and cultural identity and its emblematic figures are firmly back on the agenda while gender has been most certainly added to it. And if heroes speak to anything, it is to this. For we are dealing here with males and with idealised forms and styles of masculinity varying according to the national culture in which they were framed and performed. Heroes were men whose actions were aimed at other men – and boys. Yet for the champion to become a hero required the consent of a far wider group than the immediate, largely male audience. Women admired Borotra's suave image and antics on the court; Bartali was a much photographed man of striking looks, whilst Fausto Coppi's liaison with 'The White Lady' made the headlines and cricketers were often more aware of their impact on the ladies than they admitted. Female reaction to male sporting heroes is 'virgin' territory, while the history of sporting heroines, and *inter alia* the obstacles they have had to overcome in terms of male (and often female) attitudes, is an important subject in its own right in modern society. This history is just starting to be written. However, what is true of European male biography is ever more true of female biography. The field is wide open for the historians of tomorrow. It is hoped that they will pick up where the historians of today in this volume have left off – and that the academic study of heroes and heroines of sport becomes an integral part of the history of sport.

NOTES

1. R. Samuel and P.Thompson (eds.), *Myths We Live By* (London: Routledge, 1990), p.18.
2. For a good example of this see J.M. Roberts, *The Mythology of the Secret Societies* (London: Secker and Warburg, 1972).
3. Michael Novak, 'Sacred Space, Sacred Time', in David L. Vanderwerken and Spencer K. Wertz, *Sport: Inside Out* (Forth Worth, Texas: Christian University Press, 1985), p.728.
4. Marshall W. Fishwick, *American Heroes: Myth and Reality* (Westport: Greenwood Press, 1954), p.225.
5. Marina Warner, *From the Beast to the Blonde: on fairy tales and their tellers* (London: Chatto and Windus, 1994), p.418.
6. Michael Novak, 'The Joy of Sports', in Charles S. Prebish, *Religion and Sport: The Meeting of the Sacred and the Profane* (Westport: Greenwood Press, 1993), p.163.
7. See Hans Lenk, 'Herculean "Myth" Aspects of Athletics' in Vanderwerken and Wertz, *Sport Inside Out*, p.435.
8. G.S. Kirk, *Myth: Its Meaning and Functions in Ancient and Other Cultures* (Cambridge: Cambridge University Press, 1970), p.11.
9. Jonathan Swift, *Cademus and Vanessa*, 1, p.737 quoted in Harold Lubin (ed.), *Heroes and Anti-heroes* (Chicago: Chandler Publishing Company, 1976), p.4.
10. W. Lloyd Warner, *The Living and the Dead: A Study of the Symbolic Life of Americans*, V. P.14 quoted in Lubin, *Heroes and Anti-heroes*, pp.3–4.
11. Wiley Lee Umphlett, *The Sporting Myth and the American Experience* (London: Associated University Presses, 1975), p.170.
12. Michael Oriard, *Dreaming of Heroes: American Sports Fiction, 1868–1980* (Chicago: Nelson Hall, 1982), p.26.
13. Ibid., pp.126–32
14. Ibid., p.39.
15. Ibid., pp.48–9 and p.51.
16. Ibid., p.55.
17. John M. MacKenzie, 'Heroic Myths of Empire', in John M. MacKenzie (ed.), *Popular Imperialism and the Military, 1850–1950* (Manchester: Manchester University Press, 1993), p.110.
18. See Alan Massie, 'The Scars of Battle that Centuries Have Failed to Heal', in *The Sunday Times*, 17 Sept. 1995, pp.2–3.
19. MacKenzie, *Popular Imperialism and the Military 1850–1950*, p.111.
20. Arthur Schlesinger, 'The Decline of Heroes', in Lubin, *Heroes and Anti-heroes*, p.348.
21. Thomas Carlyle, *On Heroes, Hero-Worship and the Heroic in History* (London: Chapman and Hall, 1904), p.11.
22. Ibid., p.13.
23. Ibid.
24. Ibid., p.223.
25. Fishwick, *American Heroes*, p.4.
26. Kirk, *Myth*, p.xx.
27. Fishwick, *American Heroes*, p.3.
28. Ibid., p.224.
29. Theodore L. Gross, *The Heroic Ideal in American Literature* quoted in Umphlett, *The Sporting Myth and the American Experience*, p.169.
30. Fishwick, *The Hero: American Style*, p.9.
31. Ibid., p.245.
32. Daniel Boorstin, 'From Hero to Celebrity: Human Pseudo-event', in Lubin, *Heroes and Anti-heroes*, p.333.
33. Harold Lubin, 'New Heroes for a New Age', in Lubin, *Heroes and Anti-heroes*, p.314.
34. Boorstin, 'From Hero to Celebrity ...', in Lubin, *Heroes and Anti-heroes*, p.339.
35. Ibid., p.327.
36. G. Vigarello, 'Les héros du Tour de France: les transformations d'un mythe', paper presented to the seminar 'Les héros sportifs dans l'Europe contemporaine', European University

Institute, Florence, 19–21 March 1992; this section of the Prologue owes much to Professor Vigarello's excellent contribution which was not available to be included in full.

37. R. Barthes, *Mythologies* (Paris: Edition du Seuil, 1957), p.111.

38. Cited in Vigarello, op.cit.

39. G. Nicholson, *The Great Bike Race* (London: Magnum Books, 1977), pp.91–6; there is a large literature in French but this work offers the best account in English of the heroic qualities of the Tour.

Charismatic Nationalist Leader:
Turnvater Jahn

CHRISTIANE EISENBERG

Introduction

Sporting heroism presupposes the existence of sportsmen or sportswomen who successfully participate in contests as well as the existence of a public to observe and appreciate their success. A person's elevation to heroism results from the particular relationship between these two elements; this interaction is also the process through which the criteria of hero worship (achievement, success, manliness, courage, etc.) are defined. Thus the vehicle for the fame of W.G. Grace as a hero in Victorian England was based on the game of cricket, a game which embodied moral as well as athletic values highly appreciated by the Victorians of all classes. At the same time cricket was unparalleled as a summer spectator sport and was spread ever more widely amongst the general public by the press.[1]

In early nineteenth-century Germany, all these preconditions of sporting heroism were absent. There were no sports contests and 'public opinion' in the modern sense was only in an embryonic state; and, of course, no interaction could occur. These unfavourable conditions for hero worship were a result of three German historical characteristics:

1. Commerce and industry were underdeveloped, not only in comparison to England but also by the standards of other Western European countries. The economy was predominantly based on agriculture. Most artisan trades were organized in guilds, producing for local customers, and only a few entrepreneurs supplied the national and international markets. Large parts of the working population were paid in kind, and the cash nexus was weak.

2. There was a general lack of good communications. Germany was not a unified national state but consisted of many autonomous monarchies and duchies spread over an area several times the size of England, the 'motherland of sport'. The movement of traffic was arduous not only because of the bad roads but also because of the great number of customs barriers. The 'publishing revolution' that took place in eighteenth-century England failed to materialize in Germany owing to the absence of a capital, of parliamentarianism and of an indigenous

anti-absolutist revolt such as took place in France.
3. The social structure of the German states was not fluid; the elite was not relatively 'open' along British lines. The ranks (*Stände*) of the aristocracy, the clergy and the middle class (*Bürgertum*) were separated from each other, their boundaries being defined by law and custom. To a large extent, the lower classes were dependent on feudal forms of domination. In so stratified and fragmented a society a common preference for a sport or a sporting hero was hardly to be expected.

Yet from about 1810, this backward society witnessed the rise to national fame of a completely unknown person. Friedrich Ludwig Jahn (1778–1852), later called '*Turnvater*', attained an unusual popularity particularly among the younger generation of the rising middle classes, i.e. among students and young skilled artisans. Jahn was not a sporting hero according to the definition proposed at the outset but he achieved a degree of long-lasting fame which was quite remarkable and almost unkown amongst other sporting heroes. 'Mythos Jahn' – the 'myth of Jahn' became a subject of interest for generations of academics as well as for others who took an interest in the recreational and cultural life of Germany. Even today there are streets, squares, schools and stadiums in most German towns named after Jahn, not only in the Federal Republic but in the former German Democratic Republic as well. This is particularly remarkable, since Jahn is often regarded as a progenitor of the *völkisch* and fascist w*eltanschauung*.[2]

This article, however, will not deal with Jahn as a myth but as a real person. What did he do *himself* to contribute to his long-lasting fame is the question posed here. In order to find an answer Jahn will be examined as an inventor of *Turnen*, the German equivalent of English sport at this time, stressing the role of the *Turner* as a social movement. The conceptual tools for this attempt are derived from Max Weber's theory of charisma.

The Concept of the Charismatic Leader

In his sociology of domination Weber proposes four elements in the definition of charismatic authority.[3] First, there is the belief in the exceptional qualities of an individual. This belief calls for absolute trust in the leader and makes recognition of his legitimacy a duty. Second, the influence of the leader rests on his charismatic qualities as proved by his success. His chances of achieving recognition are increased psychologically by personal devotion on the side of the followers, arising out of enthusiasm, despair and hope. Sociologically, these chances are determined by a crisis, in which the leader is forced to prove his qualities. Third, the realm of this authority is a charismatic community, not a firmly institutionalized organization. The administrative staff consist of trusted agents, who have either been provided with charismatic authority by the leader or possess charisma of their own. There is no bureaucratic organization, no principle of formal rules, no supervisory or appellate body. Fourth, the economic basis is not derived from systematic economic activities but rests on booty or voluntary contributions.

Since social relations based on the charismatic type of domination are dependent on a single – mortal – person, they are by definition unstable. According to Weber, there is either the possibility of transformation into a type of domination which is based on the legitimacy of 'holy' traditions, or into a type of rational, bureaucratic domination.

The Making of a Charismatic Leader

Jahn as an Early Nineteenth-Century Prussian

From his early youth, Friedrich Ludwig Jahn, the son of a protestant preacher, was known for his volatility and lack of discipline.[4] This characteristic remained with him as he grew up. After attending no less than ten universities, Jahn was finally expelled from the University of Halle in 1803 because he was lazy, in debt and had some fierce and violent arguments with the old-fashioned and politically reactionary students' societies, the so-called *Landsmannschaften*; these societies were organized according to regional origin and espoused the duel as a test of a person's honour and capacity for 'giving satisfaction' to defend it. The University's 'consilium abeundi' came to the conclusion that 'it would have been better if Jahn had never been accepted as a student'.[5]

This view is understandable in terms of the general characterization of Jahn as an odd, isolated and unusual young man by sport historians.[6] However, those judgements are misleading. Jahn was not the only student who at the turn of the eighteenth and nineteenth centuries had conflicts with university authorities. He was a supporter of a reform movement composed of politically aware students who wanted to free university life from aristocratic and feudal elements. His particular kind of restless, unsettled nature was typical of the Romantic period.[7]

When Jahn left the university he regarded himself as a failure. He had achieved nothing except a linguistic article on the origins of High German; when this was published in 1806 it brought acknowledgement by Johann Gottlieb Herder but no money.[8] The general labour market for academics being unfavourable, Jahn had to earn a living as a private tutor. This subordinate and poorly remunerated position was depressing for him particularly since he was eager to get married.

Jahn's personal crisis coincided with the political crisis of the ancien régime in Prussia. In 1807 the Peace of Tilsit had sealed the disastrous defeat of the Prussian army by Napoleon in the previous year. It was widely felt that the Prussian State needed complete modernization. The leading Prussian reformers were the government minister Karl Freiherr vom und zum Stein and Staatskanzler Karl August Freiherr von Hardenberg. Both politicians initiated measures to ameliorate agriculture and industry in order to put state finances on their feet again, to reform the schools and, most important, to reconstruct and revitalize the army.[9] To promote their reforms, which were by no means to everybody's advantage and highly controversial, Stein and Hardenberg tried to inflame their Prussian subjects with a sense of nationalism. This was easier said than done. The French occupation had by no means been rejected by all Prussians and, encouraged by the propaganda of the occupiers, the bust of Napoleon became a best-selling article in 1806–7; many Prussians were eager to be told the recent news from Paris by French officers.[10]

It was in this context that Freiherr vom Stein asked poets and intellectuals, who were sympathetic to their politics, to support the Prussian reforms. These new patriots were expected to be activitists, not only to agitate in speech and writing but also to give moral and cultural leadership by personal example. Among the persons who were asked for cooperation were Johann Gottlieb Fichte, a well-known philosopher, Friedrich Schleiermacher, a theologian, Heinrich von Kleist, a popular dramatist – and Friedrich Ludwig Jahn, known as an ardent patriot and fanatical Prussian. His enthusiastic nationalism was such that, allegedly, his hair became white overnight after he had oberserved Prussians in retreat near Jena.[11] The crisis of the state, therefore, became intertwined with Jahn's personal difficulties and provided him with a way to solve them. Not only did the offer of the Prussian reformers satisfy his need for recognition, it also promised a solution to his financial problems. No person involved in the conspiratorial and risky enterprise of 'nationalising the masses' was expected to co-operate without remuneration.[12]

While the other intellectuals were expected to address the educated middle class, Jahn's job was to agitate among the lower middle class, particularly among the younger generation. His contribution to building the 'myth of a nation', in the words of Otto W. Johnston,[13] and thus to the success of the Prussian reforms, was twofold.

First, he wrote a book entitled *Deutsches Volkstum*. In this book, which was first published in 1810, he developed some general ideas about the hypocrisy and vices of the aristocracy, expressed his strong anti-semitism and advocated his notion of a standardized High German language. But the book was also designed to promote the official reform movement: Stein's propositions to renew the educational system; the division of a future united Germany into provinces designed by the poet Ernst Moritz Arndt; the ideas of the leading officers von Scharnhorst and von Gneisenau to reorganise the army, and so on. A key concern of *Deutsches Volksthum* was to spread the idea of an army recruited from the people (*Volksheer*), not from mercenaries paid by the dukes, and thus to prepare *mentally* for a revolt against Napoleon's forces of occupation.[14]

Jahn's second contribution to the awakening of a national consciousness among the German people was the *practical* preparation of a revolt against Napoleon, which brings us to the central point of this study: the emergence of *Turnen* as a paramilitary method of physical exercise. If we consider that the Peace of Tilsit had reduced the Prussian army to 42,000 soldiers, the strategic significance of this measure becomes immediately evident. Not surprisingly, it was only developed after prior consultations with the civil service and the army.[15]

'Turnvater' Jahn

From the historian's point of view Jahn's task was particularly demanding, because he had to fulfil the function of an 'inventor of traditions' in the sense Eric Hobsbawm has used this term.[16] Of course, gymnastics can be traced back to the Ancient Greeks. Some enlightened educationalists had been recommending them since the late eighteenth century, the most important of whom was Johann Christoph Friedrich GutsMuths, a philanthropic teacher at an elite school in Thuringia whom Jahn had met shortly before he launched the *Turnen* project.[17] But these exercises were only practised by a small elite of well-educated persons. To the great majority of Prussians gymnastics were unknown; as, of course, were sports and games.

Turnen began in the summer of 1810 when – with a little help from his highly placed political friends – Jahn was employed as a teacher at a private boarding school in Berlin; this school was dedicated to the educational ideas of Pestalozzi and also served as a cover for secret organizations.[18] In his official function as teacher, Jahn led some of his students to a hilly area near one of the gates to the city of Berlin to play games and to exercise twice a week. After some time students from other schools joined in as well. As interest in these exercises continued over the winter, when nothing but indoor fencing was possible, Jahn decided to institutionalize the gatherings in 1811. Within walking distance of the city-walls, on a drill ground of the Prussian army called *Hasenheide*, several acres were enclosed and climbing frames, ditches for jumping, entrenchments and a running track were built.[19] The area was very popular as a place for the citizens of Berlin to stroll in and the numbers of spectators and participants increased dramatically. For instance, in 1813 it is alleged that 10,000 watched a demonstration of *Turnen* by about 500 young people.[20]

The number of active participants grew steadily. Most of them were students from the rising middle classes as well as from the aristocracy. But after 1812, when the *Turners* began to exercise on Sundays, young clerks and journeymen also joined in.[21] From the beginning every participant voluntarily paid a small sum as a membership fee but the largest donations came from outside patrons. After 1815, when hundreds of Berlin *Turners* had volunteered for the war of liberation against Napoleon, there were additional donations from the *Generalstaatskasse*. The state also paid a generous salary to Jahn, the head of the Hasenheide *Turnanstalt*, as well as to Ernst Eiselen, who was employed as a special *Turnlehrer*.[22] In 1817 the *Turnanstalt* was so well established that between 1,400 and 1,600 young people could do their exercises at the same time.[23] About this time, the movement had already spread to about a hundred other places in Prussia and soon it counted about 6,000 followers; and there were *Turner* societies in other German states, too.[24]

The warm reception of Jahn's invention was based on several preconditions. First of all it should be stressed that the exercise and games practised under his direction had nothing in common with military drill. This characteristic of *turnen* was due to the Prussian reformers' conception of army-reconstruction, which was strictly opposed to feudal traditions. In addition, the absence of drill elements was a precautionary measure to prevent the French occupation forces from intervening.[25] But most of all it can be regarded as an expression of Jahn's honest conviction that German youth should be offered a playful, free and easy method to develop bodily strength as well as the spirit of achievement and self-discipline. With respect to the exercises he taught, Jahn remained a civilian and did not add a militaristic note to the recommendations of the enlightened and humanist educationalists he relied on. Never would he have allowed the *Turnkunst* to be something other than a component of the 'whole person's' education, and he argued against alternative concepts of physical culture.[26] However, as a contemporary newspaper report made clear, the public was very conscious of the subliminal military and patriotic motivation: 'If young people are trained in climbing, jumping, carrying weights, keeping their balance, wrestling, running and playing war games, they will also be able easily to learn shooting and striking at an opponent, marching, wheeling and holding the line'.[27]

A hidden militaristic note came in through the new name, which Jahn gave to the exercises: *Turnen*. This measure was the second precondition for the success of his initiative. *Turnen* itself was a brand new word invented by Jahn from his linguistic studies in the history of High German as well as in the regional dialects of his own times. According to Jahn 'torner' was an old term to denote a warrior; he hoped that the new word would stir memories of the tournaments of the middle ages ('Turnier').[28] Although it is doubtful whether the public was able to comprehend these considerations, the creation of the verb *turnen* was an important means of disseminating this new patriotic concern with physical exercise. Traditional words for exercising such as 'spielen', 'Gymnastik' or 'Leibesexercitia treiben', 'den Körper ausbilden', 'formen', 'geschickt machen' were ambiguous and long-winded. *Turnen*, on the contrary, was short, catchy and could easily be put into print. Within a few years about 60 words with the prefix *Turn-* were current among *Turners*, among them *Turnerehre* [Turner honour], *Turnerstolz* [Turner pride], *Turnerfreundschaft* [friendship] and so on. Many of these words were constructed by the linguistically talented young men whom Jahn appointed to an expert council, the so-called *Turnkünstlerrat* (the Turner cultural council). In this council a special language was developed, systematized and put into publications for a larger public.[29]

The members of this council also defined new terms to denominate particular exercises and their respective gymnastics apparatus. In this respect, they used two methods: First, they translated foreign words into German. Most important was the substitution of the French vocabulary derived from the courtly exercises of the aristocracy which were now integrated into the canon of *Deutsches Turnen*. 'Croisé' was translated into 'Scheere', 'rapier' into 'Fechtel', 'balancer' into 'schweben' or 'schwebegehen', 'faire de la voltige' into 'schwingen'. In addition, the linguistic experts incorporated terms from daily life and work into the language of the *Turner*, for example 'Holm' and 'Bühne' from the language of miners and carpenters, 'Gaffel', 'Reede', 'Rust' and 'Tau' from the vocabulary of sailors, 'anschultern' and 'anfußen' from hunters.[30]

These examples demonstrate that there were motives other than 'hyper-Germaness' and anti-French feelings behind Jahn's invention of the *Turner* language.[31] The development of a technical language, which was in touch with real life and intelligible to all, was necessary to disseminate a complete new physical culture. Seen from a longer perspective in time, these new linguistic forms were also a precondition for the acceptance of *Turnen* as a part of the social life of the rising middle class because they disguised the aristocratic and courtly origin of many of the newly popular exercises such as balancing acts or performing on the back of a wooden horse.

A third way in which Jahn endeavoured to make *Turnen* a social movement was his attempt to incorporate participants into an egalitarian community. In order to disguise the social distance between individuals of different origin, Jahn required the young men to address each other as 'Du' and not to use the more formal 'Sie' which was indicative of social distance. They were also to wear a common uniform. This so-called 'Gleichtracht' was made from simple, unbleached linen which was not only a most durable but also a very cheap fabric and at the same time was the only one available throughout Germany. Other fabrics would have had to have been imported from foreign countries and might have prevented poorer young men from joining the *Turner* 'army'.[32] As recommended by Jahn, this linen costume could also be used in civil life; in fact, it soon became fashionable outside the *Turnplatz*, particularly among the younger generation of Prussians.[33]

Jahn's pronounced egalitarianism was a concomitant of the attack on formal social hierarchy which was part of the 'Zeitgeist' but also, of course, a means to make the *Turner* army powerful. For these purposes, the mass of young recruits were divided into squads ('Riegen') which, technically, can be regarded as counterparts of the English idea of a sports 'team'. Both, squads or teams, opened up the possibility of retaining the specific character and ethos of the movement independently of its growth into a mass organisation.[34] One method was to build new squads with some of the members of older ones as the number of participants became more numerous. Team spirit could also be inculcated by a certain measure of competition; this happened, for example, with practising at the horizontal bar ('Reck') which allowed the counting of the pull-ups and swing-ups and therefore became the most popular exercise of the early nineteenth-century *Turner*. Squads also varied in the types of exercise they favoured, arising from the tendency of individual *Turners* to specialise in order to be accepted by Jahn and their peers.[35]

To guarantee discipline and to avoid squads breaking away from the movement, Jahn also used techniques of divide and rule. One of these techniques was the organisation of competitive games and matches between squads as well as between the members of individual squads. When Jahn learned that the competitions had the unexpected side-effect of producing vanity and egoism among individuals and groups, he began to refrain from this measure or at least tried to guarantee that these competitions took on the character of an organized spectacle or a carefully controlled examination.[36]

The alternative technique of *divide et impera* clearly preferred by Jahn was to single out certain chosen squad leaders: the so-called *Vorturner*. He called this elite together regularly to give them special training and to discuss with them general issues in the *Turner* movement.[37] These meetings had the function of channelling and coordinating initiatives from below. In addition, Jahn had the opportunity of imparting his own ideas and directives to the rank and file. One of the *Vorturner*, Christian Eduard Leopold Dürre, recorded in his autobiography that Jahn was such a talented manipulator of an audience that he could easily succeed in making someone believe that it was not Jahn's idea which he wanted to implement but his own.[38]

Jahn's delegating skills were crucial to maintaining the enthusiasm of the *Vorturner* elite. Another precondition was Jahn's talent for orchestrating the experience of community, particularly by means of long walks through the country in order to disseminate *Turnen*. During these walks, the so-called *Turnfahrten*, Jahn led the *Vorturner* to striking landscapes and to famous battlefields where he said prayers, sang songs and told stories of heroic ancestral deeds. The solemn, quasi-religious mood nurtured in this fashion generated the desire of the young men to go out and do heoric deeds themselves.[39]

The wish to become a hero was further encouraged by a particular notion of manliness, which Jahn communicated to the *Vorturner*. It was based on the assumption that chastity, the major virtue to be expected of a young man, became manifest in a strong body as well as in the healthy and joyful appearance of the 'whole person'. Masturbation as well as sexual intercourse with women, on the contrary, were associated with moral weakness and were regarded as ruinous to the body. In the *Turner* discourse the danger of corporeal deterioration and the French invasion into Prussia were described by the same metaphors of castration.[40] Thus, the ethos of manliness was a means of transforming the subliminal homo-eroticism of a 'Männerbund' into moral and political categories.[41]

The prototype of the 'Deutscher Mann' was a blond youth named Friedrich Friesen, a teacher colleague of Jahn and a member of secret societies.[42] After Friesen was killed in 1814 in a battle against the French, it was Jahn himself who most consistently displayed this particular *Turner* style of manliness. He was a tall man with long hair and a huge beard; he had a strong body and, of course, was an excellent *Turner*. He also played his role as the 'Deutscher Mann' convincingly. When invited to dinner by Staatsminister von Hardenberg, Jahn did not hesitate to appear in a simple dark suit similar to the *Turner* uniform. He was the only person to wear boots, which were so dirty that one of the other guests wondered 'whether this was part of his normal appearance or whether he had deliberately made himself dirty just as others had consciously smartened themselves'. Whatever the motive, it had the desired effect, raising even further Jahn's reputation for charisma. Hardenberg's guests were deeply impressed by Jahn, particularly since he gave a short speech in which his independent opinions and uncompromising nature were displayed to the full. Even Wilhelm von Humboldt, who was also present at the dinner, was eager to introduce himself to Jahn.[43] Another guest later speculated about the possible danger resulting from the irrational fascination of Jahn's personality.[44]

If intellectuals were amazed and won over, it is hardly surprising that the

Vorturner were captivated. Whoever was chosen by Jahn to become an emissary of *Turnen* in the provinces was inspired by the charismatic leader. Young men who absorbed Jahn's words as 'the words of an oracle' ('Orakelsprüche') and kept those 'golden phrases from Father Jahn' ('Goldsprüchlein aus Vater Jahns Munde') as a precious treasure found they were confirmed in their belief that they belonged to the chosen and had charismatic qualities of their own. If Jahn inspected a *Turnplatz* built by such a disciple and called this place 'the third most beautiful of its kind in Germany', this was a kind of recognition which the recipient could recite and live off even in old age.[45]

Although most emissaries of *Turnen* seemed to have gone off to spread the word in the provinces believing themselves specially chosen,[46] the charismatic aura of the *Turnvater* was not the only reason for the succes of this method of expansion. Jahn also offered material rewards.[47] Acting on behalf of the Prussian government, he could successfully prepare the ground for *Turners'* subsequent professional careers. His acquaintance with the leading reform politicians and civil servants enabled him to arrange that these young men received scholarships for their university studies, or – this was the most frequent method of promotion – that they were accepted for teacher training which had just begun to be institutionalized at this time. Several of the elite *Vorturner* whom he was able to place in the civil service or the military went on to obtain the positions of *Geheimer Finanzrat, Justizrat, Landrat,* or *Generalmajor*. Others served as missionaries abroad, or as officers, even in the prestigious cavalry. Most *Vorturner* became teachers and *Turnlehrer*, some of them ending their careers as heads of schools.[48]

From Charisma to Bureaucracy: The *Turner* Movement after Jahn

In 1817–18, Jahn was at the peak of his career as an agitator on behalf of the Prussian Reformers. Gymnastic instruction was introduced into the curriculum of Prussian schools (as well as into the schools of some other German states) with Jahn's and Eiselen's *Deutsche Turnkunst* as the official textbook. There were no doubts about the military use of *Turnen* in the newly-founded Kultusministerium dealing with education and culture. While Jahn's colleague Ernst Eiselen organized the instruction courses for future *Turnlehrer* [teachers of *Turnen*], Jahn himself was the state inspector of the *Turner* movement for all of Prussia. He advised local governments how to build new *Turnplätze* and acted as an employment agency for *Turnlehrer*.[49]

However, this extraordinary early expansion was short-lived. The cultural ascendency of *Turnen* came to an end when the political climate changed as Metternich's reactionary aristocratic policies made themselves felt. In 1819 Jahn was imprisoned for six years and lost contact with his followers. He never succeeded in fully regaining control. Although *Turnen* was still taught in schools, it was now suppressed as a social movement (the so-called *Turnsperre*). To exclude the public, exercises were no longer permitted in open-air grounds but banished to covered halls.

It was an attenuated and adapted form – the 'civilized' model of *Turnen* – that was incorporated into the associational life of rising liberalism and became a part of popular culture in Germany from the 1840s on. But the greater the popularity of *Turnen* in the course of the later nineteenth century, the more it deviated from Jahn's early ideas. Covered gyms were soon accepted as the appropriate places for exercising, for they opened up the possibility of practising regardless of the weather and the season and allowed the working population to take part after dark. In addition, urbanization and rising land prices made it increasingly impossible to switch back to the open air for clubs and associations composed of the popular classes. The problems resulting from the consequent tendency of the gyms to be crowded were partly solved by the introduction of the drill element which was regarded as a means of managing the crush of bodies and keeping discipline. Contrary to the wishes of Jahn, there was less scope for personal initiative and hardly any chance for heroes to arise from *Turnen* any more.

It is a historical irony that the rise of athletics and other 'English sports' which, with regard to the free and easy manner of exercise, can be regarded as a revival of *Jahnsches Turnen* were fought off in the name of Jahn. An emotional controversy of *Turnen versus Sport* developed and reached its peak in the years before the First World War when the *Deutsche Turnerschaft*, the umbrella organisation of *Turnvereine* founded in 1868, exceeded a million members. This controversy had been started in the 1880s by many an elderly *Turnlehrer* who regarded himself as a disciple of Jahn.[50] The sport movement, on the other hand, had to invent its own tradition of heorism. This new tradition became very similar to Jahn's heroism after the defeat of Germany in the First World War. But a hundred years after Jahn's time the means to disseminate it was not personal charisma but the popular press.

NOTES

1. Cf. W.F. Mandle, 'W.G. Grace as a Victorian Hero', *Historical Studies*, XIX (1980/81), 353–68.
2. The best overviews on the changing Jahn-image are by Reinhard K. Sprenger, *Die Jahnrezeption in Deutschland 1871–1933. Nationale Identität und Modernisierung*

(Schorndorf ,1985), and by Hajo Bernett, 'Das Jahn-Bild in der nationalsozialistischen Weltanschauung', *Stadion* IV (1978), 225–47.

3. Max Weber, *Wirtschaft und Gesellschaft. Grundriß der verstehenden Soziologie* (Tübingen, 1976, 5th ed.), pp.140–6, 654–87.

4. About Jahn as a person, see Wolfgang Meyer, *Friedrich Ludwig Jahn. Ein Lebensbild aus großer Zeit* (Berlin, 1904); Ernst Frank, *Friedrich Ludwig Jahn – ein moderner Rebell* (Offenbach, 1972); and Günther Jahn, *Friedrich Ludwig Jahn. Volkserzieher und Vorkämpfer für Deutschlands Einheit* (Göttingen, 1992).

5. Quoted from Edmund Neuendorff, *Geschichte der neueren deutschen Leibesübung vom Beginn des 18. Jahrhunderts bis zur Gegenwart*, vol.2, Dresden, no year, p.25.

6. Cf. Horst Ueberhorst, *Zurück zu Jahn? Gab es kein besseres Vorwärts?* (Bochum 1969). The same interpretation is to be found in the Jahn-special volume of *Stadion* IV (1978). For the tradition of this interpretation in the historiography of the *Turner* movement, see Sprenger, *Jahnrezeption*, pp.191 f.

7. For the context of the student movement, see Wolfgang Hardtwig, 'Krise der Universität, studentische Reformbewegung (1750–1819) und die Sozialisation der jugendlichen deutschen Bildungsschicht', *Geschichte und Gesellschaft* XI (1985), 155–76; Hardtwig, 'Auf dem Weg zum Bildungsbürgertum: die Lebensführungsart der jugendlichen Bildungsschicht 1750–1819', in M. Rainer Lepsius (ed.), *Bildungsbürgertum im 19. Jahrhundert, pt. 3: Lebensführung und ständische Vergesellschaftung* (Stuttgart, 1992), pp.19–42. For Jahn's activities in the student movement, see Helmut König, *Zur Geschichte der bürgerlichen Nationalerziehung in Deutschland zwischen 1807 und 1815*, pt. 2 (Berlin DDR, 1973), pp.85 f. For the influence of the romantic period, see Klaus Zieschang, 'Vom Schützenfest zum Turnfest. Die Entstehung des Deutschen Turnfestes unter besonderer Berücksichtigung der Einflüsse von F.L. Jahn', Ph.D. Thesis (Würzburg, 1973), pp.170 ff.

8. Friedrich Ludwig Jahn, *Bereicherung des Hochdeutschen Sprachschatzes versucht im Gebiethe der Sinnverwandtschaft, ein Nachtrag zu Adelung's und eine Nachlese zu Eberhard's Wörterbuch* (Leipzig, 1806), reprinted in Jahn, *Werke*, ed. Carl Euler, vol.1, Hof (1884), pp.23–128.

9. For a summary see Hans-Ulrich Wehler, *Deutsche Gesellschaftsgeschichte*, vol.1 (Munich, 1987), pp.397–485.

10. Cf. Otto W. Johnston, *Der deutsche Nationalmythos. Ursprung eines politischen Programms* (Stuttgart, 1990), p.31.

11. This episode is reported in an autobiographic piece published under a pseudonym: Karl Schöppach, *Denknisse eines Deutschen oder Fahrten des Alten im Bart*, Schleusingen, 1835, reprinted in Jahn, *Werke*, vol.1, p.474. Under another pseudonym, O.C.C. Höpffner, Jahn had published a patriotic article already in 1800: *Ueber die Beförderung des Patriotismus im Preußischen Reiche. Allen Preußen gewidmet* (Halle, 1800), reprinted in ibid., pp.3–22.

12. In his 'Notizen zur Erinnerung, auf Befehl seiner Excellenz des Herrn Staatskanzlers aufgesetzt' Gneisenau wrote: 'Der Privatgelehrte Jahn ist durch eine Pension für seine patriotische Gesinnung und für sein Aufregen anderer zu gleichem Zwecke zu belohnen'. Quoted from Neuendorff, *Geschichte*, vol.2, p.51. On the remuneration of the agitators in general, see Johnston, *Nationalmythos*, pp.27 ff., 65 ff., 175.

13. This is the title of the English edition of the book by Johnston.

14. For the incorporation of these and other reform concepts into 'Deutsches Volksthum', see Johnston, *Nationalmythos*, pp.170–5. The correspondence of the educational reforms is also revealed by Karl-Ernst Jeismann, *Das preußische Gymnasium in Staat und Gesellschaft. Die Entstehung des Gymnasiums als Schule des Staates und der Gebildeten, 1787–1817* (Stuttgart, 1974), p.246. For further correspondences, but also characteristic differences, with respect to the army reform see Michael Antonowytsch, *Friedrich Ludwig Jahn. Ein Beitrag zur Geschichte der Anfänge des deutschen Nationalismus* (Berlin, 1933), pp.20–5.

15. This is proved on the basis of archival studies by Karl-Heinz Schodrok, *Militärische Jugend-Erziehung in Preußen 1806–1820* (Olsberg, 1989), insb. pp.111 ff., 181–91. See also Wolfgang Eichel u.a., *Geschichte der Körperkultur in Deutschland von 1789 bis 1917* (Berlin GDR, 1965), pp.71 f.

16. Cf. Eric Hobsbawm, 'Introduction: Inventing Traditions', in Eric Hobsbawm and Terence

Ranger (eds.), *The Invention of Tradition* (Cambridge, 1983), pp.1–14.

17. Cf. Johann Christoph GutsMuths, *Gymnastik für die Jugend. Enthaltend eine praktische Anweisung zu Leibesübungen. Ein Beytrag zur nöthigen Verbesserung der körperlichen Erziehung* (Schnepfenthal, 1793), reprinted Dresden (1928); see also Hajo Bernett, *Die pädagogische Neugestaltung der bürgerlichen Leibesübungen durch die Philanthropen* (Schorndorf, 1971, 3rd ed.). About the visit of Jahn to GutsMuths see Jahn's letter to Georg Siemens, 7 July 1807, in *Die Briefe F.L. Jahns*, ed. Wolfgang Meyer (Dresden, 1930), pp.39 f.

18. About this school: König, *Geschichte*, pp.144–51; Karl Wassmannsdorff, 'Nachrichten über das Turnen in der Stadt Berlin vor und nach Jahn', *Deutsche Turnzeitung* No.17 (1871), .95 f.; No.18 (1871), 102–6.

19. Sketches from this time are to be found in Gerd Steins, *Wo das Turnen erfunden wurde... Friedrich Ludwig Jahn und die 175jährige Geschichte der Hasenheide* (Berlin, 1986).

20. Cf. Dieter Düding, *Organisierter gesellschaftlicher Nationalismus in Deutschland (1808–1847). Bedeutung und Funktion der Turner-und Sängervereine für die deutsche Nationalbewegung*, Munich, 1984, p.56; Carl Cotta, *Die Frühlingszeit des deutschen Volksturnens* (Leipzig, 1913), p.81.

21. Vgl. Johann Jakob Wilhelm Bornemann, *Lehrbuch der von Friedrich Ludwig Jahn unter dem Namen der Turnkunst wiedererweckten Gymnastik. Zur allgemeinen Verbreitung der jugendlichen Leibesübungen* (Berlin, 1814, reprinted Münster, 1981), pp.44, 47, quotation p.44; Düding, *Nationalismus*, p.55.

22. Cf. Rudolf Körner, 'Friedrich Ludwig Jahn und sein Turnwesen', in *Forschungen zur Brandenburgischen und Preußischen Geschichte* XXXXI (1928), 70; Cotta, *Frühlingszeit*, p.84; Schodrok, *Jugend-Erziehung*, p.183. - The salaries were higher than those of other Berlin teachers. Cf. Detlef K. Müller, *Sozialstruktur und Schulsystem. Aspekte zum Strukturwandel des Schulwesens im 19. Jahrhundert* (Göttingen, 1977), p.192.

23. Cf. Steins, *Turnen*, p.42.

24. Outside Prussia there were about 50 societies, most of them in northern Germany. Only in exceptional cases did Turner societies develop in Saxony or southern Germany. Cf. Düding, *Nationalismus*, p.67.

25. Cf. Bornemann, *Lehrbuch*, p.99.

26. Cf. Jahn's letter to Schulrat Vieth in Dessau, 11 April 1818, in *Briefe*, p.123. A similar position is Jahn's disciple adopted by Franz Passow, *Turnziel* (Breslau, 1818), p.227.

27. J.W. v. Archenholz, Über die von Herrn Jahn in Berlin eingeführten gymnastischen Übungen der Jugend, *Minerva - ein Journal historischen und politischen Inhalts* 1812, p.18.

28. Friedrich Ludwig Jahn, supplement to a letter of Wilhelm Harnisch to the medical doctor Feuerstein, 25 July 1811, in *Briefe*, p.57. See also Jahn's letter to Ernst Moritz Arndt, 4 November (1811): 'Stur, Kampfstark; ansturm, mit einem Kampfblick ansehen; Sturm, die höchste Kraftäußerung lebender und todter Gewalten, sind ja bei uns noch Erinnerungen aus alter Zeiten. Im Allemannischen heißt *Torner* (Tyro) ein Kriegslehrling. Turner ist ein bekanntes Deutsches Geschlecht'. This letter is quoted by Hans Langenfeld u. Josef Ulfkotte (eds.), *Unbekannte Briefe von Friedrich Ludwig Jahn und Hugo Rothstein als Quelle zur Frühgeschichte des Turnens*, Oberwerries 1990, p.31.

29. Cf. Johannes Zeidler, *Die deutsche Turnsprache bis 1819*, Halle, 1942, pp.37, 44, 55 f. See also Jahn's 'Prüfregeln' for successful 'Kunstwörter', in Vorbericht of Friedrich Ludwig Jahn/Ernst Eiselen, *Die Deutsche Turnkunst zur Einrichtung der Turnplätze* (Berlin, 1816), pp.XLIV f. – For the 'Turnkünstlerrat': ibid., pp.VI, XLI ff., as well as Ernst Dürre, Dr. Chr. Eduard L. Dürre. *Aufzeichnungen, Tagebücher und Briefe aus einem deutschen Turner-und Lehrerleben* (Leipzig, 1881), p.96.

30. The examples are from Zeidler, *Turnsprache*, pp.43–51, and Josef Göhler, 'Die Leibesübungen in der deutschen Sprache und Literatur', in Wolfgang Stammler (ed.), *Deutsche Philologie im Aufriß*, Bd. 3 (Frankfurt, 1962), pp.2293 ff.

31. This is the Interpretation by Ueberhorst, *Zurück zu Jahn?*, p.22, und by Dieter Langewiesche, '... für Volk und Vaterland kräftig zu würken ..'. Zur politischen und gesellschaftlichen Rolle der Turner zwischen 1811 und 1817, in Ommo Grupe (ed.), *Kulturgut oder Körperkult? Sport und Sportwissenschaft im Wandel*, Tübingen, 1990, p.33. As a general overview on the movement for language reform in early nineteenth-century Germany, see Joachim Gessinger,

Sprache und Bürgertum. Zur Sozialgeschichte sprachlicher Verkehrsformen im Deutschland des 18. Jahrhunderts (Stuttgart, 1980), pp.149–52.

32. Cf. Jahn/Eiselen, *Turnkunst*, p.226.

33. Quotation: ibid., p.226; Friedrich Ludwig Jahn, *Das Deutsche Volksthum*, Lübeck 1810, p.314. On the popularity of the uniform, see Wolfgang Kaschuba, Deutsche Bürgerlichkeit nach 1800. Kultur als 'symbolische Praxis', in Jürgen Kocka (ed.), *Bürgertum im 19. Jahrhundert. Deutschland im europäischen Vergleich*, Munich, 1988, vol.3, p.28. Martha Bringemeier, *Ein Modejournal erlebt die Französische Revolution* (Münster, 1981), pp.44 f., explains the origin of this dress.

34. Cf. Georg Simmel, *Soziologie. Untersuchungen über die Formen der Vergesellschaftung* (Berlin, 1983, 1908), p.94.

35. 'Einer lernte vom andern, und wenn eine neue Übung erfunden war, geschah dem Erfinder die Ehre des Gedächtnisses seiner Erfindung im Andenken der Genossen'. Cotta, *Frühlingszeit*, p.26, see also pp.24 ff.

36. Cf. Zieschang, *Schützenfest*, pp.213–22. Quotation: Jahn/Eiselen, *Turnkunst*, p.170.

37. Cf. Jahn's report on *Turnen* in 1818, quoted in Cotta, *Frühlingszeit*, p.84.

38. Dürre, Aufzeichnungen, quoted ibid., p.49.

39. Cf. Düding, *Nationalismus*, pp.83–109; Erich Geldbach, *Sport und Protestantismus. Geschichte einer Begegnung*, Wuppertal,1975, p.171; Alfred Richartz, 'Turner, Auf zum Streite! Die Bedeutung von Gruppenphantasien für die frühe Turnbewegung', in Gunter Gebauer (ed.), *Körper- und Einbildungskraft. Inszenierungen des Helden im Sport* (Berlin, 1988), pp.87 f.

40. Cf. Alfred Richartz, 'Sexualität – Körper – ...Öffentlichkeit. Formen und Umformungen des Sexuellen im Sport', *Sozial-und Zeitgeschichte des Sports* IV/3 (1990), 56–72.

41. Up to now there is no serious research on the question of homoeroticism in this 'manly' community. The only empirical study is from a national socialist: Karl M. Bungardt, 'Die männerbündischen Gründungen Friedrich Ludwig Jahns. Versuch ihrer Deutung als Bestandteile einer 'Nationalpolitischen Erziehung', *Leibesübungen und körperliche Erziehung* LV (1936), 530–37.

42. Cf. the characterization of Friesen by Jahn, 'Vorbericht', in Jahn/Eiselen, *Turnkunst*, p.VII. See also Wilhelm Harnisch, 'Friedrich Friesen als Erzieher und Lehrer', in Der Erziehungs-und Schulrath an der Oder, reprinted in Cotta, *Frühlingszeit*, pp.51 f.

43. Karl August Varnhagen von Ense, quoted from A[lexander] v. Gleichen-Rußwurm, *Geselligkeit. Sitten und Gebräuche der europäischen Welt 1789–1900* (Stuttgart, 1909), p.116.

44. Henrich Steffens, *Was ich erlebte. Aus der Erinnerung niedergeschrieben*, vol.8, Breslau 1843, pp.314, 320. See also Düding, *Nationalismus*, pp.82 f., and Cotta, *Frühlingszeit*, pp.28 ff.

45. Cf. Rückerinnerung des Oberlehrers Ender, *Deutsche Turnzeitung* (1867), p.323.

46. This is a result of the studies by Düding, *Nationalismus*, p.65.

47. On the importance of this factor, see Weber, *Wirtschaft*, 145.

48. Cf. Düding, *Nationalism*, pp.65 ff., Cotta, *Frühlingszeit*, p.70. See also Hans Langenfeld, 'Jahns Einfluβ auf die Entwicklung der körperlichen Erziehung im bürgerlichen Zeitalter', *Stadion* IV (1978), 28, which has a list of the fathers' occupations and supports the impression that the *Turners* were social climbers.

49. Cf. Schodrok, *Jugend-Erziehung*, p.189.

50. For example, this was the case with Wilhelm Angerstein, 'Die Bedeutung der Leibesübungen – Turnen, Sport Berufsgymnastik – für die Kulturentwicklung', *Monatsschrift für das Turnwesen* VII (1888), 289–97, 332–9.

'Muscular, Militaristic and Manly': The British Middle-Class Hero as Moral Messenger

J.A. MANGAN

Rider Haggard dedicated his story of African adventure *Allan Quartermain* to his son with the words:

> In the hope that in days to come he and many other boys, whom I shall never know, may in the acts and thoughts of Allan Quartermain and his companions, find something to help him and them to reach ... the highest rank whereto we can attain – the state and dignity of an English gentleman.[1]

In fact, Quartermain was not the perfect exemplar of the late Victorian gentleman. He lacked the honours and titles of the period 'blood', the public school and Oxbridge athletic hero of the late nineteenth century. Furthermore, since the spread of the public schools to the 'Celtic Fringe' the concept of the gentleman sportsman was a *British* ideal, if only as a means to imperial employment. Jeffrey Richards is of the view, and he is unquestionably correct, that the gentleman 'is a species not just endangered but verging on the point of extinction'. His values have passed out of fashion: his behaviour is an object of derision. The ideology he exemplified is therefore a virtually defunct ideology, a fit subject for historians.[2]

The late nineteenth- and early twentieth-century gentleman was essentially the product of the public school and its obsession with games and the games-fields as the heart of the curriculum, the source of masculine virtue and the instrument of imperial domination. The public school 'blood' was a descendant of an earlier Corinthian tradition, as Philip Mason reminds us, but by the 1880s the tradition had been sanitised for public consumption in an era of middle-class evangelism and public school expansion. The earlier indulgent, anarchic and widely admired image of the gentleman-sportsman, who had replaced the restrained Mr Darcy, was Bludyer, Thackeray's friend, brave, athletic, partial to a 'mill' (a fist fight) and frequently arrested.[3] Lawlessness was part of the Georgian manly gentleman's charm.

The early nineteenth-century gentleman sportsman is well, if not completely, personified in the person of Thomas Assheton-Smith

(1776–1859). And he timed his exit well. He died at almost the very moment when his image was being reconstructed, his masculinity redefined and his manners modified by middle-class sensibilities. In the era of British history when fox-hunting grew to be 'almost a religion, with high priests'[4] Assheton-Smith, in the words of no less an admirer than Napoleon, was 'le premier chasseur d'Angleterre'. As Philip Mason acidly remarks, 'the English have usually been able to persuade themselves that there is a serious moral purpose behind what they enjoy'.[5] The ethical role of fox-hunting was made clear by Assheton-Smith's biographer, Sir John Eardley-Wilmot. Fox-hunting, he wrote, 'serves to retain the moral influence of the higher over the lower classes of society ... and is one of the strongest preservatives of that national spirit by which we are led to cherish, above all things, a life of active energy, independence and freedom'.[6] Clearly it was a small price for a fox to pay to stimulate such qualities! And that was not all: the sport ensured hardihood, nerve and intrepidity in the young and confirmed and prolonged the strength and vigour of manhood!

In fact, Assheton-Smith was also a link between the 'unrestrained' schoolboy athlete of the first half of the nineteenth century and the later 'restrained' version of the second half of the century. He was at Eton for eleven years between 1783 and 1794 and boasted, in keeping with the times, that he learnt nothing but he did enjoy his cricket, rowing and boxing. And in a proper manly tradition he earned lasting fame for his bloody hour-long fist-fight with a fellow pupil, Jack Musters. Musters, another Corinthian of distinction, in his prime, according to Nimrod, 'could have leaped, hopped, fought, danced, played cricket, fished, swam, shot, played tennis and skated with any man in Europe'.[7] Not too much time for the intellect in all that effort.

The bruises of fist-fighting seemed to be the almost obligatory cast-marks of masculinity of the early nineteenth-century gentleman, and Assheton-Smith displayed a 'fierce readiness to show himself as good as any man with his fists' outside the ring! Giving away three stone in weight, he fought a coalheaver in the main street of Loughborough for flicking at his horse and in old age knocked down a young solicitor's clerk for bringing him an 'impertinent and dishonest' letter.[8] To an extent, Assheton-Smith failed to live up fully to the hedonistic Corinthian image of the time: he did not bet, he drank little and apparently was no womaniser. Moreover, he was a hard-working and successful businessman, but in one capacity he was a moral exemplar: he was fearless, bold and confident; a true 'male'. These were the qualities the 'blood' of later times displayed, or was expected to display, in his leadership not only of the 'lesser classes' of Britain but the 'lesser breeds' of Empire.

David Newsome has remarked in his famous study of Victorian

adolescent males that Manliness, as the Victorians understood it, was a much-used term, so much so that it is reasonable, he states, to conclude that 'manliness' was one of the cardinal virtues of the time.[9] Newsome discerned a sea-change in the meaning of manliness mid-way through the nineteenth century. He was among the first of modern commentators to describe a shift in the meaning of manliness from spiritual morality to muscular morality: 'we see the distinctive features of two opposing schools of Victorian idealists, represented by the followers of Coleridge and Arnold, on the one hand, and by the 'muscular Christian' school of Charles Kingsley and Thomas Hughes on the other'.[10] The suggested polarity is to over-simplify reality. There was, as we shall see, an even more influential school – the school of Darwinian realists, who embraced 'muscularity' as a moral ideal but were not greatly exercised if it lacked a religious component. Social Darwinism is every bit an appropriate analytical 'blade' for dissecting the body of public school mores as muscular Christianity – in fact, it is in all probability ever more apposite.[11]

Prior to 1850 life in the public schools, to recycle an adaptation of the classic Hobbesian expression, was nasty, brutish and certainly for some not short enough.[12] These schools were often godless, hedonistic, harsh and brutal places. Eton, arguably the most famous, was a microcosm of a macrocosm – the external upper-class world beyond the school walls; a world of hard-drinking, horse-racing, gambling, blood sports, prizefighting and sexual indulgence. John Chandos, in his *Boys Together: The English Public School 1800 – 1864*, graphically records the public school world of the period and its social warts – debauchery, savagery and cruelty.[13] Before the middle of the nineteenth century, as a result of conditions within the schools, rebellions were not uncommon events. Bored and brutalised boys occasionally turned on their official tormentors with explosive resentment. However, the last notable rebellion at Marlborough College occurred in 1850. The date is significant.[14] This last rebellion brought about an educational revolution in the schools – the advent of compulsory team games – as an antidote to uprisings, the creation of extensive and expensive playing fields and the establishment of cups and cup-ties, leagues and league tables – and the construction of the attendant myth of the gentleman sportsman endowed with a national instinct for 'fair play'.

The innovation contained the seeds of a problem: the possibility of anarchic, undisciplined brutality on the new games fields as a continuation of a similar and earlier behaviour in school yards, streets, lanes and countryside. A new code of conduct had to be clearly defined, demonstrated and enforced by the new athletic masters recruited to the schools. The generic name of that code was: 'fair play'. The genesis of 'fair play' lay, therefore, not in nobility but in savagery. Fair play was not the instinctive behaviour of gentlemen but the acquired behaviour of roughnecks, albeit of some social standing. It was cultivated carefully as a practical tool.[15] It was a means of ensuring controlled confrontation in physical struggle on the new playing fields. Around the concept of fair play a mythology grew. It was required. The image of the schools had to be redeemed. Evangelicalism had sobered some of the upper classes; survival now demanded a reciprocity in the upper-class schools. A necessity now became a virtue.

Public school life of the post-1850 period frequently remained hard, harsh and brutal reflecting 'the imperatives of Spencer and Sumner as often as the exhortations of Kingsley and Hughes. Attitudes were often secular not spiritual, beliefs were often materialistic not realistic, custom was often callous not Christian'.[16] By the 1880s there can be no doubt that a new morality was being successfully preached to the young public school gentlemen of Britain but it is not quite accurate to state that the ideals of Godliness and Good Learning were fading and the ideals of muscular Christianity was emerging. The truth was more secular in intent and outcome. The crucial point was that the new masculinity was a continuation of an Adamite rather than a Pauline ideal. Those who espoused Newsome's Godliness and Good Learning were something of upper middle-class misfits – a minority of 'Holy Joes' in a majority of Tom Jones, rather than Tom Browns, muscular and irreligious rather than muscular and religious; and so it was to remain. But for all that, these latter-day 'Tom Jones' were *moral* icons, symbols of a manliness which eventually owed more to rugby or cricket boots than to riding boots and very little to biblical studies, church services or Christian conscience. And their games, their leagues, their cup ties were instruments of Social Darwinism as much as anything else, more secular and less spiritual in philosophy or practice than Newsome suggests.

Newsome attributes the rise of the new moral ethic of godliness and manliness to the 'forceful and didactic writings' of Charles Kingsley, who was obsessed with the 'poison of effeminacy' of Tractarian 'unmanliness' which he saw as a composition of emotionalism, asceticism, celibacy and hagiography.[17] He was fortunate in his timing as Tractarianism took on its 'Puseyite' image in the 1850s, as it embraced 'Catholic' ritual and church and clerical ornamentation and adornment. 'Puseyism' offended many Anglicans who found security in its antithesis, Kingsleyian 'healthful and manful Christianity ... which does not exalt the feminine virtues to the exclusion of the masculine'.[18]

Kingsley was the prophet of a revolution in educational idealism, but he gave away nothing to Thomas Hughes in his proselytism. Hughes, in fact, was in his way another bridge between manliness past and future, between 'Corinthians' of the early and late nineteenth century! It was Hughes who defended the famous fist fight between Tom Brown and Slogger Williams with this passionate apologia: 'Fighting with fists is the natural and English way for English boys to settle their quarrels. Learn to box, then, as you learn to play cricket and football. Not one of you will be the worse, but very much the better for learning to box well. Should you never have to use it in earnest, there's no exercise in the world so good for the temper, and for the muscles of the back and legs'.[19] And it should not be overlooked, incidentally, that Hughes was an energetic and enthusiastic advocate of the Volunteer Movement.

The ancient universities, then finishing schools for upper-class boys, also embraced the new morality in Christian, agnostic or atheistic form. Leslie Stephen was the foremost catalyst of the new muscular morality at Cambridge. Newsome claims that he made 'a fetish of his athleticism'[20] (the term by which the new morality eventually became known). He rowed, he ran, he walked, he climbed – enormously. He sought out the athlete; he coached the boats; he patronised the Volunteers. He epitomised the new cult of muscular moral manliness: 'There was a moral value in hard walking'.[21] It thwarted any tendency to sanctimonious effeminacy and it reduced exuberant vandalism. He won a following of 'manly, affectionate young fellows'. Perhaps, all the more so, because he 'outgrew his Christianity', while his 'muscularity lasted longer'.[22]

These zealots – Kingsley, Hughes and Stephen – preached and practised 'the moral and physical beauty of athleticism; the cultivation of all that is masculine and the expulsion of all that effeminate, and excessively intellectual'.[23] They were harbingers of a Golden Age of a militant masculinity and a moral manhood that in time owed far more to the playing field than the pulpit and to the cricket square than the classroom. Nevertheless the image of masculinity exhibited a continuity. The rumbustious Englishman of the eighteenth century renowned for his aggressive temperament and his physical fearlessness[24] now became the 'play the game' Briton, renowned for his decent bravery, confident demeanour and straight back.

How this came about has been fully recorded.[25] Therefore it is, of course, more than a little simplistic to assert the Edward Thring of Uppingham was the headmaster 'who most determined the shape of things to come'.[26] Determination, in its opening moments, was shared by certain headmasters of old and new public schools.[27] However, it was eventually a system rather than any single man, or indeed any group of men, that produced the product. The system fitted functionally into the times. Eton, the most prestigious of all the public schools, offers evidence of the system's birth, growth and maturity:

> In the 1850s Eton showed few signs of what was to come. Games had little organisation and their staff stood aloof from what little there was.

There was no Rifle Corps, no house matches; a little rowing and less cricket. Within a decade the whole spirit changed. There was a flourishing Rifle Corps ... house cricket trophies, and activities on the river were 'revolutionised'. The Eton Boating Song was written in 1863.[28]

Some thirty-five years later the system had grown to maturity. There were: 'fifty fives courts where before there was one; twenty games or thereabouts of cricket as against three; compulsory football for every house four or five times a week; to say nothing of beagles and athletic sports in the Easter Term, and rowing and bathing daily through the summer'.[29] There were house colours for football and school colours for football, cricket, rowing, racquets; and a range of challenge cups, senior and junior. In a colourful metaphor, it was further recorded that: 'What is true of Eton ... is true, *mutatis mutandis*, of the other great public schools; the comprehensive net of athletics has closed around them all, sweeping in our boys by shoals, and few are the puny minnows that swim through its meshes. And yet the whole system is entirely modern, most of it a development of the last forty years.'[30]

This system successfully transformed middle-class British hooligans into imperial heroes – sometimes in fact if more often in fiction. Both the exposition and the exercise of a moral muscularity was easier in annuals, novels and comics.[31] Nevertheless Thring , if he did not determine it, certainly endorsed the new masculinity. He once wrote: 'The learning to be responsible, and independent, to bear pain, to play games, to drop rank, and wealth, and home luxury is a priceless boon – the public schools are the cause of this "manliness".'[32] By the 1880s, therefore (Newsome selects a decade earlier), the pursuit of the new manliness had become 'something of a cult'. Newsome offers this reason: the development reflected the views of the upper middle classes saturated with imperialistic notions, attracted by the spirit of aggressive patriotism which allayed fear of German militarism and successful foreign commercial and industrial rivalry. There is truth in this but the whole truth is more complex. Wellington College, in the 1880s, reflected the new manliness mores perfectly. To quote the historian of the school, G.F.H. Berkeley, 'Wellington was ... a splendid institution for the Nation and the Empire' with its fundamental purpose of producing 'a handy and dashing breed of young officers'.[33] However these future officers had first to be brought under control. Sport as an instrument of social control was the precursor of sport as moralistic imperial masculinity.

In no time at all 'fair play' became a 'traditional' aspect of upper-class schooling and allegedly an 'instinctive' Anglo-Saxon attribute. A Rev. Dr S.R.P. Slater once paraded its essentials:

We would rather lose a game than win it unfairly. We would rather
respect the spirit of the law than its letter. We would exact a spirit of
absolute obedience to the authorities set over us, never questioning the
umpire. We would desire in a race or a game, to go on if we can till
we drop dead. We would hope that the spirit would be developed
amongst us which is not so very greatly concerned for itself, so long
as the side on which we are is successful.[34]

The ideal of fair play won international praise. This exuberant comment by
the American Price Collier is quite typical of the foreign attitudes of the
time.

If I were an Englishman I should pray God that my countrymen might
never play less so long as they played the game. It is the men in the
closets, not the men in the fields and on the seas, who breed sorrow,
suspicion and envy; and the Englishman is not so dull as it might
appear when he pins his faith to the out-door man. He is not far wrong
in his belief that: *Ceux qui manquent de probité dans les plaisirs n'en
ont qu'une feinte dans les affaires.*[35]

Fair play won the admiration of many Europeans including, of course,
Pierre de Coubertin. Coubertin was a man of aristocratic prejudice,
historical misconception and utopian idealism: in his view commercialism
was ungentlemanly, fair play was a natural quality of the English gentleman
and sport, as played by the English public schoolboy, was a means of
promoting international harmony. The *real* origins of the concept of fair
play (so dear to his heart) were wholly misunderstood by him. The concept
was a utilitarian rather than an idealistic instrument. It is no accident that the
close connection between the concept of fair play and games is about one
hundred years old. The term, as used by Shakespeare in 1595, had no
association with sport; by 1880 it represented upright conduct in a game.[36]
It was closely linked to the games field, the prevention of anarchic action
during the game, and the maintenance of social order after it.

    Fair play quickly became equated with moral 'manliness' – the robust
manliness of imperialists. As I have written elsewhere, the term was 'a
substantive widely favoured by prelates on speech days and headmasters on
Sundays [which] embraced antithetical values – success, aggression and
ruthlessness, yet victory within the rules, courtesy in triumph, compassion
for the defeated'. The combination aroused the wonder and envy of the
contemporary world. Many came to believe that 'by virtue of their play
sense the English have acquired certain qualities which are as precious to
themselves as they are pleasing to others ... remarkable moral gifts, the
result of team work, that is to say, manly rivalry under "the aegis of fair

play"'.[37] Yet the simple reality was that fair play was less a moral ideal than a practical need. In the middle of the nineteenth century it served the most basic of social functions – social cohesion. It was practical, sensible and valuable. It promoted social integration not social disintegration – on and off the playing field! And the image of the upper-class 'blood' was transformed – from metropolitan hooligan to imperial hero. Now the young upper middle-class schoolboy became 'John Bull' – with better manners – in cricket whites or football shorts, a mythical hero – at home and abroad and the embodiment of an ethical ideal – 'fair play'. This had the result that late Victorian and Edwardian headmasters, who almost to a man exuded self-confidence, exuded a similar confidence in the sterling make-up of their protégés, who almost to a boy were 'muscular, moral and manly'.[38] The famous headmaster of Shrewsbury, the Reverend H.W. Moss, for example, asserted that the public schoolboy of his period of office was 'as manly, as public spirited, as devoted a lover of justice and fair play ... as those who had gone before him'.[39]

There were two stages to promotion to the pantheon of heroes 'who played the game': heroism in immaturity and heroism in maturity. As John Lowerson has so shrewdly observed: 'It was ... the printed word which created the aura of heroism, and this aura was dependent on the ascription of moral values by mediators.'[40] This was crucial. These values, as Lowerson rightly recognises, were constructed 'for a constituency whose creation has been well charted, at least in terms of its core, the burgeoning schools and colleges of the late Victorian middle classes',[41] but they were also diffused among a metropolitan and imperial clientèle which embraced schools, colleges and clubs. The diffusion was both outward and downward from the 'reformed public schools and their imitators'.[42] This diffusion, in time, spanned the nation and the globe – and the mythical hero personifying public school 'manliness' was to be emulated east, west, north and south. And while he may be in short supply in the 1990s, his ethic is proclaimed loudly in the most popular of modern professional sports – association football. Posters, banners, and electronic boards urged 'fair play' on players from five continents in the recent Fifth World Cup – and delightfully – for exactly the same reasons as it was projected in the Victorian public schools – to prevent anarchic turbulence on *and* off playing fields. Practical tools of social engineering, it seems, do not go out of fashion!

It is worth recalling that Arnold Lunn, in *The Harrovians,* drawing on his personal experiences as a schoolboy at Harrow at the turn of the century, wrote that 'under the elms is the real temple of the school'.[43] He added for good measure that Jesus Christ would have had a hard time of it in the *fin de siècle* public school![44] In the late Victorian and Edwardian eras, as a consequence, the mythical hero of the public school system was the 'blood', the games aristocrat. Lunn, in his recollections of Harrow schooldays, called these 'bloods' 'Homeric heroes'. Their adolescent battlefields were playing fields. There they displayed their mythical qualities: courage, stoicism, stamina and determination. There they achieved what mattered most to most staff and pupils – victory in league and cups. There they demonstrated the morality of 'muscularity' and asserted moral ascendancy. There they perfected the muscular, moral virtues which would often serve them well as adults – as soldiers, administrators, educators and entrepreneurs in empire. That at least was the theory – and it worked, to an extent, in practice.[45] The games system not only assured control over the children of the middle classes within the schools, in due course it was believed, it also assisted those children in their attempts to control in turn the native 'children' of the Empire.

> Realise the importance of games. It's in football and cricket and rowing that Englishmen get that splendid moral training which no other nation gets. Germany and France overwork their boys, ... nearly always they are stunted and weak. None of them get that magnificent sporting instinct which is the real foundation of our great Empire. So what I want to say to you boys is: 'Play up and play the game'. Be proud of your reputation for efficiency in games – it is the source of ... higher imperial efficiency.[46]

National mature mythical heroes of imperialism, it is sometimes overlooked, were not infrequently immature mythical heroes – during the period of their preparation for imperialism. In the 1960s, in a developing age of popular culture and an atmosphere of anti-elitism, Newsome was bold enough to find virtue in both Godliness and Good Learning and muscular Christianity. He wrote that both ideals were grand conceptions, and we deluded only ourselves if we laughed them to scorn: 'Both enunciated a code of living which was unselfish, active, honourable, useful and good. Both suffered in application from ruthlessness, arrogance, lack of sympathy and perhaps an undue emphasis on the virtues of success.'[47] All this is true. Then he asserted, somewhat pompously,[48] that the worst feature of the earlier ideal was a tendency to 'make boys into men too soon' while the worst feature of the later ideal was to fail 'to make boys into men at all'! In fact, he wholly fails to appreciate that manhood is capable of various functional definitions. The Victorian upper middle classes were more than satisfied with the militaristic masculinity they so successfully inculcated in many young public schoolboys.[49] It served the times extremely well. In Newsome's own words: 'Its code of living became so robust and patriotic in its demands that it could be represented as reaching its perfection in a code of dying.' Exactly![50]

The process of transforming metropolitan hooligan into imperial hero was sustained, unrelenting and extraordinarily successful. And this success certainly owed much, to return again to Lowerson, to the written word and, to a degree, to the many versifiers of the period,[51] who, among many others, attempted to create a consciousness of collective purpose,[52] to preach both the moral necessity of, and the moral superiority inherent in the masculinity they praised and perpetrated. These men were 'the troubadours of a once powerful and now ridiculed ethic. They recorded *and* shaped it..... They carefully depicted archetypes, priorities and possibilities'.[53] They were high priests. They comprised a sacred elite – ' "guardians" of ideals ... expositors of principle ... repositories of tradition'. They were 'a choric group acting as the conscience of the community echoing its deepest convictions'.[54]

In any consideration of the public school 'blood' as a moral messenger it is imperative to include probably the most famous of all the poets of Victorian and Edwardian public schools, Sir Henry Newbolt, rarely considered today, and look at his world of school heroes and the morality they personified, and through his verse transmitted to generations of aftercomers. In the making of the mythical imperial heroes of the playing fields, his voice was the loudest in volume and most passionate in conviction.

Time and again in his verse Newbolt depicts the public school 'blood' as sacrificial warrior and as moral icon demonstrating his taught talents, transferring these talents from the games field to the battlefield and inspiring his successors by this demonstration of lessons well learnt. Newbolt was a 'media voice' of his era – one without wireless, television, video or film. His audience was world-wide. His influence was pervasive.[55] If Edward Bowen's 'Tom' was a model for Harrovian peers,

> When there are bruises to add to;
> Why did he crush Jack with a rush?
> Only because that he had to!
> Base is the player who stops
> Fight, till the fighting is o'er;
> Who follows up till he drops,
> Panting and limping and sore?
> Tom![56]

Then Newbolt created an 'army' of 'Toms' mapping the world of experience of his public schoolboy heroes for heroes yet to come. Like Tom these boys were abstractions in concrete 'for an unsophisticated audience with a restricted frame of reference',[57] whose role was 'to channel emotion, mobilise the will, direct energies and determine action'.[58] Newbolt shared with many other late Victorian versifiers, who celebrated imperial glory and grandeur, a conviction shared with the early philosophers of Homeric Greece, that 'the greatest heroes were men of action', who like the Greeks sought honour, in the absence of war and as a preliminary to war, in their games:[59] 'self-sacrifice was the presiding principle of their verse and gives it a coherence and purpose. They saw poetry as the 'magister vitae'. They enunciated moral laws and '... interpreted the moral world for their charges. In their verse they were concerned with the problem of how to live and die correctly'.[60]

Newbolt was a myth-maker of extraordinary potency. He reconstructed the ageless sacrificial warrior for the British imperial era. He understood perfectly that 'mythology is ... a historical artefact ... a collective dream of one particular culture'.[61] He also fully appreciated that a mythology has 'its particular features' but also that 'it is based on elements which recur in other historical situations'.[62] With good reason – mythology is a response to a need to master reality, to interpret events, to make them intelligible and acceptable.[63] 'Man constructed the myths', states Terence Hawke in his *Structuralism and Semiotics*, 'and in so doing he constructs himself'.[64]

Newbolt was, like numerous poets, versifiers and songsters[65] of the age of the New Imperialism, a fierce patriot:

> Praise thou with praise unending,
> The Master of the Wine;
> To all their portions sending
> Himself he mingled thine.[66]

Equally he was a proud Imperialist and loyal Victorian. In his 'Victoria Regina', which formed part of the 'Cycle of Song' offered to Queen Victoria on the occasion of her second Jubilee in June 1897, he celebrated

> A thousand years by sea and land
> Our race has served the island kings,
> But not by custom's dull command
> Today with song her Empire rings.[67]

Newbolt himself 'sang' continually, if not exclusively, of war and its inevitability:

> Think that when tomorrow comes
> War shall claim command of all,
> Thou must hear the roll of drums,
> Though must hear the trumpet's call.
> Now before they silence ruth,
> Commune with the voice of truth;
> England! On thy knees tonight
> Pray that God defend the Right.[68]

its ecstasy:

> So shalt thou when morning comes
> Rise to conquer or to fall,
> Joyful hear the rolling drums,
> Joyful hear the trumpets call.
> Then let Memory tell thy heart;
> 'England! what thou wert, thou art!'
> Gird thee with thine ancient might,
> Forth! and God defend the Right![69]

and, as in his 'The King of England', his nation's enviable capacity to wage it successfully:

> Unarmed he rode, but in his ruddy shield
> The lions bore the dint of many a lance,
> And up and down his mantle's azure field
> Were strewn the lilies plucked in famous France.[70]

The 'King of Kings' Himself was to be relied upon 'in the time of War and Tumult' to support the race 'that strove to rule Thine earth, with equal laws unbought' and which uniquely possessed 'The love that loved the slave':

> Thou wilt not turn Thy face away
> From those who work Thy will,
> But send Thy strength on hearts that pray
> For strength to serve Thee still.[71]

In his verse Newbolt carefully sets the scene for schoolboy sacrifice with selected moments of imperial warfare in which a brave death is inevitable and welcomed. In his description, for example, of the famous death charge in 'The Guides at Cabul', the last surviving English officer after exhorting his men to 'Never give in', then 'grappled with death as a man that knows no doubt', while, shortly afterwards with 'the joy that spurs the warrior's heart' the remaining Guides, stoically dressed their slender line,

> And will never a foot lagging or head bent,
> To the dash and clamour and dust of death they went.[72]

This 'deed of an alien legion', Newbolt states in the opening stanza, should stand as a lesson to 'Sons of the Island Race' everywhere, who recount their father's battles 'with lips that burn',

> To fight with a joyful courage, a passionate pride
> To die at the last as the Guides at Cabul died.[73]

In 'Sacramentum Supremum', which depicts another heroic imperial event at Mukden in March 1905, Newbolt again took the opportunity offered to make the moral message plain:

> Draw near, my friends; and let your thoughts be high;
> Great hearts are glad when it is time to give;
> Life is no life to him that dares not die,
> And death no death to him that dares to live.[74]

Newbolt, perhaps had himself in mind, from 'a race high-handed, strong of heart ... conquerors, builders in the waste',[75] when he described 'The Non-Combatant' 'no man's chosen captain' and 'a name without an echo', yet who in his own way, as a man fully conscious of his heritage, 'fulfilled the ancestral rites, and kept alive the eternal fire' chanting 'the old heroic names' conscious of the fact that some, at least, hearing him 'hummed his music on the march to death'.[76] Newbolt certainly had William Cory, the Eton master and composer of the 'Eton Boating Song', in mind in his 'Ionicus' when he wrote of him 'with failing feet and shoulders bowed' walking unsteadily and unrecognised in the suburban streets of outer London

> But still through all his heart was young,
> His mood a joy that nought could mar,
> A courage, a pride, a rapture, sprung
> Of the strength and splendour of England's war.[77]

Cory's heart, Newbolt wrote, was 'high to the end' and he dreamed, as all stalwart in emotion if not in body, should dream of 'the sound and splendour of England's war'.[78]

Newbolt had a triple obsession: with schooldays and school playing fields, with sacrificial schoolboys, and with subaltern's wars. His alma mater, Clifton College, 'The Best School of All', remained vivid in his memory throughout his life:

> We'll honour yet the School we knew,
> The best School of all:
> We'll honour yet the rule we knew,
> Till the last bell call.
> For, working days or holidays,
> And glad or melancholy days,
> They were great days and jolly days
> At the best School of all.[79]

especially, of course, the gamesfield and its associations:

And where's the wealth, I'm wondering,
Could buy the cheers that roll
When the last charge goes thundering
Beneath the twilight goal?[80]

It was, in this poem, to 'the land of youth and dream', that Newbolt touched
upon the self-assured and self-effacing qualities of the school 'blood' that
would serve him in his calm and confident soldiering in empire:

The stars and sounding vanities
That half the crowd bewitch,
What are they but inanities
To him that treads the pitch?[81]

It was this mythical hero who attracted some of his most impassioned verse
in which he described the 'progression from anticipation to fulfilment ... in
the most complete sense, from playing field to battlefield'.[82]

Our game was his but yesteryear;
We wished him back; we could not know
The selfsame hour we missed him here
He led the line that broke the foe.

Blood-red behind our guarded posts
Sank as of old the dying day;
The battle ceased; the mingled hosts
Weary and cheery went their way:

'Tomorrow well may bring', we said,
'As fair a fight, as clear a sun'.
Dear lad, before the word was sped,
For evermore thy goal was won.[83]

In fact, in his verse 'games of cricket and football were interwoven with the
greater game of war. The garment was seamless. Nostalgic memories of the
fierce moments of a keenly fought house match provided the spiritual
resource to face the tests of the morning's bloody conflict.'[84]

When the chance was offered individual heroes found themselves
acknowledged in his verse. Major N.H. Vertue killed in the battle for Spion
Kop in the Boer War earned this valete:

Foremost of all on battle's fiery steep
Here VERTUE fell, and here he sleeps his sleep.
A fairer name no Roman ever gave
To stand sole monument on Valour's grave.[85]

Newbolt caught to perfection the Darwinist ethic that frequently characterised life in the public schools of Britain in the late nineteen and early twentieth centuries and the associated concept of fair play practised there, in his 'Clifton Chapel'.

> To set the cause above renown,
> To love the game beyond the prize,
> To honour, while you strike him down,
> The foe that comes with fearless eyes;
> To count the life of battle good,
> And dear the land that gave you birth,
> And dearer yet the brotherhood
> That binds the brave of all the earth.[86]

The poem describes a visit by a father with his son on the occasion of the boy joining the school. In the school chapel, the father confides to his son that some day soon 'you too may speak with noble ghosts of manhood'. He would one day recall, the father declares, 'the vows of war he made before the Lord of Hosts'. The final words of fatherly advice concern the beauty of the destiny of true heroes:

> Among the lights that gleam and pass,
> You'll live to follow none more pure
> Than that which glows on yonder brass.
> *'Qui procul hinc'*, the legend's writ, –
> The frontier-grave is far away –
> *'Qui ante diem periit:*
> *Sed miles, sed pro patria'*.[87]

This destiny is, of course, spelt out in the much-quoted, now often mischievously if not maliciously, 'Vitaï Lampada' which brings together in a single poem the fearless schoolboy 'blood', the courageous young subaltern and the efficacy of the ethic of fair play:

> There's a breathless hush in the Close to-night –
> Ten to make and the match to win –
> A bumping pitch and a blinding light,
> An hour to play and the last man in.
> And it's not for the sake of a ribboned coat,
> Or the selfish hope of a season's fame,
> But his Captain's hand on his shoulder smote –
> 'Play up! Play up! and play the game!'

> The sand of the desert is sodden red, –
> Red with the wreck of a square that broke; –
> The Gatling's jammed and the Colonel dead,
> And the regiment blind with dust and smoke.
> The river of death has brimmed his banks,
> And England's far, and Honour a name,
> But the voice of a schoolboy rallies the ranks:
> 'Play up! Play up! and play the game!'[88]

This is the word, declares Newbolt, that every son of the school 'must hear', must never forget, must 'bear through life like a torch in flame'.

> And falling fling to the host behind –
> 'Play up! play up! and play the game![89]

Battlefield and playing field fuse together in the consciousness of Newbolt's schoolboys – during and after schooldays as in 'The School at War'.

> All night before the brink of death
> In fitful sleep the army lay,
> For through the dream that stilled their breath
> Too gauntly glared the coming day.
>
> We heard beyond the desert night
> The murmur of the fields we knew,
> And our swift souls with one delight
> Like homing swallows Northward flew.
>
> We played again the immortal games,
> And grappled with the fierce old friends,
> And cheered the dead undying names,
> And sang the song that never ends;[90]

and in 'He Fell Among thieves', which describes the nostalgic thoughts, in his last hours before execution, of a young officer captured by brigands on the North West Frontier:

> He saw the School Close, sunny and green,
> The runner beside him, the stand by the parapet wall,
> The distant tape, and the crowd roaring between
> His own name over all.
>
> He saw the dark wainscot and timbered roof,
> The long tables, and the faces merry and keen;
> The College eight and their trainer dining aloof,
> The Dons on the dais serene.[91]

Newbolt's infatuation with war and the warrior seems perfectly illustrated in his short poem 'Peace' written in 1902 at the end of the Boer War:

> No more to watch by Night's eternal shore,
>   With England's chivalry at dawn to ride;
> No more defeat, faith, victory – O! no more
> A cause on earth for which we might have died.[92]

The British mythical heroes discussed in other chapters in this volume are representatives of other athletic subcultures. The numerical dominance of those chapters reflect contemporary fashion. The middle classes and the middle-class mythical heroes are firmly out of fashion. It is salutary, therefore, that they have a recorder. It ensures historical balance, rescues from conscious neglect a section of society which contributed hugely to national and world sport as a political, cultural and social entity, and arguably it avoids justifiable accusations of contemporary 'inverted snobbery'! In a period in which it is modish to embrace anti-elitism and eschew elitism it is important in the interests of historical completeness that the middle- class athletic hero is not written out of cultural history.

Newbolt's schoolboy 'bloods' translated into sacrificial subalterns were mythical heroes – actual and fictional – with a moral message for their times. Newbolt was a didactist. For him gamesfields were moral arenas with metaphorical meanings, but they were also locations where Tom Jones became not Tom Brown but Harry Desmond.[93] On these fields the manners of the eighteenth-century gentleman-sportsman were modified, restrained and redirected. This transformation reflects *both* continuity and change in British cultural history. It is also a significant part of that history.

Newbolt, himself, was part – an influential part – of an extensive movement which created a 'rhetoric of jingoistic conceit in poetry, prose and picture'.[94] It involved major and minor prose writers, poets and painters, who undertook the cultural indoctrination of the young upper middle class male into a chivalric, militaristic manhood, who depicted brave and cool public school 'bloods' taking their playing field courage, determination and confidence onto imperial battlefields – in the service of the imperial community. Their image-makers consciously constructed 'inspirational stereotypes embodying self-sacrificing service, personifying national nobility, justifying the grandeur of imperialism'.[95]

Newbolt, therefore, was one of many high priests of a cult which constructed, interpreted and sustained a myth. These priests 'mastered the presentation of a powerful and simply iconography and passed it passionately from one generation to the next'.[96] With the result, as Sir Derek Birley, among many others, has noted: 'The rush to the colours was led by the sport-mad leisured classes, the "flanneled fools and muddied oafs" ....

The public school men were imbued with the spirit of Newbolt'.[97] Their influence cannot be measured with precision but their efforts at making mythical heroes can be traced in detail. In any study of European mythological heroes they cannot be omitted. Their influence was extraordinary and extensive.[98] Arguably, Newbolt is the best known of them in modern Britain and yet is little known in modern Europe. For his contribution to the making of mythical heroes in the culture that gave most of today's global sports to Europe and the World he deserves mention.

NOTES

1. Quoted in Jeffrey Richards, 'The English Gentleman', *The Listener*, 6 May 1982, 6.
2. Ibid.
3. Philip Mason, *The English Gentleman: The Rise and Fall of an Ideal* (London: Deutsch, 1982), p.82.
4. Ibid., p.83.
5. Ibid.
6. Ibid.
7. Ibid., p.85.
8. Ibid., p.86.
9. David Newsome, *Godliness and Good Learning* (London: John Murray, 1961), p.195.
10. Ibid., p.197.
11. Ibid., p.199.
12. See J.A. Mangan, 'Social Darwinism and Upper Class Education in Late Victorian and Edwardian England', in J. A. Mangan and James Walvin (eds.), *Manliness and Morality: Middle-Class Masculinity in Britain and America, 1800 –1940* (Manchester: Manchester University Press, 1987), pp.135–59.
13. This state of affairs is briefly discussed in J.A. Mangan, *Athleticism in the Victorian and Edwardian Public School: The emergence and consolidation of an ideal* (Cambridge: Cambridge University Press, 1981). See especially Chapter One.
14. John Chandos, *Boys Together: The English Public School 1800–1864* (London: Yale University Press, 1984), is outstandingly good on the conditions of vice and violence which characterised the pre-1850 unreformed public schools.
15. See Mangan, *Athleticism in the Victorian and Edwardian Public School*.
16. For an outline of the utilitarianism of the concept of 'fair play' and possibilities regarding its modern relevance, see J.A. Mangan, 'Sport: Competition, Fair Play, Commercialism'. Presentation delivered at 'The Sports Business in Tomorrow's World', an international conference on world sports management organised by Georgia Institute of Technology at Atlanta, Georgia, October 1994.
17. See Mangan, 'Social Darwinism and Upper Class Education...', pp.152–3.
18. Newsome, *Godliness and Good Learning*, p.197.
19. Ibid., p.210.
20. Quoted in Newsome, *Godliness on Good Learning*, p.213.
21. Ibid., p.215.
22. Ibid., p.216.
23. Ibid.
24. See John Lucas, *England and Englishness* (London: The Hogarth Press, 1990), p.76.
25. See Mangan, *Athleticism in the Victorian and Edwardian Public School*, p.26.
    Newsome, *Godliness and Good Learning*, p.226.
27. See Mangan, *Athleticism in the Victorian and Edwardian Public School*, Chapters One to Four.

28. Newsome, *Godliness and Good Learning*, pp.224–5.
29. Mangan, *Athleticism in The Victorian and Edwardian Public School*, p.68.
30. Ibid.
31. See J.A. Mangan, 'Duty unto Death: English Nationalism, Militarism and Masculinity in the Era of the New Imperialism', in J.A. Mangan (ed.), *Tribal Identities: Nationalism, Europe, Sport* (London: Frank Cass, 1995), for a discussion of the role of juvenile literature in this transformation.
32. Quoted in Newsome, *Godliness and Good Learning*, p.221.
33. Ibid., p.201.
34. Quoted in Mangan, 'Sport: Competition, Fair Play, Commercialism', 4.
35. Price Collier, *England and the English from an American Point of View* (London: Duckworth, 1913), p.213.
36 See Mangan, 'Sport: Competition, Fair Play. Commercialism', 1.
37. Ibid.
38. Mangan, 'Social Darwinism and Upper Class Education', p.135.
39. Ibid.
40. John Lowerson, *Sport and the English Middle Classes* (Manchester: Manchester University Press, 1993), p.70.
41. Ibid., p.72.
42. Ibid., p.73.
43. Arnold Lunn, *The Harrovians* (London: Methuen, 1913), p.110.
44. Ibid., p.140.
45. See, for example, the description of the Sudan Political Service, Chapter Four, J.A. Mangan, *The Games Ethic and Imperialism* (Harmondsworth: Viking/Penguin, 1986).
46. From Francis Duckworth, *From a Pedagogue's Sketch Book* quoted in James A. Mangan, 'Ethics and Ethnocentricity: Imperial Education in British Tropical Africa', in William J. Baker and James A. Mangan (eds.), *Sport in Africa: Essays in Social History* (New York: Holmes and Meier, 1987), p.138.
47. Newsome, *Godliness and Good Learning*, p.238.
48. Ibid.
49. See Mangan, 'Duty Unto Death', passim.
50. Ibid., passim.
51. See 'Duty Unto Death', passim. See also J.A. Mangan, 'Gamesfield and Battlefield: A Romantic Alliance in Verse and the Creation of Militaristic Masculinity', in J. Nauright and T. Chandler (eds.), *Making Men: Rugby and Masculine Identity in Britain and Its Empire* (London: Frank Cass, 1996).
52. J.A. Mangan, 'Moralists, Metaphysicians and Mythologists: the "Signifiers" of a Victorian and Edwardian Sub-Culture', in Susan J. Bandy (ed.), *Coroebus Triumphs* (San Diego: San Diego, University Press, 1988), p.143.
53. Ibid., p.144.
54. Ibid.
55. Just how pervasive is illustrated by the description provided by my wife Doris Mangan of her aunt, Margaret Collins, who as socialist Lord Mayor of Newcastle once made it her 'party piece' at an official banquet and declamed it with pride and passion!
56. 'Tom' in Rev. The Hon. W.E. Bowen, *Edward Bowen: A Memoir* (London: Longmans, Green and Co., 1902), p.404.
57. See J.A. Mangan, 'Philathlete Extraordinary: A Portrait of the Victorian Moralist, Edward Bowen', *Journal of Sports History*, 9, 3 (Winter, 1982), 34.
58. Mangan, 'Moralists, Metaphysicians and Mythologists', p.146.
59. Ibid., p.159.
60. Ibid., p.161.
61. J.M. Roberts, *The Mythology of the Secret Societies* (London: Secker and Warburg, 1972), p.347.
62. Ibid.
63. Ibid., p.349.
64. Terence Hawke, *Structuralism and Semiotics* (London: Methuen, 1977), p.4.

65. See especially in this context Mangan, 'Duty Unto Death', passim.
66. 'England' (first verse) in Henry Newbolt, *Poems: New and Old* (London: John Murray, 1912), p.103.
67. 'Victoria Regina' (first verse) in Newbolt, *Poems: New and Old*, p.104.
68. 'The Vigil' (second verse), in Newbolt, *Poems: New and Old*, p.80.
69. Ibid. (fifth verse), p.81.
70. 'The King of England' (second verse) in Newbolt, *Poems: New and Old*, p.105.
71. 'Hymn' (seventh verse) in Newbolt, *Poems: New and Old*, p.211.
72. 'The Guides at Cabul' in Newbolt, *Poems: New and Old*, p.66.
73. Ibid. (first verse), p.65.
74. 'Sacramentum Supremum' (first verse) in Newbolt, *Poems: New and Old*, p.75.
75. 'The Non-Combatant' in Newbolt, *Poems: New and Old*, p.74.
76. Ibid.
77. 'Ionicus' (first verse) in Newbolt, *Poems: New and Old*, p.72.
78. Ibid., p.73.
79. 'The Best School of All' (chorus) in *Newbolt, Poems: New and Old*, p.101.
80. Ibid. (second verse), p.102.
81. Ibid. (second verse), p.101.
82. See Mangan, 'Moralists, Metaphysicians and Mythologists', p.146.
83. 'The Schoolfellow' in Newbolt, *Poems: New and Old*, p.89.
84. Mangan, 'Moralists, Metaphysicians and Mythologists', p.146.
85. 'On Spion Kop' in Newbolt, *Poems: New and Old*, p.90.
86. 'Clifton Chapel' (second verse) in Newbolt, *Poems: New and Old*, p.76.
87. Ibid. (fourth verse), p.77.
88. 'Vitaï Lampada' (first and second verses) in Newbolt, *Poems: New and Old*, p.78.
89. Ibid. (third verse), p.79.
90. 'The School at War' (first, third and fourth verses) in Newbolt, *Poems: New and Old*, p.91.
91. 'He Fell Among Thieves' (seventh and eighth verses) in Newbolt, *Poems: New and Old*, p.70.
92. 'Peace' in Newbolt, *Poems: New and Old,* p.94.
93. Harry Desmond is the schoolboy hero in H.A. Vachell, *The Hill*, a novel of schoolboy life at Harrow just prior to the Boer War. Desmond dies in the war, bravely leading his men in a charge.
94. See Mangan, 'Duty unto Death' for a consideration of this combined 'rhetoric' and its influence.
95. Mangan, 'Duty unto Death'.
96. Sir Derek Birley, *Playing The Game: Sport and British Society 1914–1945* (Manchester: Manchester University Press, 1995).
97. See Mangan, 'Duty unto Death'.

Cricket and Englishness:
The Batsman as Hero

RICHARD HOLT

Cricket in England, though not elsewhere in the United Kingdom, was far more than a game. This sport, which spread widely in nineteenth-century England, baffled Europeans. It was something uniquely English, shared only with those who had left the mother country for remote parts of the Empire or like Indian princes had been educated at public schools. There was more to cricket than a technical appreciation of its complex tactics and peculiar terms. Understanding the centrality of cricket in English culture, especially from the late nineteenth century to the 1960s, meant understanding something significant about the Englishness of the male half of the population, though cricket attracted female spectators too. For a young man wishing to make his way in the English sporting world, cricket offered a unique route to national renown.[1]

Why cricket? Why 'unique'? Cricket, it must be stressed, was unlike other sports not only in the way it acquired a moral vocabulary and called up images of a vanishing pastoral England but because by the later nineteenth century it was no longer confined to certain social groups or regions. It was *the* English national sport. Cricket spread from the eighteenth-century gentry and their country house teams of servants to the growing Victorian middle classes and industrial workers of the cities, covering most of the country. The winter sport of football was divided from the outset into 'association' and 'rugby' codes whilst rugby itself was further split both socially and regionally in the 1890s into northern working-class and southern middle-class formations; and association football for all its great success did not attract a significant non-working-class audience until well after the Second World War. Cricket was the universal English summer game and great cricketers were truly national figures in a way other sportsmen were not. The English Eleven were far more closely and widely followed than national football or rugby teams. Cricket was to the English what rugby came to be for the Welsh – a way of defining their identity and knowing themselves.[2]

Only certain kinds of cricketer could become heroes. There was an unfairness at the heart of this sport that came to pride itself on its sense of fair play. Those who toiled long and hard as bowlers seldom received the kind of acclaim enjoyed by batsmen, especially the opening batsman, who strode majestically from the pavilion to the wicket in his whites with bat in hand. The name of probably the greatest English bowler of all time, S.F. Barnes, is little known to later generations of cricketers let alone to the general public. Why were batsmen the heroes when the best cricket brains knew it was bowlers who won matches? Partly, of course, as in baseball where the hitters also fared better than the pitchers, it was the man with the bat who had to face the combined might of the fielding side; it was the man with the bat who could play the graceful, attacking strokes or resolutely defy the collective will of the opposition; it was the man with the bat who had to face a hard leather ball often at very high speed hurtling at him with no protection for the upper body. Batting called for bravery, as any schoolboy who had walked out to the wicket knew – and a large proportion of the modern audience for cricket was made of up those who had played the game at school. And a man who could not only tame the ferocity of a fast bowler but keep a calm and graceful demeanour whilst doing so was the stuff of English heroism. Batting required more courage and less strength than bowling and predictably batting came to be much more closely associated with the social elite than bowling. Batting acquired public school prestige. The English heroic ideal in cricket, despite regional variations which were especially important in Yorkshire, gradually came to require a man to display grace, quiet authority, unruffled calm under attack, elegance, modesty and integrity.[3]

The cricketer as hero did not spring fully formed into the English cultural landscape; there were three broadly distinct but overlapping eras of English cricket, during which both the game itself and the heroic ideal were defined and elaborated. First, there were the pioneer figures, the folk heroes not just of cricket but of pugilism and horse-racing whose names were well known before the era of the mass press, especially those mid-Victorian cricketers like William Clarke, Alfred Mynn and George Parr; it was W.G. Grace, the great hero of English cricket but far from its subsequent heroic ideal, who bridged the gap between the first and second ages of cricket as the sport was taken over by a mixture of upper- and middle-class amateurs who elaborated new rules and codes of conduct between the 1860s and the 1880s; the late Victorian and Edwardian years were the age of the amateur hero *par excellence*, of C.B. Fry, A.C. MacLaren, 'Ranji', F.S. Jackson and others; this era ended after the First World War as 'gentlemen' gave way to 'players' as the best batsmen. Yet this new breed of professional hero was a man whose example showed his respect for the forms and values of the preceding amateur age. These men – Hobbs, Woolley, Sutcliffe, Hammond, Hutton and Compton, for example – were symbols and role models of a new suburban England. The English gradually came to like their heroes to be unexceptional people, modest, respectable and rather ordinary off the field but calm and courageous with an aristocratic sense of command and grace when playing – a peculiar accommodation between the aristocratic and democratic principles which ran widely through English life. It was the relationship between the two that gave the English sporting hero his distinctiveness, and this was true not only of great batsmen, of course, but of footballers such as Stanley Matthews and Bobby Charlton too.

Early Sporting Heroes

It had not always been thus. Earlier cricketers, despite considerable fame, had not enjoyed the wide public esteem characteristic of national heroes. Cricket was less central to the emerging national identity in its first century as an organized sport than it was to become in the late Victorian and Edwardian 'Golden Age'. The heroes of Georgian and early Victorian England – and, as Linda Colley has powerfully argued, of an emergent sense of Britishness – were mostly military: Wolfe at the battle for Quebec, Nelson at Trafalgar and Wellington triumphant at Waterloo.[4] Great sporting figures were of some limited patriotic significance but they were not required to be virtuous; pugilists like Jack Broughton, who introduced gloves, 'rounds' and other changes in the eighteenth century, may have been England's first national sporting hero. But neither he nor his successors, such as 'Gentleman' Jackson, who would hold an opponent's hair with one hand and pummel his face with the other, could be described as 'Arnoldian' embodiments of decent manliness. Pierce Egan's *Boxiana*, however, did much to establish boxers as national celebrities and revealed the importance of the pen in the business of making heroes.[5] Jockeys could hardly be called moral heroes but their fame was indisputable within the aristocracy and the gambling public. Fred Archer was nearly as well known as W.G. Grace in the 1880s. His wedding in 1883 was attended by thousands and, according to *The Times*, Archer's suicide after the early death of his bride produced a 'sense of shock and almost personal loss to millions'.[6] There were regional heroes like the Tyneside oarsman Harry Clasper, whose races were followed avidly on the banks of the Tyne and whose funeral filled the streets of Newcastle to capacity; and Abraham Cann, from a Devonian wrestling family, whose exploits were famous throughout the south-west and who counted Lord Palmerston among his admirers.[7]

It was out of this world of essentially local heroes that the early cricketers emerged. At first they were only known in their counties but over the course of the first half of the nineteenth century, notably from the 1840s onwards, they began to acquire national status as the new rail network facilitated the movement of teams and the distribution of newspapers.

Originally cricket was a 'patronized' sport like pugilism and racing where gentlemen would put together teams to challenge others, often for quite high stakes. The intermittent nature of matches and the amounts wagered were not conducive to creating heroes. Some of the outstanding aristocratic players were notorious rather than celebrated in a positive heroic sense. The Reverend Lord Frederick Beauclerk was the best player of the early nineteenth century but was arrogant and said to be willing even to back the opposition against his own team to win a bet.

John Nyren, the first chronicler of cricket, came closest to creating the first folk heroes in his famous account of *The Cricketers of My Time, or Recollections of the Most Famous Old Players* which was published near the end of his life in 1833 and recalled the great days of the Hambledon club in the later eighteenth century. A mixture of nobles and local farmers rub shoulders in a work which at a very early stage showed the importance of the pen in creating as well as chronicling the sporting hero. In this case the cricketers were an intriguing collection of 'characters' who played for what was the leading club side of the day: Tom Walker 'with skin like the rind of an old oak', John Small, Tom Suter, George Lear, the long stop, 'as sure of the ball as if he had been on a sand bank' and Harris 'the best bowler who ever lived'.[8]

Nyren was the first of a series of cricket writers stretching through to the interwar years and Neville Cardus, who made it their business to present cricketers as heroic figures, casting their reflections in a nostalgic, elegiac tone. Most famous of the mid-nineteenth-century chroniclers was Nicholas Wanostrocht, better known as 'Felix', a schoolmaster and fine left-handed batsman who played for Kent and for the Gentlemen against the Players in the 1830s and 1840s. *Felix on the Bat* appeared in 1845 and helped publicise Alfred Mynn, a large and genial man, the fourth son of a gentleman farmer, whose performances as an all-rounder brought him fame. Playing for the South against the North in 1836 – a popular fixture at the time which gave a national dimension to individual fame – he made 146 despite being so grievously hit on the unpadded front leg that it was feared the leg might have to be amputated. Mynn's reputation as good humoured and unflappable made him perhaps the first popular cricketing hero.[9] He was a majestic twenty stone man, the subject of the game's first verse panegyric and the only cricketer to have been heard of in France, where he was allegedly hailed, 'Voila le Grand Mynn'.[10]

Of those born around the turn of the century like Mynn, there were several others who approached similar levels of public recognition. Fuller Pilch, the son of a Norfolk tailor, who began playing for the Bury St. Edmund's Club but moved to Kent in 1835, was probably the best batsman of his day and could draw crowds of up to twenty thousand; then there was Frederick Lillywhite, known as the 'Nonpareil', the outstanding bowler of his age, who first came to Lord's when he was past thirty and enjoyed a further twenty or so seasons conceding no more than seven runs a wicket. Perhaps most influential of all, if not the most heroic performer, was a former bricklayer, William Clarke of Nottingham, who in 1846 formed the first All England Eleven – a team which played exhibition matches throughout England and brought the names of Pilch and others to a wider public. Clarke made the name of George Parr, Pilch's successor as the leading English batsman, very well known in the mid-Victorian period. Parr, one of nine children of a Nottinghamshire yeoman farmer, took over running the All England Eleven on Clarke's death in 1856 and led the first overseas cricket tour in 1859 to the United States and Canada. Just as 'Felix' helped to make the name of Mynn, so Richard Daft, who played with Parr, later recorded his achievements in books of early cricket reminiscence. From the start, great cricketers needed cricket writers to transform great performances into heroic myths. With *The Doings of the Eleven, Being a true, full and particular account of the campaigns of 1851 and 1852*, a collection of articles from *Bell's Life*, 'Felix' did for cricketers what Egan had earlier done for the pugilists.[11]

Rapid technological change and declining folk traditions combined to prepare the way for cricketers to emerge as heroes in a more mobile, urban, literate society where the oral transmission of the heroic was giving way to the written. Within a generation Mynn, Pilch and others would find their way into Sir Leslie Stephen's *Dictionary of National Biography* – cricketers with 26 entries, well ahead of boxers with 21 and jockeys with 13. Though nationally known, these early players were strongly rooted in their counties, transitional figures tending to be seen either like Mynn or Parr as countrymen, tall, broad, decent, 'Roast Beef of Old England' specimens or the skilled, wily, supremely determined players like Clarke and Lillywhite who had risen from humble origins. Though not yet expected to be the moral figures of late Victorian legend, the pressure of public scrutiny, which so moulded the behaviour of so many later players, was already there. Fame had its price, as 'Felix' observed in his farewell speech at Lords in 1851. 'Though strange it may appear', he wrote, 'the more you succeed by a principle of action unimpeachable and true, just so will you provoke the envy and slander of your fellow creatures'.[12] Being a hero was never easy and there were always those waiting to knock the hero off his pedestal. But these early Victorians had less far to fall. It was the next generation who made cricket into a test of national character and placed the performer on a moral pinnacle.

The Amateur as Hero

The rise of the cricketer as an English heroic type – or more precisely of the gentleman batsman as hero – was in one sense almost a by-product of Splendid Isolation. The detachment of Britain from a military role in Europe led to a shift from a focus on great soldiers who fought the French or politicians who stood up to them – like William Pitt whose legend inspired the foundation of the patriotic Pitt Clubs – to the growth of Empire based on good colonial government and the spread of British values. Of course, Victorian public school sportsmen were a robust lot who valued strength and were quite prepared to fight.[13] Newbolt's famous Edwardian poem 'Vitaï Lampada' was an explicit recognition of the value of cricket for training in battle, and sport was saturated with expansionist imperial and Darwinist concerns. However, these underlying concerns were increasingly mixed with ideals of sporting morality and fair play, which were most fully developed in the game of cricket. Cricket was a form of highly organized competition in which the rules of play and its etiquette were elevated into a new civic ideal of vigour, integrity and flair. Underlying this efflorescence of the amateur was what Veblen aptly named 'the leisure class'. The astonishing growth in the economy and population of western nations, especially in Victorian Britain, had created a large new group of young men with the time and money for serious play. There were jobs in the City, openings at the public schools, journalism, and other avenues along with the frequent availability of family funds, all of which permitted a gifted sportsman to continue his enthusiasms at the highest level. The importance of this, as we shall see, became fully evident in the changed economic circumstances of the interwar years when a combination of wartime inflation and recession contributed to the decline of amateurism. Conversely, the amateur batsman enjoyed a final Indian summer in the persons of May, Cowdrey and Dexter in the more affluent 1950s before the formal distinction between amateurs and professionals was abolished in 1963.

The amateur ideal developed with the growth of public school sport in the late Victorian years and its finest exponents were not seen until the 1890s. From then until the outbreak of the first World War, a succession of gifted amateur players established themselves as the schoolboy heroes of what came to be known as 'The Golden Age'.[14] This was a world of standardized rules, 'immaculate' whites and rolled pitches; a world in which the gamesmanship of earlier times survived amongst professionals but was overtaken by the new imperative of 'playing the game' not just to the letter but in the spirit of the law, 'walking' from the wicket without questioning the umpire and generally acting with magnanimity in victory and graciousness in defeat, playing in an entertaining, attacking style without gambling on the outcome or receiving payment. Such was the full blown amateur ideal, ingeniously combining older notions of honour and chivalry with an evangelical belief in the purity and moral purpose of competition and physical endeavour.

Spanning the earlier Victorian exploits of Pilch and Parr and the turn of the century years of Fry, Ranji and Archie MacLaren, a single figure bestrode cricket like a colossus: Dr W.G. Grace. For once the cliché seems apt and unavoidable. Grace, probably the most famous of all English sportsmen and certainly the first national sporting hero, provided the perfect link between the early years of bumpy pitches, colourful clothing and professional touring teams and the new world of amateur cricket. Grace played his first game for the Gentlemen against the Players in 1865 at the age of 16 and his last in 1908 at the age of 58. In the 1870s he was still playing games for wagers with a touring side whilst turning out for his county as an amateur. Grace eventually qualified as a doctor and made a living partly from medicine and partly from the fees for overseas tours and generous expenses he was paid. He was never quite a gentleman himself, occasionally refusing to abide by an umpire's decision and forever chattering away in a high-pitched voice to the irritation of the opposing team.[15]

Grace was a hero through the sheer force of his achievements, his personality and his extraordinary longevity. He was far from the *beau idéal* of the perfect Englishman like Fry but rather a 'Grand Old Man'– his nickname in later years – a founding father, and both the pioneer and supreme all-round exponent of the modern game. For Grace was not simply the best batsman of his age; he was also one of the best bowlers. Lapses from the amateur code may have cost Grace the knighthood *Punch* and *The Times* demanded for him, but they endeared him to the wider cricketing public for whom he was both a great cricketer and a great character; he was instantly recognizable, 'one of the best known men in England', who represented a robust kind of old world Englishness of sturdy yeomen and hunting squires. His roots in deepest Gloucestershire and his vast, bearded, portly, scruffy presence offered a reassuring link with the past at a time of unprecedented social upheaval. A career of nearly fifty years during which he scored around 100,000 runs and took 7,000 wickets made him more than a hero; he was an English institution.

Although Grace was not a public schoolboy, he sent his son to Cambridge and in his later years fell out with his county over his affection for the purely amateur player. Yet Grace was equally at home with professionals and was one of the few amateurs to give them credit for their achievements. For the mythologists of this era of English sport, the officials and writers who both responded to public feeling and also shaped it, did not favour the top professionals who served their country well over many years. Leading professionals were left out of the unfolding story of sporting greatness in England's imperial heyday. Great batsmen like Arthur Shrewsbury of Nottingham, to whom Grace paid the singular compliment of saying 'Give me Arthur' when asked who of all his many batting partners was the best, was never lionized by the cricketing establishment or press. Similarly Bobby Abel of Surrey, who along with Shrewsbury was the most reliable and prolific opener available, was overlooked. The 'Little Guv'nor', as the Surrey crowd called him, was the son of a lamplighter from Rotherhithe. At one point only Grace had scored more first-class runs than Abel and yet neither Shrewsbury nor Abel made the *Dictionary of National Biography*, which, however, managed an entry for Allan Gibson Steele, who played well for Marlborough and Cambridge and appeared in a couple of early Test matches against Australia. W.W. Read, the Surrey amateur who played alongside Abel and was assistant secretary of the County for some time, was similarly noticed when the 'Little Guv'nor' was not.

Class division lay at the heart of amateur cricket in the Golden Age and set the terms upon which heroism was bestowed. The oral transmission of legend and the actual contemporary reputation of great players amongst the general public is now beyond our knowledge. We must hope the public was fairer and less prejudiced than the MCC or the cricketing and quality press staffed with men such as Frederick Gale, who had played cricket at Winchester before becoming a parliamentary clerk and spending much of his time writing on cricket for *Punch* or *The Cornhill* as 'The Old Buffer'. Equally influential in fostering the amateur ideal of greatness was William Justice Ford, a former Marlborough schoolmaster, standing six foot three and weighing seventeen stones, who once scored 44 runs in 17 minutes for Middlesex against Kent. He later wrote widely in works of reference like *Wisden*, founded in the 1860s, and was soon accorded almost scriptural authority in the assessment of a player's reputation.

Who, then, were the men from whom the myths of the Golden Age were made? After Grace, that looming presence from another age, there was the brilliant C.B. Fry who played for Oxford and England at cricket and headed the batting averages for several years. Fry also represented England at association football and earned a Cup Final medal with Southampton, played international rugby and jointly held the world long jump record for 21 years. Versatility in sport was particularly prized amongst amateurs for whom being a 'natural' was supremely important. Gentlemen were not supposed to toil for their laurels or at least not to make it too obvious. In fact, Fry worked very hard at his game as he did at his books, to become a sound Oxford classical scholar. The cricket historian H.S. Altham wrote that 'Fry could, alike in form and feature, have stepped out of the frieze of the Parthenon'.[16] He was a sharp critic of professionalism, although a great admirer of professional cricketers like Jack Hobbs who played in the amateur spirit. In his view professionals cared too much about winning whereas the amateur player should attack with a mixture of vigour and elegance. Above all – and this is a matter of prime importance – Fry was a master of self-presentation. For many years he ran a magazine which even bore his name. Whilst adopting the self-effacing outward form obligatory for the gentleman amateur, he assiduously cultivated his own legend and openly presented himself as a role model for the nation's youth through his association with the naval training ship *Mercury*, which he ran for nearly fifty years with his wife. Fry outlived his glorious youth, even meeting Hitler and expressing some sympathy with his racial ideas. He took the responsibilities of heroism seriously. He should have been content to let his remarkable cricketing achievements, which included six consecutive centuries and 3,147 runs in 1901, speak for themselves. But he blew his own trumpet and knew how to get others to play the same tune. This brought him great fame at first but became somewhat embarrassing later. Heroes have to know when to be quiet.[17]

Fry was a self-proclaimed *Boys' Own* hero who was apparently offered the throne of Albania after the First World War – an honour he both refused and publicized. No less remarkable in his way and a good deal more exotic was his batting partner at Sussex, the Indian Prince, Kumar Shri Ranjitsinhji, known to all as 'Ranji'. Ranji, who was a friend and admirer of Fry, learned his cricket late as an undergraduate at Trinity College, Cambridge, where he won a blue. He qualified for Sussex in 1895, scored 77 at Lord's against the MCC in his first match and became the first batsman after Grace to score a century in his first Test match against Australia; he topped the averages in 1896 and again in 1900 with 3,065 runs at a quite extraordinary average of over 87 runs a match. Statistics, however, no more account for the fascination with Ranji than they do for Fry or for Grace for that matter. It was the manner in which the scores were made that created the aura of greatness which solidified into heroism: the latent racism of imperial England was held in suspension by the glamour of his family and the brilliance of his style. For Ranji was supremely elegant: his 'leg glance' – a stroke he was said to have invented – was one of the great sights of turn-of-the-century cricket and turned by cricket writers into a myth of the Golden Age. 'From the moment he stepped out of the pavilion he drew all eyes and held them', wrote Gilbert Jessup in later years.[18] Ranji became an icon of Edwardian England, a symbol of how the spirit of the gentleman amateur could transcend racial if not social barriers. Ranji's status as an English hero was part of a reassuring and self-reinforcing cycle of mutual congratulation which bound the indigenous rulers of Britain's prize possession to the mother country. The fact that new research suggests Ranji neither paid his debts nor was quite honest in his dynastic claims only shows how effectively the Golden Age mythology took hold.

If Fry and Ranji have survived as the best-known Golden Age heroes, other amateurs were no less revered within cricket though rather less well known in the wider world. For heroism has its gradations and by definition extremely few can stay for long in the public mind. Among the ranks of cricket lovers, Archie MacLaren, was a compelling and charismatic figure. A cricket prodigy at Harrow, he went on to captain Lancashire and England. A.C. MacLaren was a commanding opening batsman, who scored a record 424 in a county match, and was famed for his attacking flair. Tall, handsome, even patrician, in appearance and autocratic in manner; he was a great player against Australia in Australia and a symbol of English energy. Though autocratic – his haughty manner angered the great professional bowler Sydney Barnes – he had a suitably modest side that showed itself on one occasion when he said of himself in relation to Victor Trumper, the marvellous Australian batsman, that 'he was an honest selling plater in the company of a Derby thoroughbred' – a suitably equestrian analogy for the patrician world from which he came. Like other legendary players, he lasted a long time, taking an MCC team to New Zealand in 1922, scoring 200 not out at the age of 51 though in the process sustaining an injury that forced his retirement. This was myth-making stuff and myths were duly made, notably by Neville Cardus, who confessed to experiencing 'the Grace of Art' through the vision of a single MacLaren off drive, thus ensuring that 'from MacLaren to Wagner the romantic gesture would henceforward be a sure and natural transition'.[19] Rarely has the process of hero worship been made so transparent.

Stanley Jackson had been MacLaren's contemporary at Harrow, where Winston Churchill was his 'fag'. As MacLaren was unfortunate in his business affairs, so Jackson – or 'Jacker', as he was known to his friends in the Oxbridge slang of the day – was triumphant, combining an exceptionally successful cricket career with becoming a colonel, an MP, Chairman of the Conservative Party and Governor of Bengal. He played for Cambridge and intermittently for Yorkshire, captained England to victory in the 1905 Test match series, and headed the batting and bowling averages for the series in what came to be known as 'Jackson's Year'.[20] A major factor in Jackson's popular success was that he played his best cricket against Australia, though like C.B. Fry, he was too occupied to tour for his country. Such was the paradox of the amateurs; they were loved for their selfless patriotism but frequently refused to play for their country when touring conflicted with their private business or personal interests. The public was supposed to feel gratitude that they gave freely of themselves when they could and were not supposed to mind that they could not always make themselves available. A strange sort of hero, perhaps, but the standards applied to amateurs were different; it was as if the public should be grateful that such accomplishments were even possible; the grace and spontaneity of the amateur exempted him from the more humdrum responsibilities of the professional, at least in the eyes of the educated classes.

Amongst others who achieved almost equal renown there was A.E. Stoddart, a tall, athletic stockbroker from Hampstead, who made his debut for Middlesex in 1885 at the age of 22 and scored 485 for Hampstead the following year. The season 1894–95 was a great one for 'Stod', who successfully captained England against Australia as well as the England rugby team; he was also good boxer, golfer, tennis and hockey player and horseman. Rarely has one man combined so many of the physical enthusiasms of land and money. 'In his small corner of the last decade of the nineteenth century, he was an idol; the choice of music hall songsters and light versifiers as the image of cricket'. If anyone had the makings of a hero it was 'My dear victorious Stod', as one ballad began, but his mother died while he was on tour in Australia and he later announced he was 'tired of first class cricket', left the game in 1900 with his health and business interests in decline and shot himself in 1915. The true English hero was not supposed to retire early or commit suicide and Stoddart's name declined into embarrassed obscurity. His sad end spoiled the legend as did the suicide of the greatest professional batsman of the Golden Age, Arthur Shrewsbury. For those like Cardus, whose poor Mancunian childhood was spent in awe of 'Archie' MacLaren and his like, the subsequent 'Golden Age' mythology, much of it emotion recollected in interwar tranquillity, was not to be sullied with suicide. Only the durable endured and 'Stoddie' slipped from hero to celebrity to has-been, marrying an Australian widow in 1906, taking a paid job at the Queen's Club' in 1907, running to fat – 'the ageing sportsman was simply an ageing sportsman'.[21] Athleticism and dignity in later years were vital to the true hero and batting heroes were supposed to grow old gracefully and rather slowly.

Gilbert Jessup saw no such diminution of his powers, and in his case power was precisely the word. 'The Croucher', as he was known on account of his squat, menacing stance at the wicket, was the most spectacular player of a spectacular age, scoring faster than any other leading player; his 53 centuries were made at the amazing rate of almost 83 runs an hour. Playing for 20 years from 1894 to 1914 he moved from Cambridge to Gloucestershire where he was the young partner of the ageing Grace. He was a competent fast bowler, too, opened the bowling against Australia at Lord's in 1899 and was one of the greatest fielders and throwers of a ball of all time. Jessup was not a classic amateur in the stylistic sense; but he fulfilled to perfection the requirement that a batsman should be exciting, and played one of the greatest Test match innings ever when England were in a desperate position against Australia at 48 for 5 with 273 needed to win. He came in and made 104 in 75 minutes to put his country in a winning position.[22]

Yet Jessup was no mere 'slogger'. Sheer power was not enough and the Croucher's agile footwork was famous. Attack with style was the watchword. Reggie Spooner was a great favourite with the crowds and the critics despite the fact that business commitments meant he never played in Australia and was often unavailable at home. He was the epitome of the public school sportsman who played rugby as well as Test cricket for England. From Marlborough he went to Lancashire where Cardus in his youth watched the man who could hit the most perfect cover drive – a stroke that must have been much in evidence when Spooner and MacLaren scored 368 in their opening partnership against Gloucester in 1903, a score which remains a Lancashire record.[23] Reginald Foster was yet another double international, who captained England at football and cricket, the only man to have done so,. He was the third of seven sons of a Malvern clergyman, who all played for Warwickshire – or 'Fostershire' as it was known for a while. Like Spooner, his hallmark was a seemingly effortless virtuosity. He scored 287 on his Test debut at Sydney in 1903–4, the highest score made in Australia by an Englishman at that time. Like Stoddart, business and illness intervened and he died young of diabetes but left a legacy of great stroke play that was assiduously polished in later histories.[24] Similarly, Lionel Palairet, another tall, poised public schoolboy, joined Somerset straight from Oxford and at the age of 22 shared a partnership of 346 against Yorkshire, driving the ball into the river and the churchyard at Taunton in a cavalier fashion that brought him immediate acclaim.[25]

Here were amateurs who could often keep professionals out of the national side. This is the essence of what the 'classes' admired about the Golden Age. In an era when the 'masses' were battering on the door of democracy, and organized labour was challenging private enterprise, when there were acute fears of economic and naval competition from Germany and nagging doubts about Darwinist racial deterioration, the cream of amateur cricket was a reassuring sight. In cricket the classes and the masses seemed by mutual consent to occupy their rightful respective places whilst the Empire was strengthened by sporting contacts. Professionals might provide muscle and consistency but amateurs were supposed to have the flair, the sense of command, the wider vision and aesthetic appreciation. They also practised a lot, or a lot more than they sometimes admitted. Truth soon became clouded in a haze of myth-making, myths largely made by the educated classes for the educated classes but which despite a blatant neglect of the best professionals contained a grain of truth; never before or since has the game been played with quite the same beauty and apparent abandon. For myths may well to have some basis in fact, especially in sport where performances cannot be faked; there is an intrinsic integrity in the spectacle. Fry, MacLaren, Ranji, Jackson, Jessup and company were great players of what was the first generation of mature Test and county cricket. But were they greater than the professionals like Hirst and Rhodes? Perhaps not, but they were not professionals. That was the point. They were supposed to be private middle-class citizens with the talent and energy to play as well as professionals, role models for the ambitions of the common middle-class man.

The Professional as Hero

A 'return to normalcy' was the cry after the horrors of the Great War, and not just for the currency. As England went back to the Gold Standard in 1925, so the myth of 'The Golden Age' was made. Neville Cardus explored the relationship between the 'style and personality' of the great batsmen and remembered MacLaren 'dismissing balls from his presence with the wave of an imperial bat'; Cardus's myth-making began in the *Manchester Guardian* and influential books of cricket essays began to appear in the mid-1920s just as the post war years saw an abrupt change in the fortunes of the gentleman cricketer of the Golden Age.[26] Yet the supremacy of the amateur was maintained in terms of the structure and conventions of interwar cricket. The sharp social distinctions between amateurs and professionals remained. There were petty differences such as the placing of initials after the name and separate dressing rooms and, more seriously, the unwritten rule that a professional could captain neither his county nor his country. The amateur retained the outward forms of superiority but the professional donned the game's heroic mantle.

The Great War, in Keynes famous phrase, spelled the 'euthanasia of the rentier'. Inflation, recession and not least the disproportionate loss of life and limb amongst junior officers robbed the amateur game of some of its most promising recruits. Of course, the greatest of all modern batsmen was an amateur and played from 1927 to 1949. But he was an Australian: Bradman, the torment of England teams; not an English hero but an intermittent idol of the English, whose duck in his final Test innings robbed him of a Test average of over a hundred and reduced the Oval to silence. England revered Bradman, who became the first active cricketer to receive a knighthood.

But the greatest interwar English cricketers were all professionals. Wally Hammond, the supreme attacking talent of the 1930s, renounced his professional status after eighteen seasons to captain England in 1938 but he can hardly be classed as an amateur in the true sense. Nor, for all his aggression and brilliance, did Hammond endure as an English hero, although he was a celebrity who played some heroic matches on his day. He eventually emigrated to South Africa, 'where he died, sadly a rather faded star'. 'See him while you can', *Picture Post* told its readers in 1946 when after more than a quarter of century in the sport he headed the batting averages with almost 85 runs an innings.[27] 'Lets go to see Hammond' was a familiar phrase and yet he did not endure as a hero. He was autocratic, too unpredictable a Test player and had a failed marriage and money troubles to boot. He was also socially insecure, the son of an indigent army officer, a grammar schoolboy, without the resources for private education or Oxbridge but 'choosing his friends among the amateurs, [he] distanced himself from his fellow-professionals and found it a financial struggle to keep up standards of dress and entertaining in the social ranks to which he aspired'.[28]

English heroes had to be at ease with themselves and the undisputed hero of English cricket – and of a broad swathe of the Home Counties – for much of the first half of the century had none of these problems. John Berry Hobbs, known universally as 'Jack', arguably fitted the particular English criteria for heroism more perfectly than anyone else before or since. He was as exceptional on the field as he was unexceptional off it; he played with perfect grace and unhurried effortless efficiency at all times against all kinds of bowling on all kinds of wickets; he broke almost all the records and often said cricket would be a better game if they were not kept. 'The Master', as he was sometimes called, was quiet, modest, elegant, dignified but not pompous; he was shy with a dry sense of humour and a taste for practical jokes; respectable without being stuffy, an Anglican but no evangelical he developed a successful sports business in Fleet Street; he was just the sort of man parents wanted their daughters to marry and in fact he enjoyed a long and happy marriage himself, caring for his wife, Ada, devotedly when her mind began to wander at the end of her life. He was neither clever nor especially articulate; Victorian melodramas were his preferred reading; he liked the music hall but drank very little.[29]

Hobbs was man of suburban virtues and a hero of suburbia, coming not from the ranks of northern industrial workers but from the southern manual service class – a neglected group in English social history – the eldest of twelve children of the groundsman of Jesus College, Cambridge. He was the first professional sportsman to enjoy the awe and respect of his fellow players, the liberal professions and the grandees of the MCC alike. He played cricket for Surrey from 1905 to 1934; he was the outstanding batsman of his age, scoring even more freely than Grace, whose total of centuries he passed in 1926 when well into his forties and toasted at Taunton with a glass of ginger beer. Jack was loved – the word here is not lightly chosen – both by his fellow cricketers and by the cricket public. 'Despite all the fuss and adulation made of him he was surprisingly modest and with a great sense of humour' was how his Surrey partner for so many years, Andrew Sandham, recalled him, whilst his Surrey captain Percy Fender called him the 'most charming and modest man anyone could meet'.[30] Fender's greatest problem with Hobbs was that Hobbs as a dutiful professional always insisted on due deference to an amateur captain calling him 'Sir' or 'Mr'. In the summer of 1926 when Britain was split by a General Strike, Hobbs in his mature later years and his new England partner, Herbert Sutcliffe, born in Pudsey near Leeds, the orphaned son of a publican brought up by his aunts, who played his first cricket in Methodist teams, were a reassuring sight, a relief from the strife and a cohesive force, a visible reminder of the shared bonds of an English sporting culture.[31] They were a pair whose virtues of northern grit and southern grace seemed to combine the perceived characteristic regional virtues of the English perfectly.

Hobbs was the first English professional sportsman to be knighted. The next was still a boy when Hobbs was at the wicket with Sutcliffe and remarkably came from the same small Yorkshire town as Sutcliffe. Len Hutton was the first professional to be allowed to hold the key position of moral and tactical authority within the team – an honour not awarded until 1953, the same year Hobbs was knighted. Hutton had established himself as an English sporting hero earlier than any other player when at the age of twenty-two he broke the record for the highest individual score in a Test match with 364 against Australia at the Oval. Hutton broke Bradman's record in the summer of 1938 at a time of mounting international tension. The sight of the Australian players clapping and gathering round to congratulate him, which filled the papers, offered a comforting spectacle of imperial solidarity. Here was an ordinary young Englishman at the heart of things, strong enough to bat on for thirteen hours. With the massive sport and leisure programmes of fascist Italy, twice winners of the football World Cup and Hitler's 'Strength through Joy' movement culminating in the Nazi Olympics, the English needed reassurance of their sporting superiority. Whilst Hutton's career was interrupted by the Second World War and the effects of a broken arm sustained as an army physical training instructor, he became the rock around which the post-war England team was built, winning the captaincy as class divisions finally began to break down. He looked the part, lean and distinguished, but this is where his resemblance to the amateur ideal ended. He was a professional to the core, ruthless in his pursuit of victory, not afraid to slow a game down to avoid defeat, a player in gentleman's clothing with just the blend of style and efficiency that England required. And in due course 'Len' became 'Sir Leonard'.[32]

It was, perhaps, easier to be a hero then than now. Reviewing the press coverage of cricket between the wars, Gerald Howat has observed that 'compared with a later age the press was more ready to create heroes than to destroy reputations'.[33] Cardus supremely but others, too, like J.M. Kilburn in the *Yorkshire Post*, a great supporter of Hutton, produced an influential collection of articles in 1937, which despite being less florid in style than Cardus was in its way no less elegiac.[34] The young E.W. Swanton began a cricket writing career in 1929 that spanned sixty years and there were the retired amateurs headed by none other than C.B. Fry, who wrote numerous articles and several influential books on the game. Writing cricket books became a thriving sub-genre of publishing, led by *Wisden*. Cricket fans would accumulate lovingly its yellow and brown bindings, a permanent record of the doings of the great men of the game. The pundits in their turn became heroes. Cardus had such a place and more recently, John Arlott, the former Hampshire policeman turned BBC poetry producer, wine enthusiast, promoter of English cheeses, biographer of Hobbs and a voice on radio and television that was synonymous with cricket for thirty years from the late 1940s. Brian Johnston ('Johnners'), the cheery boyish enthusiast, was another of these BBC personifications of Englishness; his recent death provoked an outpouring of genuine national regret led by the Prime Minister. These men were heroes of a kind and there was some ill-feeling when Arlott's son published a less than adulatory memoir of his father.[35] The BBC commentary teams came to be as much a part of the English summer as the BBC itself became part of English life, defining and shaping sporting values from the 1930s through to the 1960s, after which the increasingly sensational tabloid coverage of sport changed the terms of the debate.

Earlier heroes had the advantages without the disadvantages of extensive media coverage. From the 1920s on Hobbs, Sutcliffe, Hammond and the rest could be seen on the news reels that accompanied films or in the 'news theatres' that sprang up all over the country and heard on the radio – a prime topic for future research. The press, film and the BBC brought the deeds of others to a wider public, too; Patsy Hendren of Middlesex was a great favourite, a jokey cockney of Irish descent, who scored 170 centuries as a mainstay of Middlesex and England for a great many years. A superb sportsman, he played football for Brentford and Manchester City and once for England in the Victory international of 1919. Too stocky and unorthodox to look like a classic amateur, he caught the attention of the public as a character, a reversion to the older kind of folk hero, a clown, a stout performer and a nice man. Hendren was much loved though he did not fit the mould of the classic hero.

On the other hand, Frank Woolley, the tall and handsome Kent left hander, who played from 1906 to 1938 in a graceful cavalier fashion and scored nearly 60,000 runs, was a more striking figure. Beginning his career as Woolley departed, Denis Compton, another dashing batsman of striking good looks, who played, like an amateur of the Golden Age, not just marvellous cricket but on the wing for Arsenal and England, caught the public eye. His 3,816 runs at an average of over 90 in the summer of 1947 came to be seen as symbol of a post-war English renaissance.[36] His partner for Middlesex and often for England was Bill Edrich, who scored almost as freely as Compton and managed to open as a fast bowler as well. David Frost, the television personality and entrepreneur, remembered seeing them destroy the South Africans: 'Compton was a tremendously elegant figure, handsome, debonair...But Bill Edrich was my hero...short, stockily built, gutsy...I knew everything about him, in the way that children memorise statistics and facts'.[37] Cricket had heroic partnerships as well as heroes. Hobbs and Sutcliffe, the southern willow and the northern oak; Compton and Edrich, the professional as amateur and the professional as professional. Six years later in the Coronation year, Edrich was at the other end of the wicket when Compton scored the winning runs against Australia to take the Ashes for the first time in twenty years. The crowds flooded on to the Oval, and tens of thousands more watched for the first time on television, standing in little groups around the shop windows where the new sets were on show or clustering in darkened livings rooms as the monochrome images 'flickered to and fro'.

These cricket heroes were ordinary men. Few of them had notable war records; Hobbs did not enlist for service citing responsibilities to his widowed mother and large family as a reason and eventually was conscripted as an aircraft mechanic. Sutcliffe was in the Green Howards but never saw action and Hammond was just too young. There is no suggestion here of lack of patriotism; it is the lack of patriotic display set against the conscious imperial relish that accompanied earlier amateur heroes that was striking. In the Second World War the best players were often used as physical education instructors with plenty of opportunity to play in matches to keep up morale on the home front and there were plenty of propaganda photos of sportsmen in uniform. Denis Compton, for example, played for Arsenal and for England as a footballer as well as displaying his batting talents. Hutton broke his arm not in battle but in the gym. There were, of course, plenty of fine cricketers who performed heroically in war; Hedley Verity, the supreme slow bowler of the age, for example, died heroically under fire in Italy in 1943. It is rather that a man no longer *had* to prove himself in battle to be a model for manhood. Sport was more or less demilitarized and distinct from training for war; in Britain the two had for long been more loosely associated than in continental Europe where the link was made more explicit and the military honours of sportsmen more prominently advertised.

The English batsmen who claimed so much of the public attention's attention between the wars and into the 1950s were distinctive in other ways, too: as men, in business, in their social attitudes and way of life – aspects which have naturally been more or less neglected in the sizeable literature that has accumulated on their play. What did they look like? Their physique, their faces, their clothes? For this group of great batsmen were for the most part strikingly handsome. Woolley was tall and looked like a film star; Hammond was handsome, divorced and said to be 'a bit of a ladies man'; Edrich drank very heavily – he was once carried home 'paralytic'at 5a.m. on the fourth morning of a Test – married four times and, in the euphemism current at the time, 'lived life to the full'.[38] Not all English heroes were as prim as Hobbs but little of this ever got into the papers which drew a discreet veil over the alcoholic and sexual exploits of leading players.

Physical beauty was mentioned, albeit in a brisk, dismissive masculine fashion. It was important that this attractiveness appeared quite natural; any hint that such a man had preened and manicured himself to appeal to women would have made him the immediate object of ridicule. Unlike their male counterparts in the cinema, sporting heroes could never be intentionally erotic; this was the province of a Valentino, a Fairbanks and Flynn and of women stars. And yet consideration of the attention paid to hair and clothes reveals a covert element of sex appeal which was passed off as good grooming or a proper fastidiousness. To admit they had appeal for women – as several of them undoubtedly did – would have been to forgo the image of decent manliness which they had inherited from the Golden Age. The Englishmen who modelled themselves on cricketing heroes by and large had a profound distaste for what was perceived as the Mediterranean style of male affectation; the physically robust but embarrassed and restrained Englishman was the antithesis of the gigolo. So cricketers like Sutcliffe became half acknowledged male icons of the interwar years. 'There was Herbert, black and blue and not a hair out of place', as Hobbs is said to have remarked, after a particular battering at the hands of the Australian attack.

Denis Compton, who treated the importance of his image as a male symbol with appropriate masculine contempt, nevertheless 'used to wonder how' his Australian friend and adversary Keith Miller 'got his hair so smooth as he brushed it back with that characteristic gesture of the hand ... until I discovered he had a tiny comb, about three or four inches, which he could hold in the palm of his hand as he smoothed back his hair, cleverly concealing it from the spectators and the players'.[39] A photo of Len Hutton's wax model being prepared in Madame Tussaud's revealed an assistant hard at work on parting the hair with the precision that male fashion required whilst another adjusted the blazer. Hutton, who came from the same town as Sutcliffe, could hardly match the 'glossy black hair and twinkling deep set eyes' of this Yorkshire Clark Gable, who according to his biographer, 'was worshipped by the girls'.[40] Yet Hutton, too, had a winning smile.

The dress code and etiquette of cricket allowed these men, and the countless others who watched them, to dress in a smart, casual summer style associated with wealth, good birth and leisure whilst not appearing to dress up. This killed two birds with one stone, advertising not just a man's physical vigour and attractiveness but suggesting a certain social distinction. 'Whites', as they were known, were all important and the adjective 'immaculate' the most frequently used to describe them. Playing in dirty or crumpled whites was unthinkable for the great players. Hobbs was always beautifully turned out and Hammond abhorred collecting green marks on his flannels but no-one carried the cult of the immaculate cricketer further than Sutcliffe. Hutton recalled how Herbert would 'arrive with a flat case in addition to the old-fashioned cricket bag so that flannels and shirts were kept spotless and creases remained razor sharp'; he even ordered 'consignments of silk from Thailand to make up into cricket shirts'.[41]

However attractive these cricketers were as men, it was crucial for their public image not be seen as 'womanisers' or 'philanderers'. Hammond lost public sympathy over his divorce and Sutcliffe bristled at a fellow player who hinted even remotely at infidelities on tour.[42] As relatively humble inheritors of the revived code of chivalry that underlay nineteenth-century amateurism, these men had not only to be 'sans peur' but also 'sans reproches'. The intense respectability of much of English life, especially in the broad spectrum of skilled worker, shopkeeper and amongst the middle classes meant that family values had to come first. Here Hobbs excelled above all others. His devotion to his wife Ada was well known and he looked after her lovingly and without much help towards the end of her life when she suffered mental illness. The only time he ever crossed swords with the authorities was when he asked for her to be allowed to accompany him to Australia at his own expense. Hutton had a long and seemingly happy marriage, too, and both expressed satisfaction that their knighthoods – the only two of the period – gave recognition to their wives. Sutcliffe's wife had been the secretary to he local mill owner and played an active part in his life. Hobbs was an Anglican and Hendren a Catholic and both went to church whilst Sutclifffe and Hutton were both brought up in the traditions of the Pudsey chapel. Swearing and drunkenness were taboo and Hobbs was known to discipline fellow professionals if they transgressed.

These men were perhaps unintentionally models of social mobility. Their wages were decided by their counties and well in excess of anything a skilled working man or even a good professional footballer could make if benefit matches, endorsements and other earnings were taken into account.

Hobbs ran a successful shop in Fleet Street and a telling photo of him leaving his house in Clapham shows a city gent on his way to the City.[43] Hendren, at the height of his career, was making as much as £1,500 a year and Hobbs in excess of this, at a time when £1,000 a year was considered a very good middle-class income. Sutcliffe also set up a shop but diversified into other business and made a good deal of money, buying a Rolls and a grand house on the hill overlooking his old home. Hutton moved south from Pudsey settling eventually in the London stockbroker belt and taking up golf, embodiments of that wider change which saw a gradual shift from the North to the South, from manual into service sector employment, and the certain self-conscious refinement that went with it. This was most apparent in Sutcliffe and Hutton, both from deepest Yorkshire. Hutton's 'polished tones' were evident in his Oval acceptance speech as captain of the England team in 1953 and Sutcliffe before him had surprised C.P. Snow who remarked to him that 'one would never know you had not been to public school and Cambridge'.[44]

Of course, these great players were quite unrepresentative of most professional players; their higher earnings enabled a significantly different lifestyle which removed them from the ranks of manual workers where most professional players remained. Nevertheless their status as professionals remained 'inferior'. It was widely believed in the 1920s that if Hobbs had let it be known that he wished to have the England captaincy, it would have been difficult to refuse him. Percy Fender, his county captain at Surrey, said as much. But Hobbs never asked either for the county or the England job despite having as shrewd a tactical brain as any in the game. Perhaps he simply did not want the responsibility; more likely he felt it was not 'his place' to hold such an office – and the son of a Cambridge college servant knew his place was to serve the Gentlemen, not to lead them. When Hutton was made captain of England for the 1953 series, he was still ineligible to captain his county; an absurd situation, which nonetheless Hutton accepted philosophically, commenting that Lord Hawke, who had run Yorkshire cricket for fifty years, had done 'much to set standards that the game would be ill-advised to despise'.[45]

These men were deeply conservative, attached to the rituals of the game and its divisive social traditions. At Middlesex, who played at the 'Headquarters' of the sport, Hendren thought that 'amateurs and professionals mix splendidly' and Compton, who followed him, observed, 'I never felt or minded the distinction though it was there quite precisely and I don't remember other pros minding it either'.[46] Although Sutcliffe made a good deal of money, kept servants and could have easily afforded to play as an amateur, he never did. But neither did he buy land and try to turn himself into a squire as was often the way with new money. Rather, like Hutton after

him, Sutcliffe sent his son to public school and it was William Herbert
Hobbs Sutcliffe ('Billy') who led the county as an amateur captain in 1956
and not his more famous father. Acceptance of the social order was central
to the status of English hero: Sydney Barnes and Cecil Parkin, both great
players who openly denounced deference, were too divisive. The
professional hero, as defined in the press and endorsed by the amateur
establishment of the game and its wider public, required and received
respect but he did not agitate for the removal of discrimination; several even
expressed some regret when the old arrangements were finally changed in
1963 and all players were henceforth just 'cricketers'.[47]

The English expected their heroes to be modest, reserved and thoroughly
respectable, preferably with long, stable marriages, sensible but not too
clever, prudent financially without ever being greedy or allowing the mere
pursuit of money to interfere with their loyalty to club or country. During
the first half of this century they have preferred placid heroes who did not
create scenes, decent and fair people; supremely talented and stylish on the
field and quite ordinary off it; the sort of steady man you might like for a
next door neighbour or a prospective son-in-law; working men who had
risen into the ranks of the middle classes, not rich but comfortably off. It had
not always been so. The early heroes of the game were more shadowy
figures, folk heroes who were only expected to be remarkable cricketers not
necessarily good men as well. It was the rise of the gentleman amateur and
the cult of fair play that turned sport into a form of moral education and set
up the batsman as a kind of idealized Englishman, striding to the wicket in
his whites, wearing the colours of his county or his country, to do battle as
knights of a new kind of chivalry. These were men who were self-
consciously unspecialised, often showing as much virtuosity off the field as
they did on it whether in other sports or in other walks of life. Dr Grace was
both the exception and the link, bestriding both ages, the father of the
modern game, a technical pioneer with sporting values that preceded the
rise of the public school model. The modern working professional, the
county or occasional Test match player owed perhaps more to the earlier
tradition than to his immediate amateur predecessors. Yorkshire cricket, for
instance, was a famously hard and gritty business which produced many
great players but it was only Sutcliffe and Hutton who fully transcended
their northern origins to become national heroes. The professional batsmen
who became model Englishmen in the first half of this century combined the
efficiency of the professional with the appearance of the amateur, drawing
selectively on both traditions to create their own distinctive style. Since
then, of course, the world has moved on. Sponsorship, media marketing,
perhaps even the public itself, no longer really want ordinary, solid chaps
who happen to be great cricketers.

NOTES

1. Cricket has a vast and rich literature in comparison to other popular English sports; there are many sound histories of the playing side of the game and numerous well-written biographies; however, there is no comprehensive social history and much of the literature is too concerned with the creation of Englishness through cricket to stand back and explore the process; Derek Birley, *The Willow Wand: Some Cricket Myths Explored* (London, 1979) remains a pioneering effort; C. Brookes, *English Cricket: The Game and Its Players through the Ages* (London, 1978) has a historical context and R. Sissons, *The Players: A Social History of the Professional Cricketer* (London, 1988) is valuable; the essays by Jeff Hill and Jack Williams in R. Holt, *Sport and the Working Class in Modern Britain* (Manchester University Press, 1991) are written from the social history perspective whilst W. Vamplew, *Pay Up, Pay Up and Play the Game* (Cambridge University Press, 1989) covers the earnings of players; the recent social history of *Victorian Cricket* by K. Sandiford (Scholar Press, 1995) extends the author's important work on crowds but appeared too late for consideration here.
2. D. Smith and G. Williams, *Fields of Praise: The Centenary History of the Welsh Rugby Union* (University of Wales, Cardiff, 1981) remains the classic analysis of a sport as the expression of national identity.
3. Derek Hodgson, *The Official History of Yorkshire CCC* (Crowood Press, Marlborough, 1989) is an excellent work of reference full of the distinctive myths of the county.
4. L. Colley, *Britons: Forging the Nation, 1707–1837* (Yale University Press, 1992).
5. D. Brailsford has written extensively and well on this, notably, 'Morals and maulers: the ethics of early pugilism', *Journal of Sport History*, 12 (Summer 1985).
6. Cited in R. McKibbin, 'Working Class Gambling in Britain 1880–1939', *Past and Present* (Feb. 1979), 174.
7. For Clasper see E. Halladay, *Rowing in England: A Social History* (Manchester University Press, 1990), p.19; for Abraham Cann, see entry in *Dictionary of National Biography* (Oxford University Press, 1921–2 ed.).
8. Passages from Nyren are quoted from A. Ross (ed.), *Penguin Cricketer's Companion* (Penguin, London, 1981).
9. P. Morrah, *Alfred Mynn and the Cricketers of his time* (London, 1986).
10. *Carr's Illustrated Dictionary of Extra-Ordinary Cricketers* (Quartet London, 1983).
11. R. Sissons, *The Players*, pp.15–27, covers Clarke, Pilch, Parr and 'Felix'.
12. Ibid., p.317.
13. J.A. Mangan's extensive body of work provides the evidence for this, notably *Athleticism in the Victorian and Edwardian Public School* (Cambridge University Press, 1981), but see also *The Games Ethic and Imperialism* (Penguin/Viking, 1986).
14. 'The Golden Age' was partly a literary creation as Birley observed in *The Willow Wand*; C. Brookes, *His Own Man: The Life of Neville Cardus* (London, 1985) explores a key mythologist and G. Plumtre, *The Golden Age of Cricket* (Macdonald Queen Anne London, 1990) is a well-illustrated short account.
15. W.F. Mandle, 'W.G. Grace as Victorian hero', *Historical Studies* (April 1980) summarizes much of the extensive literature on Grace; E. Midwinter, *W.G. Grace: His Life and Times* (London, 1981) is useful; see also E.W. Swanton's short essay in P. Hayter (ed.), *Cricket Heroes* (Bloomsbury/TCCB, London, 1990).
16. Cited in Martin-Jenkins, *The Complete Who's Who of Test Cricketers Revised* (Macdonald Queen Anne Press, London, 1987).
17. C.B. Fry, *A Life Worth Living* (London, 1939); see also Hayter, *Cricket Heroes*, pp.80–3 for a sharp profile by Alan Ross.
18. S. Wilde, *Ranji: A Genius Rich and Strange* (London, 1990), p.1 for a critical account; the standard work is A. Ross, *Ranji* (London, 1983); for a fascinating fictional recreation of the relationship between Fry and Ranji see Ian Buruma, *Playing the Game* (London, 1991).
19. M. Down, *Archie* (London, 1981); for Cardus see Brookes, *His Own Man*, pp.83–4.
20. A. Gibson, *Jackson's Year* (London, 1965).
21. J. Arlott, *John Arlott's 100 Greatest Batsmen* (Queen Anne Press, London, 1989), pp.245–7.
22. Hayter, *Cricket Heroes*, pp.138–42.

23. Plumtre, *The Golden Age*, pp.69–71.
24. Ibid., pp.77–8.
25. D. Frith, *The Golden Age of Cricket 1890–1914* (Omega, London, 1983), p.87.
26. Brookes, *His Own Man*, pp.96–7.
27. G. Howat, *Cricket's Second Golden Age*, p.279.
28. Ibid., p.270
29. R. Mason, *Jack Hobbs: A Biography* (London, 1960) gives a first hand sense of the adoration Hobbs inspired; John Arlott's *Jack Hobbs, Profile of the Master* (London, 1981) completes the process of canonization concisely.
30. Benny Green (ed.), *The Wisden Papers of Neville Cardus* (London, 1989), pp.103–4.
31. A. Hill, *Herbert Sutcliffe: Cricket Maestro* (London, 1991), ch.5 for the partnership with Hobbs; Hill gives a fuller picture of his subject than most cricket books do.
32. G. Howat, *Len Hutton: The Biography* (London, 1988) gives a full account which can be supplemented by Donald Trelford's impressive *Len Hutton Remembered* (London, 1992) and Hutton's own *Fifty Years in Cricket* (London, 1984).
33. Howat, *Cricket's Second Golden Age*, p.272.
34. J. M. Kilburn, *In Search of Cricket* (Pavilion,. London, 1990).
35. John Arlott, *Basingstoke Boy: An Autobiography* (London, 1990); Timothy Arlott, *John Arlott: A Memoir* (London, 1992) and D.A. Allen, *Arlott: The Authorized Biography* (London, 1992) attest to his continued significance.
36. Denis Compton, *End of an Innings* (Pavilion, 1988 with intro. by Benny Green).
37. *The Independent*, 11 October 1993, p.13 on the publication of *David Frost: An Autobiography* (London, 1993).
38. Cited in a review of A. Hill, *Bill Edrich: A Biography* in the *Times Literary Supplement*, 14 July 1995, p.12.
39. Compton, *End of an Innings*, p.105.
40. Hill, *Herbert Sutcliffe*, pp.97–8.
41. Hutton, *Fifty years in Cricket*, p.21; Hill, *Herbert Sutcliffe*, p.97.
42. Ibid., p.98
43. *Carr's Dictionary of Extra-Ordinary Cricketers*, Hobbs.
44. Hill, *Herbert Sutcliffe*, p.87.
45. Hutton, *Fifty years in Cricket*, p.139.
46. Compton, *End of an Innings*, p.194.
47. For a wider discussion of the amateur/professional relationship see M. Marshall, *Gentlemen and Players: Conversations with Cricketers* (London, 1987).

'Our Stephen and Our Harold': Edwardian Footballers as Local Heroes

TONY MASON

In the spring of 1948 the British actor Tyrone Guthrie went to see the Manchester derby.[1] He had never been to a football match before but he was impressed by the skill, speed and beauty of the spectacle. He was struck by the similarity between team games and the ballet, both dependent on the 'deployment of figures into a conventionally prescribed space'. In the case of ballet the rhythm was supplied by the music: in football by the movement of the ball. More germane to our concerns was his realisation that, as in ballet, film, theatre or concert, one of the great attractions of football was the magnetism of its stars. To the crowd, the home side, in particular, were familiar personalities often referred to by their Christian names. Spectators exchanged gossip about their exploits, careers and mannerisms and their form was minutely and often brutally criticised. It was obvious that this element of personality, hero-worship or star magnetism was a long-standing attraction of the professional game.

Historians and teachers of history have recently been accused of ignoring the heroic figures from the British past. Heroes should not be written out of history. They provide examples to be followed, people to believe in, inspiration to contemporaries and perhaps a slice of 'necessary fantasy'.[2] Nor do they need to be Generals or Prime Ministers, or other 'great men'. Local labour movement leaders, for example, or indeed any other 'ordinary' people who could do one thing supremely well and who excited many of their contemporaries, ought to be remembered. Sportsmen in general, and footballers in particular, seem to fit this concern. This chapter attempts to explore the relationship between two Edwardian footballers and their local audience.

Star quality in football players is obviously bound up with performance. Most people remember the spectacular, which is why some players preserve their reputation long after their careers are over. The ball artists, the goal scorers and sometimes the goalkeepers can be recalled with relative ease when it is much more difficult to remember the consistent defenders or the industrious midfielders. It is also a truism that footballers with very long careers have an advantage over those with short ones, although the 'shooting star' snuffed out by injury or accident is often a figure whose tragedy imposes itself on the memory.

Before 1914 football heroes were essentially local and their loyalty, reliability and 'steadiness' were prized qualities. They were part of the urban social fabric, unlike county cricketers who appealed to wider identities both regional, due to the county championship, and national, as a result of the already well-developed system of test matches between England and Australia or South Africa. Football had its home international championship but this was less important to the English than to the Scots for whom the annual match with England helped reinforce a Scottish identity. But it was the FA Cup Final which drew the biggest crowds and club football which fed parochial and civic pride and provided towns and players with hard-won celebrity. Every town had its football team and every club its local heroes. This chapter is about two of them.

Stephen Bloomer and Harold Fleming remain synonymous with Derby County and Swindon Town even though Bloomer spent four seasons late in his career at Middlesbrough. They were not exact contemporaries but their careers overlapped and for a brief period they were in competition for the inside-right position in the England team. Bloomer played for Derby in the First Division from 1892–93 to 1905–6, Middlesbrough from 1905–6 to 1909–10 and then Derby again from 1910–11 until his retirement at the age of forty in January 1914. He played 474 league games for Derby scoring 293 goals, and 50 FA Cup ties scoring 38 goals.[3] In addition he scored 28 goals in 23 international appearances for England, a record which remained unbroken until 1956. Harold Fleming played for Swindon Town in the Southern League from 1907–8 until 1923–24, eventually reaching 226 games in which he scored 148 goals.[4] Injuries and four years lost to war restricted his opportunities. He is one of only a handful of Southern League players to be chosen for England for whom he played eleven times scoring nine goals.

Bloomer and Fleming came from different social backgrounds. Bloomer was the typical professional footballer from the manual working class having been born in Bridge Street, Cradley Heath, in the industrial Midlands on 20 January 1874, the son of Caleb, a puddler. The family moved to Derby when he was a child. Fleming was born at Downton near Salisbury in the west country on 30 April 1887. According to a Swindon newspaper he was the son of a clergyman although his birth certificate lists his father's occupation as dairyman. Perhaps he later became a clergyman in one of those dramatic Hardyesque transformations. It does seem that young Harold himself was destined for the Church but he apparently gave up training at a Warminster theological college due to ill health although he remained an active Christian all his life. This was an unconventional background for a professional football player, although a small number of clergymen played for professional clubs as amateurs before 1914, most notably the Rev. K.R.G. Hunt of Wolverhampton Wanderers. Interestingly, football did not run in either family. Bloomer's father was opposed to his playing, certain that it would lead to injury and time off work, and he never went to watch until his son first played for England, at Derby in 1895.

Both Bloomer and Fleming learned their football at school where by the 1880s and 1890s the game had become part of the sub-culture of working-class boys and youths. Bloomer played at St James Elementary School in Derby between 1880 and 1886 before moving on to local amateur clubs Derby Swifts, for whom he scored 14 goals in one match, and Tutbury Hawthorn. It was not surprising that Derby County heard of his promise and signed him up at 7/6d. a week after he had scored four times in his first match for Derby reserves. By then he was working in a local foundry. Fleming began his organised football playing in Sanford Street Elementary School and was a member of the team which won the schools' league in 1898–99. He then went on to the Higher Grade secondary school and began work as a clerk in the offices of the Great Western Railway Company in Swindon. He played for the Staff Clerks Thirds and at St Mark's Theological College, Warminster, for both the Catechism and the First Eleven. He then played three times for Swindon amateurs before being snapped up by the professional Swindon Town. That he must have had a rare talent is indicated by the fact that he played only once for the reserves before promotion to the first team. Only injury and his religious scruples – he refused to play on either Christmas Day or Good Friday – kept him out of the team.

Stardom was all about performance and as we have seen from the bare outline of their career statistics both Bloomer and Fleming were regular goalscorers, and obviously, therefore, always attracted attention. Bloomer was Derby's leading scorer in fourteen seasons and Fleming was not far behind. Perhaps that was enough to confer heroic status in their respective communities, but we must probe further. In sport one needs to develop an aura; one requires that hard-to-define 'presence' which inspires confidence in those on the field and in the stands. Bloomer did not look the part. Harry Newbould, Secretary-Manager of Derby in the 1890s, said that when Bloomer first played he was 'pale, thin, ghost-like, almost ill-looking, he caused the Derby crowd to laugh when they first saw him'.[5] But of course first appearances were deceptive. Though slender, Bloomer was also muscular and benefited from the regular training the club had only just instituted. In his second full season Bloomer's 19 goals helped Derby to finish third in the league, its best position up to that point. In 1894–95 his equaliser in the last five minutes of the match with Notts County helped Derby avoid relegation. In 1895 Bloomer first played for England against a very weak Irish side and scored two of England's nine goals. In 1896 he scored five or four, depending which of the authorities you consult, against Wales at Cardiff in a 9–1 win and in 1901 four more against the same opponents at Newcastle. In January 1899 he scored six for Derby against Sheffield Wednesday on a very heavy pitch. These were spectacular feats but there were many others. During his reign Derby reached the Cup Final three times, including two years in succession, and Bloomer's goals were often crucial, never more so than in the semi-final of 1899 against Stoke at Wolverhampton. He equalised with a spectacular back header – all his own work – gave Derby the lead with a left- foot shot from a free kick and then ran through what was left of the Stoke defence from some way out for his hat-trick. The *Athletic News*, always seduced by irony and under-statement, summed up the performance thus: 'A man who scores all three goals for his side in a match of this sort is a bit useful you know.'

It is difficult to know what the basis for Bloomer's usefulness was without having the opportunity to watch him but contemporaries praised his speed off the mark and to the ball and he said himself that 'I always try to get there first.' This pace over the first few yards, such an asset to any footballer, was allied in Bloomer's case to near legendary shooting. With both feet and from any angle or distance and, crucially, with little backlift and, according to Ivan Sharpe, a colleague in the Derby side of 1911–12, using the boot close to the toe rather than the instep, in tight situations Bloomer could accomplish shots which others could not manage. It is thus of no surprise that not only was he a great goalscorer but also a good passer of the ball, both to bring his wing partner into the game and to provide penetrative through balls for the centre-forward. The best description of Bloomer the player was probably provided by Ivan Sharpe. He was not, Sharpe thought, a subtle or scientific player 'but he had the golden gift of splitting a defence with one arrow-like, pin-pointed pass. Just as he could make this pass while the ball was moving, so he could shoot with sudden touch. He scored most of his goals by *sudden* shooting.' Bloomer had few tricks and plenty of players excelled him in the dribble but 'rare judgement, inspired raiding and passing and sudden shooting sum up the story of Steve Bloomer in football'.[6]

Harold Fleming, like Bloomer, was officially an inside-right but he also played on the right wing and at centre-forward. In fact, he was rarely confined by the dictates of position; he was a roamer, a much more unorthodox player than most of his contemporaries, renowned for his dribbling and with a body swerve which gave him the ability to leave defenders standing or lying perplexed. For the Swindon supporters at least, he provided some of the most crowd-pleasing moments in football. Ball control and balance were the core of his skill. He also scored goals, in his first four seasons with the club 18, 28, 19 and 19 goals respectively, thus playing a major part in taking Swindon Town from fifth in the Southern League in 1907–8 to successive second places in the next two seasons and to the championship for the first time in 1910–11. Like Bloomer, he was a frequent scorer of spectacular goals, such as the one against West Ham in April 1913 when he met a centre from Jefferson and 'taking the ball in the air, fired the leather into the net with terrific force amid deafening cheers from the crowd'.[7] We have Fleming's own description of a famous last-minute winning goal which he scored against Manchester United in the first round of the FA Cup in January 1914. The modest description highlights not only the skill and persistence but also the luck which even the best players need.

> ... receiving the ball near the half-way line, [I] bore out to the right corner flag and then working inwards, tried to centre it. Completely misjudging the position of the ball, I semi-topped it, with the result that it ran along the ground, hit the legs of one of the defence, but – miracles of miracles – it came back towards me as I was following up the kick. Before anyone could get to the ball I had managed to make contact and the next moment the ball was in the net ...[8]

Charles Buchan, an excellent player himself, who played with and against Fleming, was very impressed by his play and borrowed one of his tricks for his own repertoire. 'It was to get an opponent on one foot by pretending to go one way with the ball, then suddenly changing direction and slipping past him on the other.'[9] That football is a team game is one of the older clichés but in the Swindon team Fleming stood out. He became their first and only player to be selected for England, one of only a handful of Southern League players to be so honoured. His first international was in April 1909 when he was chosen as a last-minute replacement for the injured Vivian Woodward. Swindon were at home to Northampton on that day and fifteen minutes before the start 'an intimation was conveyed around the ground to the effect that' Fleming was to play at Crystal Palace, news which was received 'with loud cheers by the crowd of 8,000 ...'.[10] Fleming played eleven times for the national side, scoring nine goals, and would probably have played more often but for the rough treatment he received in a cup tie with Barnsley in 1912. He was only able to play twelve times for Swindon in 1912–13.[11] One of his team mates later said of him: 'he couldn't head and he couldn't shoot [a strange opinion, this one!] but he had the most amazing ball control and body swerve I have ever seen'.[12]

Football heroes had to produce a regular series of eye-catching performances, especially at home in front of spectators keen to idolise. Without consistent heroic performances a player could hardly achieve heroic status. But the press was important in creating the star player. It is a commonplace that newspapers both reflected the popularity of sports such as football and contributed to it. Before the match the writers picked out the 'dangermen' and told the readers what to look for and expect. After the match, they provided a detailed account of what the readers had seen or had not seen, if the game was 'away'. Their judgement of who had played well, and who badly, influenced the public perception of 'heroes' and 'villains'. Sometimes papers conducted polls among the readership to find the most popular player, such as that organised by the Manchester Sunday *Umpire* in 1904: the unsurprising result on the eve of a Cup Final in which Manchester City were to take part, from a poll of 2,000, many doubtless denizens of Manchester and district, put Billy Meredith at the top. Bloomer was second.[13]

There was some difference in coverage between local and national papers. The local press concentrated on the doings of the local team and its players. The *Swindon Advertiser*'s emphasis was on the Southern League and it covered the FA Cup in any detail only while Swindon remained in the competition.[14] Fleming's benefit against West Ham was on the same day as the FA Cup Final and was given much more space than the climax of the English season. But local papers were anxious to use the comments of the national press on their team or their man. The *Advertiser* quoted the views of a selection of London papers on Fleming's performance in his first international extensively, as did the *Football Express* in Derby after Bloomer played against Scotland in 1907. This was particularly apposite as by then Bloomer was no longer a Derby player but, as the paper said, 'we still think of him as one'.[15]

Most importantly, of course, the press was first with the news. On Friday 16 March 1906 most Derby supporters were astonished to learn of Bloomer's move to Middlesbrough and the majority received the news from the *Derby Evening Telegraph* or from someone who had read it there.[16] It was also from that paper that four and a half years later they found out that he was returning to the Baseball Ground. This was a fascinating episode and tells us much about the powerful emotions generated by the return of the local champion.

By 1910 Derby were in the Second Division and having an undistinguished season. Bloomer's first match was against Lincoln City, not particularly attractive visitors but Bloomer was a very powerful magnet in Derby and on that October Saturday afternoon the biggest crowd of the season turned out, over 14,000. It was a partly stage-managed, partly spontaneous welcome for the local hero whose four seasons away and age – he was 36 – had done little to diminish popular expectations of him. As the teams came out the band played 'See the Conquering Hero Comes' and his reception by the crowd was – wait for the understatement – 'in the highest degree flattering'.[17] When he scored after about twenty minutes the 'enthusiasm of the crowd was aroused to an extraordinary pitch'. Much in his play recalled his former brilliance, notably the delicate passes to his right-wing partner and his potency in front of goal. Of course, some of his speed had been lost 'but his mysterious command of the ball and his sudden and unerring aim in front of goal all proclaim him still to be a genius'. No understatement there. Genius was also used to describe Fleming in 1914 after Swindon had beaten Watford 3–0 and his dribbles and crosses had led to two of the goals. 'Only the genius of Fleming raised Swindon from a very ordinary side.'[18] Both players clearly possessed an ability which raised them well above the commonplace, an ability to win or turn a match by a piece of inventive individualism.

In 1911–12, Bloomer captained Derby to an exciting promotion back to the First Division. In order to go up Derby had to win their last two games. The first, against Gainsborough Trinity, was won 4–0. The second was away at Barnsley on the Monday evening after the Cup Final in which Barnsley had actually taken part. Their team had only just arrived back from London when they had to take on the promotion favourites and it was perhaps not surprising that Derby won 2–1. A large crowd had assembled outside the *Telegraph* offices in the Cornmarket and great cheers greeted the news of the goals when they were posted up in the window. The team was due to arrive back at Derby station at 10.28 p.m. A large crowd packed Station Street and the Station approaches shouting 'Are we downhearted?' and answering 'No oooooo', as a night of jubilation and festivity got under way. Not only were the streets packed but so were the windows overlooking them. The train was ten minutes late but was greeted by deafening cheers, and when Bloomer and the team were recognised they were

> bodily lifted onto the shoulders of stalwart enthusiasts. The crush was too dense for a triumphal procession but a wagonette near the station was requisitioned and the players placed on it. The horses were taken out of the shafts and scores of willing hands dragged the improvised 'coach' towards the town.

The pressure was so great the vehicle came to grief at the post office. Several of the players, including Bloomer, were carried shoulder high to the centre of the town and eventually permitted to address the crowd from the balcony of the Royal Hotel. Bloomer had by this time lost his cap and what he said was not reported.[19] The press made much of his contribution to the team's promotion. At 38 and after 20 strenuous seasons he was the leading scorer with 18 goals and, as the local paper emphasised, he had every reason to be a proud man. If his departure to Middlesbrough had eventually led to

Derby's relegation, 'he had done his part in restoring lost laurels'. The press clearly played some role in this emotionally powerful demonstration but, with few police present, it appears now to have been a largely spontaneous welcome for a team of local heroes led by the 'champion of champions'. But it was the newspapers which gave a kind of added value to the events by reporting them in such detail both informing those who did not go (but who might one day think they had) and 'embalming' the experience for those who had been there never thinking it would be one day recovered and represented as history.[20]

Neither the supporters of Derby nor those of Swindon needed to have the genius of Bloomer nor Fleming pointed out to them but it was the local newspaper which underlined, reinforced and provided a language to discuss the star quality of both men and especially in the case of Fleming, to emphasise his wider meaning in the life of the town. At the end of the 1908–9 season, for example, the *Advertiser* published the following encomium.

> There is no doubt that during the past season the Swindon Town club has been very largely indebted to the popular inside right Harold Fleming. Never before in the history of Swindon has a local player been discovered who has more fully justified the confidence placed in him. Indeed, Fleming has done more than serve his club; he has brought honour to the town of Swindon by reason of the fact that his prowess in the field favourably attracted the attention of the FA in London ...

After that successful first appearance for England against Scotland Fleming was selected for the tour to Austria-Hungary and the paper welcomed him back under the headings 'Return to Swindon of Harold Fleming. The Continental Tour. Local Hero scores 3 goals.' Many of the paper's readers were doubtless relieved that he had 'returned looking wonderfully well and highly pleased with the trip'.[21] Fleming was awarded a benefit in 1913 and took the last home game of the season and though expressed in rather pompous terms, the paper's plea to the readership was sincere enough, that the match gave them 'the opportunity of showing in tangible form that admiration and appreciation of a player who has done so much to make Swindon famous in the realm of Association Football'. A good crowd turned out paying £135 with another £133 worth of tickets sold beforehand. He had been guaranteed a minimum of £350.[22]

Of course the performance and the press often reinforced each other most notably when Swindon knocked Tottenham Hotspur out of the FA Cup in the third round in 1910. The score was 3–2, and Fleming scored a brilliant hat-trick, two of which followed the individual runs and dribbles which were his hallmark. Anyone from Swindon reading the *Daily News* must have felt some swell of local pride.

> Harold Fleming is already a Knight of Football. When he succeeds to the Peerage of the game, as he surely must, his only title can be that of Lord Swindon. Already Fleming of Swindon is becoming Wiltshire's most illustrious figure of all time ... I have seen other players his equal in skill, and many others his equal in strength, but not more than 2 or 3 in whom these qualities are so enormously developed.[23]

Perhaps there was a touch of early tabloid exaggeration but the praise was sincere. Similarly the *Athletic News* was only being partly ironic in March 1914 when it headed a report of a Southern League game between Swindon and Gillingham missed by Fleming due to injury 'Five Goals Without Fleming'.[24]

'   If the performance and media notice of it are the two most crucial elements in the elevation of the pre-1914 footballer to star status, individual character was also a factor of some importance. As Tyrone Guthrie suggested earlier in this chapter, if one watches a team on a regular basis one feels one gets to know the players, and one has insights into their individual characters. One sees them react to good and ill fortune and to the ups and downs of a physical contact team game containing a considerable element of the unpredictable. You are able to identify those who play to the crowd, the humorists, the sulkers, those who never give up and those apparently easily discouraged when circumstances conspire against them.

Of course convincing evidence about what footballers were like in themselves, of how they got on with colleagues and opponents is difficult to come by save for the small minority who leave behind letters or autobiographical writings. Even among those a kind of freemasonry is often at work with few wanting to appear critical of former colleagues. Modern, often ghost-written players' autobiographies have to be read with a lot of attention to the space between the lines. There are very few of these for the Edwardian generation of professionals. So what were Bloomer and Fleming really like?

As we have already observed Ivan Sharpe played with Bloomer towards the end of the latter's long footballing life and he wrote later that

> ... our Stephen was a tyrant. He said what he thought, and if things were going wrong his partner had no easy Saturday afternoon. 'What d'ye call that? A pass? I haven't got an aeroplane! ...' He would extend his activities to the other flank of the forward line. I was there. I know.

If, after a breakdown in attack, one studied the crowd, the sky, or any other useful object out of the line of Bloomer's glare – as was the rule in the Derby ranks of that day – he would stand stock still, in the centre of the field, strike an attitude by placing his hands on his hips, and fix the offender with a piercing eye. If this glare, as was the rule ... was still ignored, he would toss up his head, as if beseeching the recording angel to make a note of this most awful blunder, and stamp back to his position in a manner intended publicly to demonstrate his disapproval.

Quite wrong, of course. Not good for the side. Not good for the alleged offender.[25]

The language of these complaints was almost certainly rougher too. None of that ever reached the contemporary press but in 1902 the Derby County Board of Directors were moved to criticise the 'strong language' used by the players both on and off the field. The President of the club was designated to suggest to them that success was more likely if they would encourage each other rather than abuse each other. It is not known if this had any effect.[26]

One of the legends, or simply the gossip, about Bloomer was that he used to prepare for important matches at home with a few pints of beer in the Cambridge Hotel close to the Baseball Ground.[27] It is interesting to note that he and another player were reported by the trainer for neglect of training and, 'attending at the ground when under the influence of drink' and suspended until further notice. But Bloomer was too important a player to be left out of the team for long and he was quickly reinstated though his colleague, Stevenson, was transferred. In February 1901 Bloomer was again admonished for neglect of training and insobriety. He promised to do better in the future and was fined £1. Later he was fined again for not training and being 'dissatisfied' and warned as to his future conduct. A month or so later he was back before the directors for a fourth time accused of insobriety and inattention to training. Once more he was severely admonished and once more he promised to do better in the future.[28] It could be that these actions were a kind of protest against the maximum wage which was instituted in 1901 and which probably cost Bloomer £1 a week, his salary of £5 being reduced to £4. It is not clear how much the regular supporter would know about this. The local press occasionally appeared to hint that all was not as it should be as on the occasion of those six goals against Sheffield Wednesday when, after pointing out that the match had been watched by the England International Selection Committee due to pick the teams for the North against South trial match, rather tartly concluded, 'it only shows what he can do when in the humour and we shall expect him to do better in future matches for the County when the International Selection Committee is not present than he has done recently'. Perhaps it was just a sour comment on the loss of form of a key player.[29]

Bloomer never said much about himself although he did put his name to several occasional newspaper columns in the 1920s. In one of these he confessed to the occasional cartwheel after scoring a goal but claimed that as he grew older he took successes and failures 'more philosophically'. It seems that he was more likely to show his frustration rather than his pleasure. When he wanted to give the impression that he *really* meant business he would further roll up his sleeves and spit on his hands. He was probably only sent off once after retaliating against Herbert Sharp of Everton, a good record when one considers the hard knocks which regularly came his way.[30]

As we have seen Fleming was from a different background, more rural and lower middle class and perhaps less subject to the frustrations of the professional footballer's lot. He was a religious man who never played on Christmas Day or Good Friday, was also teetotal and had had much more formal education than most of his Swindon team-mates. When he was first selected for Swindon Town the other players were said to have seen him as 'not of their kidney and not likely to be sociable because of his higher social status' and they had been pleasantly surprised when it did not turn out like that.[31] The evidence does suggest that 'our Harold' was a modest, unassuming, friendly chap, qualities which fit the invented character of English heroes, especially sporting ones. Although an individualist as a player, the charge of selfishness was hardly ever heard as the chairman of the club stressed to the AGM of 1909 when reporting England's 4–2 victory against Hungary in Budapest, news of which had just been telegraphed.

> And if Harold Fleming of Swindon had not scored one of those four goals he would be much surprised. At any rate, if he had not scored a goal himself, he had greatly assisted another player to score, for he was a most unselfish player (applause).[32]

There was never any suggestion that Fleming tried less than his best although he did miss a lot of games through injury. Like Bloomer he was always likely to produce the spectacular of which few others were capable.

But, as has often been remarked, the trouble with being a hero is that it does not usually last long and the fame and celebrity of most Edwardian football stars was short-lived. Moreover, nothing produces quite the same excitement and satisfaction as playing and giving up the game leaves a large gap not easy to fill. There is some evidence to suggest that Steve Bloomer did not find life after football easy to fill. He was very unfortunate in that after he had retired in 1914 at the age of 40 he was offered the job of instructor and trainer at the Berlin Britannia Sports Club. He arrived in Berlin three weeks before war broke out and stayed for three and three quarter years as internee in the Ruhleben camp. He was joined by a number of British ex-professionals as well as a range of other British and Empire citizens and a very sophisticated camp life was constructed. Bloomer and others played a very active role in the organisation of sport in Ruhleben with barracks cricket and football leagues the big attraction.[33]

After he returned to Derby he occasionally played for and coached Derby County reserves for a couple of years and then worked abroad coaching in Spain in 1924. He later worked as a 'general assistant' at Derby County which does not suggest a position of great responsibility. Rippon and Ward in *The Derby County Story* wrote that 'there were stories of heavy drinking but these were later refuted by members of his family'.[34] Mrs Bloomer died in 1935 and Bloomer himself died at the Great Northern Inn, the home of his daughter and son-in-law, on 16 April 1938. He had been unwell for some time and the then manager of Derby County, George Jobey and three other local sportsmen had organised a fund, supported by the FA and many of the clubs, which had raised over £500 to send him on a cruise with the hope of easing his asthma and bronchitis. He died three weeks after he returned from the trip. The funeral was a very spectacular one, a clear indication of the great esteem in which his football achievements were still held. Many members of the football world were there including old players like Billy Meredith. The cathedral was packed and large crowds lined the streets along which the cortege passed to the Nottingham Road cemetery.[35]

Harold Fleming had a different war to that of Steve Bloomer serving as a Captain in the 4th Transport Battalion of the Wiltshire Regiment. He was, of course, thirteen years younger than Bloomer and resumed his career with Swindon Town after an absence of four years. Along with the other teams in the Southern League Swindon were elected to the new Third Division South of the Football League. In their first match in the new league Swindon beat Luton 9–1, Fleming scoring four goals. But he only played one more full season. He remained an influential figure at the club and popular with the crowd. Although only playing five league games in 1923–24 he was brought back for each of the ties in Swindon's cup run and scored several important goals. He finally retired in 1924 at the age of 37. Readers of the Swindon *Football Pink* in all parts of Britain and the Empire contributed towards a silver salver and tea service as a retirement present. He died on 23 August 1955.[36]

Again there is a suggestion that he was not able to match his success on the football field with a similar one off it. His football boot manufacturing business failed in the depression but he opened a sports goods shop in the town which brought a modest living. He was also active as a coach to young players and made one of the early coaching films with which he toured Britain in the 1920s and which was sold to the French Football Association. Derby and Swindon were towns of similar socio-economic structures. Both were heavily dependent on the railway industry and engineering, and both had largely working-class populations. The main difference was perhaps that Derby was closer to the industrial heartlands of the Midlands whereas Swindon's hinterland was largely rural. It is not clear if that difference affected the way local enthusiasts saw the game. Both Bloomer and Fleming were essentially local men largely bred if not born in their respective towns. As we have seen, Bloomer came with his parents when he was young and Fleming was born in Wiltshire and was partly educated and for some time in his youth worked in Swindon. They were essentially local stars although both threatened to become national ones. Perhaps Bloomer, with his international records and well-known name, was a national figure by 1914. Certainly Gibson and Pickford called him the first giant of the game, although he was not invited to the FA's Jubilee dinner in 1913.[37] Fleming might have become one but for the lost years of the war. And yet it is surely no accident that they both remained closely identified with Derby and Swindon. Bloomer did move but returned to finish off his career in the town he obviously thought of as home. It would be interesting to know whether Fleming ever had the opportunity to play elsewhere. Of course, as well as economic, social and sentimental connections, the maximum wage helped to keep players 'local'. But both players seem to have identified themselves with Derby and Swindon. Those were the places in which they found fame and those were the places in which they stayed.

To local football enthusiasts they were 'our Stephen' and 'our Harold', important signs that Derby and Swindon were at least on the football map and able to attract the favourable notice of the football power brokers in London. Fleming provokes more curiosity because of his relatively unconventional background for a professional footballer. But his fame, as Nick Fishwick has pointed out, did not mean he could exert influence in other areas of life. His support for the Conservative candidate in the second General Election of December 1910 merely provoked suggestions that he should stick to football, and the Conservative lost.[38]

Fleming is remembered at the club by a small statuette made by a local sculptor which stands inside the main entrance at the football club. The inscription is revealing: 'To the inspiring memory of Harold Fleming, the great footballer and gentleman, who played for Swindon Town between 1907–1924, and was capped nine times for England'.[39] The stretch of road running from the County Ground to the Wiltshire hotel is called Fleming Way. Bloomer has no such memorials but his grandson recently sold nineteen of his international caps for £8,050 in order to start a fund to enable the local authority to erect a statue similar to those of Sir Stanley Matthews in Hanley and Jackie Milburn in Newcastle. It is not clear what the outcome will be.[40]

Edwardian professional football was an urban phenomenon and the players were local heroes representing the local community against all comers. They were part of a local, largely working-class football sub-culture from which there would be little possibility of escape until the abolition of the maximum wage, the dramatic expansion of international football and the diffusion of television. Bloomer and Fleming were essentially decent, steady, long-lasting and respectable, ordinary men with one extraordinary talent.[41] Bloomer and Fleming helped their teams to win and by their special skills made winning even more enjoyable. Perhaps the national curriculum should pay at least a little attention to local heroes such as these?

NOTES

1. The *Listener,* 29 April 1948.
2. See recent statements by Dr Nicholas Tate, the Government's Chief Adviser to the National Curriculum and Raphael Samuel in the *Guardian,* 23 September 1995.
3. He also scored 59 goals for Middlesbrough and in seven of ten appearances for England against Scotland. Most of these figures are taken from Gerald Mortimer, *Derby County: The Complete Record 1884–1988* (Breedon Books, 1988) and Anton Rippon and Andrew Ward, *The Derby County Story, 1884–1991* (Breedon Books, 1991).
4. The Southern League became the Third Division South of the Football League in 1919–20.
5. Quoted by Anton Rippon, *Derbyshire Life and Countryside,* 49 (Sept. 1984), 61.
6. Ivan Sharpe, *40 Years in Football* (1952), p.22.
7. *Swindon Evening Advertiser,* 19 April 1913.
8. Swindon Town F.C. *Handbook* (1948–49), p.12.
9. Charles Buchan, *A Lifetime in Football* (1955), p.22. Buchan's impression of Fleming's play remained strong because he included him and not Bloomer in his eleven old timers to tackle any team in the world. Buchan (1955), p.215. Interestingly, Fleming also pipped Bloomer by six selectoral votes to five for the England team against Ireland at Derby in 1911. Bloomer was then 37, Fleming 24. Rippon and Ward (1991), p.19.
10. *Swindon Advertiser,* 9 April 1909.
11. He often came in for such attention. Some Stoke fans shouted 'Knock Fleming in the bloody river' in 1912. For both of these occasions see Nicholas Fishwick, *English Football and Society 1910–1950* (Manchester University Press, 1989), p.84.
12. Quoted by Dick Mattick, *The Story of Swindon Town Football Club* (Barracuda Books, 1989), p.23.
13. John Harding, *Football Wizard. The Story of Billy Meredith* (Breedon Books, 1985), p.79.
14. Fishwick (1989), p.96.
15. *Derby Football Express,* 13 April 1907.
16. Middlesbrough were spending money in a desperate fight to avoid relegation and the previous year had paid a record £1,000 for the Sunderland centre-forward Alf Common. This led to a limit being placed on the amount that could be paid for a player. Derby received £750 for Bloomer. Middlesbrough stayed in Division One but were later fined for offering Bloomer an illegal inducement to re-sign for the 1906–7 season.
17. See *Derby Evening Telegraph,* 3 and 5 October 1910.
18. *Athletic News,* 23 February 1914.
19. *Derby Daily Telegraph,* 15 April 1912.

20. *Swindon Advertiser*, 7 May 1909.
21. *Swindon Advertiser*, 11 June 1909.
22. *Swindon Advertiser*, 19 April 1913. Swindon Town F.C., *Director's Report*, 4 June 1913.
23. Quoted by Mattick (1989), p.22.
24. *Athletic News*, 9 March 1914.
25. Ivan Sharpe (1952) quoted in Brian Glanville (ed.), *The Footballer's Companion* (Eyre and Spottiswoode, 1962), p.243. The suggestion is made in Rippon and Ward (1991), p.19, that Bloomer got through quite a number of right-wing partners because they did not come up to scratch.
26. Derby County F.C., *Minutes* of Board of Directors, 6 January 1902.
27. Rippon (1984), p.61.
28. See the Derby County F.C., *Minutes* 20 September 1898, 28 February, 15 August and 1 October 1901.
29. *Derbyshire Evening Telegraph*, 21 January 1899.
30. Rippon and Ward (1991), p.30.
31. *Swindon Advertiser*, 16 September 1910.
32. *Swindon Advertiser*, 4 June 1909.
33. *Thomsons Weekly News*, 18 July 1918. It would be interesting to know more about this. One of the inmates who later became a Canadian academic wrote a fascinating book about the camp community in which he concluded that the organisation of sports helped the internees to survive not so much by the playing and the watching but by the fact that 'they were playing their roles in a social world that had become as real and absorbing' as the one outside the camp. J. Davidson Ketchum, *Ruhleben. A Prison Camp Society* (University of Toronto Press, 1965), p.229.
34. Rippon and Ward (1991), p.19.
35. See the detailed reports in the *Derby Evening Telegraph*, 16 and 20 April 1938.
36. *Swindon Evening Advertiser*, 23 August 1955.
37. Alfred Gibson and William Pickford, *Association Football and the Men Who Have Made It* (1906), Vol.I, p.150. It is interesting that both Bloomer and Fleming were among the few professional footballers included in *Burke's Who's Who of Sport* (1922).
38. Nicholas Fishwick (1989), p.136.
39. Eleven times when the two games against Hungary in 1909 are counted.
40. *Derby Evening Telegraph*, 26 October 1994.
41. When the editor of the *Athletic News* interviewed Bloomer in 1905 he stressed the respectability, the Bloomer home 'like a palace, everything so clean and orderly' and the Bloomer daughters 'in white muslin frocks [looking], like fairies, so tastefully and daintily were they dressed'. Quoted by Anton Rippon (1984), p.61.

National Identity and the Sporting Champion: Jean Borotra and French History

JEAN-MICHEL FAURE

Between 1920 and 1932 French tennis players triumphed in all the major international championships. On several occasions, Jean Borotra, René Lacoste and Henri Cochet carried off the singles and doubles titles at the top tournaments – Wimbledon, Roland Garros, Forest Hills and the Australian international championships – and with Jacques Brugnon, their inseparable doubles partner, they won the Davis Cup five times for their country. Such a series of victories might seem quite sufficient justification for remembering them today with pride. In our view, however, more than mere sporting victories are needed for champions to acquire lasting fame. Success on the sports field is short-lived, however hard-won. Outside the narrow circle of the faithful and the initiated, champions and their exploits are easily forgotten; contrary to the accepted view, sporting heroes are by no means legion and only a few emblematic figures enter posterity. Those who are thus enshrined in the collective memory are only those who succeeded in personifying the cultural identity of an area, their behaviour, conduct and style of life embodying moral and national ideals through which certain social groups discovered and sublimated their own destinies. Pre-war tennis in France reflected the mentality of an inalienably French *bourgeoisie*, its way of life, its dreams and its curiously idiosyncratic existence, which the members of that class loved to evoke.

Our four champions all belonged to this privileged world. Jean Borotra's father was a landowner turned man of letters living in his château at Pouy d'Arbonne near Bayonne. René Lacoste's father was a powerful and energetic industrialist, while Henri Cochet was the son of a prosperous tradesman who also ran the local tennis club in Lyons, and Brugnon's family possessed substantial property. The successful careers of these champions, respectively businessmen, industrialists and senior officers, did not belie their social origins and indeed accompanied their sporting achievements. Nevertheless, despite the renown they acquired from their prowess on the courts, only Borotra really became an historical *figure*. His personal biography encapsulates the social history of his class with its associations, attachments, beliefs and values. And his singular destiny invites us to examine the forms of legitimacy which, through a process both simple and complex, transform a sporting champion into a national hero.

The Culture of the Elite

Tennis, a game invented by an Englishman, Major Wingfield, appeared in France at the end of the nineteenth century as the fashionable pastime of a patrician and patriarchial urban elite of independent means whose pleasures stretched, like its summer residences, from the Riviera – that perfect setting for 'princely extravagance' – to the Norman coast. Guy de Maupassant, a caustic observer of the new craze if ever there was one, painted a ferocious picture of his compatriots' growing infatuation with such physical activities, which he considered pathetic and ridiculous:

> One used to go to the seaside in order to bathe and swim. Now one goes there to indulge in a very different kind of exercise ... Today everyone has a racket in his hand ...These unfortunate people, the distinguishing mark of whose madness recalls the rattles of the demented buffoons of yore, are infected by a disease of English origin called lawn tennis. They have their fits in meadows because much space is required for their convulsions. Bands of them can be seen frantically bustling about, running, jumping, bounding back and forth amid loud cries, contortions, fearful grimacing and wild gesticulation ...Their leaps, gestures and sudden dashes at once reveal to the alarmed passer-by the hidden bestiality in all human faces, which always bear a resemblance to some animal type, and strangely bring to light all the body's secret tics. This is how one enjoys oneself today and it is to indulge in such daily antics that one now goes to the seaside.[1]

In the opulent lounges of the Racing Club de France at the Croix Catelan a large contemporary painting recalls the beginning of tennis in Paris. Attractive young ladies in stylish dress nonchalantly recline on the grass while a pair of young men in 'boaters' indulge in the sport before their admiring gaze, with a net stretched between two trees. The competition was clearly sartorial rather than athletic but all the same tennis did not simply identify one socially, it also encouraged flirting and therefore was linked to the marriage market. A rich iconography conveys the cosy atmosphere of these select tennis clubs together with their members' pronounced penchant for romance; for this was also the age of those quaint little poems that accompanied *billets doux* and summed up all the sentimentality of the *belle époque*:

In the shade of a leafy lane
Before venturing on the court
How sweet it was to bill and coo
And dream of derring-do
Oh! we were young and gay
And before going out to play
With rose and periwinkle o'er our heads
A long lover's kiss we exchanged.[2]

The emotional tone was that of the *bourgeoisie* which aspired to live nobly on its unearned income, including that which it derived from the land, and found its models of behaviour in the conspicuous consumption of a monied aristocracy. However, between the end of the century and the outbreak of the First World War income from real estate constantly dwindled. As the historian Y. Lequin has shown, upper middle-class wealth in France underwent considerable diversification and property was redistributed in favour of the industrialists, businessmen and members of the professions. Transferable assets tended to predominate everywhere and commercial and industrial profits to replace fixed incomes. A spirit of entreprise gradually became one of the distinguishing marks of the elite; if the latter was still defined by the social ease now displayed through increasing links with such places as tennis clubs, the references were no longer the same, as what was formerly a pleasant little beach game was no longer played in the same spirit and tended now to become a sport. On the eve of the war, an article in *Les Sports Modernes* underlined the change:

> The members of polite society are all turning into athletes, those, that is, who play lawn tennis. It is just being recognised that the latter is a sport. Until now it was held to be an innocent pastime for anaemic young men and pale young ladies. It was as familiar and easy-going as loto or whist; and if it encouraged anything in particular, it was the matrimonial ambitions of parents guided by a wise sense of domestic economy. We are about to change all that and to establish a clear distinction between this English sport and the game of shuttlecock, which seemed so much to resemble it. Because certain great players have shown that vigour, skill and stamina are all essential qualifications, we have become adepts of the spirit of athletics ... Nowadays, we no longer play lawn tennis for fun but to win championships, which is a sign of progress and, because we can no longer practise a sport except with a view to winning something, we won't deny that it *is* progress.[3]

Though distinctive, the practice of a sport was not in itself enough to confer symbolic unity on a disparate bourgeoisie uncertain of its cultural identity; but it certainly helped. Asserting a preoccupation with one's physical condition seemed to be a way to assert one's membership of a common culture. Nevertheless, this process of self-enhancement was essentially indirect; it sought and found its norms and models in the image of a remote aristocratic culture as represented in the bourgeois imagination. Whereas the *rentier* thought he was imitating the great nobleman's taste for lavish expenditure, the new bourgeoisie took as a point of reference his system of values and codes of honour. The *ancien régime* thus haunted the whole era, an obsessive phantom of what history had destroyed, flitting like a dream in and out of the plays and novels of the time. With the help of a few collections of relics, the odd remembered fragment of the past, combined with pure literary artifice, the authors in vogue constructed a contemporary fable.

The epic of *The Three Musketeers* performed the same function as the study of primitive religion undertaken a few years later by Durkheim; it traced the frontiers of a new territory, the exploration of which legitimised this symbolic representation of modernity. Published in 1844, Alexander Dumas' historical romance began an immensely long career which made it an effortless bestseller even in the late 1920s. With its thousands of published copies and numerous dramatised versions all over France, to say nothing of the serialised editions in the popular press, it possessed all the attributes of myth, i.e. a story larger than life that, as Balzac put it, 'can serve any purpose and explain everything'. In *The Three Musketeers*, each of the four heroes possesses the virtues of exceptional human beings – courage, nobility, ardour, panache, vigour and daring, intelligence and reason. Their honourable rivalry accentuates their loyalty; a common determination gives force to their designs and substance to their collective invincibility. Four such men, sharing everything, from their fortune to risking life and limb, always ready to stand by one another, never shrinking from danger, carrying out individually or as a band their joint resolutions; four such swords brandished in all directions or converging on a single point, could not but succeed in forcing their way through whether by ruse or violence, subterraneously or in the full light of day, by mine or trench, to their fixed objective, however remote or well defended.[4]

Fiction thus invaded the present, providing the historical framework which enabled the most recent exploits to take root in the continuum of time and become legend. Tennis, the protean sport of the elites, its scenic and ritualistic devices evoking the codified confrontations of the duel, composed its own historical record in accordance with traditional rules. It gave a new lease of life to the long forgotten passion of the Kings of France for the *jeu de paume* and perpetuated allegedly inherent ethnic qualities:

'quick reflexes, sharp decisions, courage, determination and that imaginative inspiration which is the characteristic mark of our national temperament'.[5] The exploits and victories of the musketeers of tennis, thus firmly anchored in history, were able to transcend the cold details of mere sporting results and gain access, with all the requisite legitimacy, to the nation's cultural heritage.

The Aristocratic Ethos

Before reaching the Davis Cup final in 1925 and winning it two years later, the French triumphed in all the big tournaments. No major title escaped them. Cochet and Borotra were the first to shine at the finals of the French military championship in Lyons. Lieutenant Borotra 'is en route for glory', said the fashionable press which noted his presence wherever tennis had become a part of a new lifestyle. From Biarritz to Etretat and from Deauville to Paris, he piled up tournament victories. 'And yet I didn't know how to play. If I had an expert eye, it came from playing pelota and my only tactics consisted in rushing up to the net. I made use of a funny kind of chop which dug the ball into the court and which I immediately followed up with a volley.'[6]

It was then that he acquired the nickname that played down his social status but popularised the acrobatic aspects of his style. With his beret screwed tight on his head, he became 'the bounding Basque', the tightrope artist of the tennis courts, whose spectacular leaps delighted the crowds. 'If', a London paper asked its readers on the Frenchman's first appearance at Wimbledon in 1924, 'you had to choose just one tennis player to watch in your lifetime, which one would it be? Borotra of course!' Returning the compliment, he beat René Lacoste in the finals. The winner possessed the indefinable qualities which, in the eyes of his contemporaries, expressed 'the profoundest tendencies of the national character'. His natural gifts enabled him to dispense with the rigours of technical perfection or asceticism. 'Streamlined features, determined mouth, penetrating look, the shoulders of a pelota player and a ballet dancer's legs, the joie de vivre of his style', his courtesy, elegance and fair play – all contributed to his aura. 'He is a prince whom only France could offer the world.'[7] At the same time, to be the object of real affection, heroes must have a few frailties which remind us that they are only human and show us how they overcome the inevitable accidents of an exceptional career. In 1926, for instance, during the decisive inter-zonal doubles final between France and Australia, Borotra suddenly collapsed when the ball struck him at point blank range on the head. There was a long interruption during which doctors busied themselves around the unconscious player. After tottering palefaced back onto the court, he dramatically won the match for France with his audacious volleys, adding to his already enormous prestige in the process.

René Lacoste's game, on the other hand, excluded all notion of risk and improvisation, produced a very precise, taut, almost austere style of play calculated according to a strict, almost mathematical logic. (Lacoste's nickname, 'the crocodile', came from his mascot, a baby alligator which he acquired in Boston and kept in his hotel bedroom throughout his first Davis Cup competition in the United States.) Stubborn, tenacious, tireless and dogged, he refused to admit defeat and never gave away a point. He proved this in a classic encounter at the French international championships in 1927; outclassed by the American giant, 'Big Bill' Tilden, he finished the match, exhausted but triumphant, with an 11–9 victory in the fifth set after a combat lasting four hours. If the French doted on Borotra, who confirmed their own image of themselves, admired the artist and magician of the courts in Cochet, and felt considerable esteem for the altruistic team spirit of Brugnon, they respected Lacoste who personified the *essential* virtues of courage and determination.

All these players, including the Americans, Tilden, 'Little Bill' Johnson and Hunter, unquestionably constituted the elite of world tennis at the time but who, asked the press in 1929, was to be hailed 'champion of the last five years' after the third French Davis Cup victory? The number of individual victories counted of course but the main criteria were aesthetic, emotional and moral and had nothing to do with formal ranking. There could be no simple statistical answer to the question and it would be anachronistic to believe otherwise. The arbiters of the decision were strict guardians of tradition and the cult of values: a champion never lost heart or gave up; he fought on and his combativeness alone won him the gratitude of his fellows. The memorable match between the great Tilden and Cochet in Paris at the end of the 1920s is a good example. 'It was said Tilden was tired, worn out, unwell after a difficult crossing, with the shadow of defeat already hanging over him and fit only to serve to a few young hopefuls. Yet against Cochet he was magnificent, patient, tenacious, full of determination, constantly at full stretch to avoid yielding an inch of ground, heroic and immense, commanding respect and arousing admiration.'[8] Each encounter was unique, the extraordinary story of a clash of equals. 'Our life-long friendship [between all of them] is due to the fact that we never cheated. We always defended the spirit of the game. Our matches were tough, with no concessions. It is all a question of fairness and honesty. We were pure amateurs.' This was how Borotra reflected upon it in an interview for this article.[9]

These contests *inter pares* were part of the strict logic of honour. The cardinal virtue was loyalty, which comprised being worthy of the demands

of the competition. The value of victory was incalculable. It bestowed
prestige but was not heroic in itself. Only a disinterested passion for the
struggle could do that. For a true amateur, tennis was a *raison d'être* not a
source of income. This philosophy cannot be explained simply by saying
that these amateurs did not need to play for money; it was much more
exacting than that and required that the pursuit of excellence be recognised
as an existential principle. The exploits of the Musketeers legitimised the
survival of aristocratic values in a culture of efficiency and progress.

There is nothing paradoxical in this. Different forms of rationality, as
defined by Max Weber, can co-exist within the same cultural configuration.
The crowd which enthusiastically acclaimed Lindbergh's record flight
across the Atlantic accorded the same kind of homage to Alain Gerbault's
solo voyage aboard his tiny yacht. The futuristic exploits of the American
aviator take nothing away from the prowess of a navigator whose skills are
essentially those of another age. A similar logic holds good for individual
actions and the values which inspire them. 'We should resist the temptation
to reduce conduct to some general *habitus* called human nature thus
justifying a kind of simplistic set of historical characteristics – the noble or
the bourgeois'.[10] The disinterested striving of the amateur finds a *modus
vivendi* with the dynamism of the entrepreneur; in Borotra the sporting
champion coexisted comfortably with the *polytechnicien*.

The Spirit of Enterprise

Lacoste gave up tennis as early as 1928 to devote himself to business and a
few years later Cochet joined Tilden as a professional. Jean Borotra played
less often but his destiny was now beginning to take shape, adding force to
the prestige won on the courts and consolidating the champion's image. In
the eyes of the elites, he represented a particularly legitimate form of the
man of action. He had volunteered at eighteen while still a schoolboy in a
classe préparatoire at the lycée Saint-Louis, was subsequently awarded the
Croix de guerre and twice mentioned in dispatches, entered the prestigious
Ecole Polytechnique in 1920, and picking up a law degree along the way left
to begin a fulfilling career in the oil industry. The press, which was busy
covering his sporting achievements, took advantage of this to remind
company managers at the same time of their duties, social mission and
responsibilities. And in August 1927, on the eve of Borotra's Davis Cup
final against the United States, *Auto* devoted two front page articles to the
Ecole des Roches, an upper middle-class secondary school founded by E.
Desmolins at the beginning of the century and modelled on a progressive
British public school. While advocating a comprehensive system of
education based on sport and handicrafts, the school drew its main

inspiration from specifically French intellectual traditions and in particular
from the Catholic philanthropy of Le Play. The task of education was seen
to be that of improving the human condition while reconciling the classes
through the work ethic.

> The old class distinctions will gradually disappear. The aristocracy is
> already no more than a fashionable label with no worthwhile
> substance. It is in full decline, having been ruined by the prejudices
> which have estranged it from the world of labour. That part of the
> *bourgeoisie* which, out of foolish vanity, still prides itself on living
> nobly, has only succeeded, for the same reasons, in declining with
> elegance. Thus today's social trends are busy raising the lower classes
> while eliminating the old upper classes. What remains to be done
> therefore is to create a method of education which will prepare the
> worker for his social elevation in the most favourable conditions. It is
> above all the employers and leaders of large-scale industry and
> commerce who are in a position to take such an initiative; they are the
> only ones who can directly influence their employees.[11]

This conception of society was by no means retricted to progressive
headmasters; it was common in managerial circles between the wars and
found further expression in G. Lamirand's work, *The Social Role of the
Engineer in the Factory.*[12] The author, a former student of the *Ecole
Centrale,* fervent Catholic and admirer of Lyautet, was directly inspired, on
his own admission, by the latter's principles: 'Meet, get to know one
another, unite and set to work'. He was in favour of a flexible version of
paternalism which would, he thought, assure the harmonious development
of a conflict-free industrial society. The engineer had to assume command,
to show and lead the way as one whose personal ethic and involvement
encouraged solidarity and participation in the common endeavour.

The opportunity of playing such a role appealed as much to the
polytechnicien as to the world champion. Borotra's professional career
began with SATAM, an oil firm which controlled a substantial segment of
the market in petrol sales in France. He soon discovered that the equipment
used was old-fashioned and set to work solving a problem that constituted
a threat to the firm's budgets.

> It was a crucial matter. We were about to install American petrol
> pumps which were still very inaccurate and made all kinds of fiddling
> and fraud possible. When I saw as much, during my first trip to the
> US, with the French national team, I realised that there was no point
> in recommending such obsolete material to my fellow
> *polytechniciens.* A solution had to be found. On my return, I tried to

find a fool-proof way of eliminating leaks and wastage. I put on overalls and went down on to the factory floor and it wasn't easy but I succeeded and we won a terrific battle because our apparatus was recognised as being the best.[13]

This success took place during a period of prosperity which reached its climax at the end of the 1930s. The French car industry was still in very good shape and held second place internationally, in front of Britain and Canada. The French oil industry had also stood up well after the Wall Street crash.[14] Borotra's petrol gauge meant a new victory for French enterprise and underlined the competence of the country's engineers, their intellectual rigour and initiative as well as the excellence of the educational system which had produced them. His contemporaries indeed never tired of celebrating the qualities of a man whose exploits and *panache* in all fields were such powerful symbols of the country's stature and vitality:

> Jean Borotra is export manager in a famous firm of petrol distributors which is the world's number one and capable of winning almost any market from the Americans... Thus it was not just the Davis Cup that the most brilliant of our Musketeers was preparing to capture from the young American republic when he set sail with his glorious comrades: he was also going to defeat them at their own game. Today, the managing director of Shell is a bosom friend, all England idolises him and the umpires at Wimbledon are prepared to delay the start of play until five o'clock if he so requires. He may have a very fast car but the dear fellow must be allowed time to get his business appointments in the City out of the way before the match begins. His astonishing career as a sportsman-cum-businessman should serve as an example to all those in France who give up or would rather wait for a miracle to happen.[15]

Borotra delighted Wimbledon again in 1930, gave his country a final Davis Cup in 1932 by winning his two singles before devoting himself to business during the years preceding the Second World War when these highly ritualised sporting contests would soon be forgotten.

The Meaning of Patriotism

Borotra was an artillery captain in the front-line near Dijon on the outbreak of war. He was captured by the Germans but escaped and took refuge in Montauban. He wrote to General Weygand asking to be demobilised and thought of making his way to England. The battle of Mers el kebir and subsequent destruction of the French fleet changed his mind and the armistice appeared as a necessary interlude to prepare for his country's revenge. He shared this view with a large section of French society which continued to trust Marshal Pétain. The old leader was still thought of as the providential architect of victory in 1918 and his prestige remained high. After the military defeat, questions were raised about the causes of the *débâcle* and numerous publications waxed eloquent at the time on the physical inadequacies of the French people and their lack of enthusiasm for sport. Undoubtedly during the interwar period spectating had been more popular than participating in sport. Very soon, advocating an authentic 'physical revolution' became one of the favourite themes of the Vichy regime. It is easy to associate such an aim with its Nazi forms but this is to obscure the specifically French dimension it had at the time. A broader sociological view requires a more nuanced approach which properly takes into account 'the values of the period which must underpin any attempt to explain particular forms of behaviour'.[16] To describe all propagandists of the cult of the body as virtual fascists is to part company with sociology, to say nothing of historical truth.

Jean Borotra, like most anglophiles, recognised that sport was an essential form of education and an excellent means of socialisation. 'It is on the sports field that the child is most likely to acquire the taste for effort, loyal and tenacious combat and team spirit which makes a community meaningful'.[17] It was because he was convinced of this that he accepted the job of Commissioner for General Education and Sport in July 1940. His mission, defined by Pétain himself, consisted in 'making a younger generation strong again, better prepared for life and ready to answer all the country's needs'. Faced with immediate criticism from the universities, which saw in this idea of education the threat of an intolerable dictatorship of body over mind, Borotra went out of his way to stress what he meant by a *complete education*.[18] The latter 'aims at the whole human being. Unlike purely intellectual disciplines on the one hand, which appeal to intelligence and character alone or, on the other the purely physical disciplines, a *complete education* for an active life involves the entire human being; this approach is necessary because a human being is not just the sum of his physical, moral and intellectual qualities but a synthesis of them'.[19]

Without going into detail, a brief summary is necessary of the content of the five hours a week which Vichy's General Secretariat for State Education reluctantly set aside for the body. Most of the time was taken up by physical education and sport: the former merely reproduced the rather arid educational principles of Georges Hébert: as for the latter, it involved a rational preparation for sport through a theoretical and practical study of gesture as well as actual participation aimed at enhancing both the moral and physical qualities of the man of action. Less stress was laid on the complementary activities of handicrafts, excursions, choral singing and first aid. This initial training, if successful, could foster the development of *sports clubs* as true centres of national revival:

> The clubs must continue to pursue their technical objectives but sport must be much more than that; it must even be more than a source of physical well-being or healthy recreation: it must become that magnificent kind of activity which enables each one of us to attain and then to maintain the full physical, moral and intellectual development which everyone owes to his country and to society and which the athlete himself has clearly in mind when he promises in his oath 'to practise sport with discipline, unselfishness and loyalty in order better to serve his country'.[20]

For Borotra, this idea of a 'complete education' was clearly a cornerstone of the National Revolution;[21] but his understanding of what this kind of renewal meant turned out to be too exclusively patriotic to have any real future. The Germans soon became worried by the multiplication of clubs and discovered obvious signs of a desire for revenge in this movement to restore France to her former glory. Accordingly they banned gliding and skiing, which clearly had a military use, and eventually exercised strict control over the statutes of all such associations.[22]

Borotra's view of sport, increasingly threatened by the forces of occupation, placed him within the sphere of influence of a form of Catholic philanthropy whose austere and puritanical disciples were actively involved in the early stages of the Vichy regime. These views dominated the General Secretariat for Young People until the spring of 1942 and the staff of the school at Uriage;[23] this latter insititution, as it turned out, was closed down only a few months later.[24] Despite the efforts and charisma of the new Commissioner, the political forces which in the course of 1942 firmly committed Vichy to a policy of collaboration with the Nazis finally got the better of Borotra and his projects. The followers of Abel Bonnard, who were also great admirers of the *Hitlerjugend*, had already decided that French youth were being offered nothing but a diet of childish games inspired by the scout movement whereas what was needed was a demanding, virile education. The turning point occurred during Borotra's tour of North Africa in April–May 1941 at the head of a delegation of 150 athletes. The mass gatherings organised for the occasion were doubtless an opportunity to reaffirm imperial unity and fidelity to the Head of State but also to revive patriotic faith in the future of the nation. For a regime which was such a stickler for orthodoxy in official declarations, certain of General Weygand's phrases were suspect. 'At time of trial, when we have to pull ourselves together, sport assumes major importance,' declared the government's delegate in French Africa, who added, 'Is there a better schooling in life than entering a sporting event with the determination to win but also the resolve to take punishment without losing heart?'[25]

His words were on everybody's lips and consequently the General was removed from office later in the year. But Borotra then took up the theme in his turn: 'Each one of us must strive to practise one of those sports which teach us how to face up to onslaughts, hard blows and danger. Remember that when a country's youth and, in particular, its elite, lose the habit of being on the receiving end and of giving tit for tat, then they must very soon expect to be dealt blows of a crueller and more painful kind elsewhere.'[26]

The champion's mission was clearly coming to an end. His most virulent critics had harsh words to say and were indignant at the intolerable poster for the North African tour showing a French athlete and 'a coloured man' side by side beneath the flag. They denounced Borotra's admiration for the work of Léo Lagrange and the fulsome homage he paid to the former Popular Front minister killed in action in June 1940. They recalled his anglophile sentiments, his British grandmother, his wife's origins (she was the daughter of an English MP who also happened to be an 'Austrian Jew') and finally his unfortunate habit of quoting 'that Jew Bergson'.

As soon as he came to power, Laval dismissed Borotra and replaced him with Colonel Jep Pascot. The latter thereupon set up the monolithic organisation which his predecessor had always refused and implemented a policy for sport which was unquestionably an attempt to militarise and indoctrinate the young.[27] In November 1942, the former Wimbledon champion was arrested by the Germans and immediately deported to Sachsenhausen whence he was transferred six months later to Fort Itter where General Weygand and Daladier as well as Léon Jouhaux were fellow prisoners. After three unsuccessful attempts to escape, Borotra was freed by the Americans in May 1945.[28] Soon after the Liberation he was awarded a second *Croix de Guerre,* the medal for deported Resistance workers and that for escaped prisoners. He was also made Commander of the *Légion d'Honneur,* Commander of the British Empire and awarded the Swedish Order of Vasa; thus is Jean Borotra's name recorded for posterity. From personal conviction, he joined that group of men who, in the context of the Second World War, based their ethical code on the idea of personal example: the officer, the engineer, the company director and the sporting champion were all destined to serve as models for the common vocation of 'serving one's country'. This mission was stronger than individual destinies and permanently established them as a group with a collective destiny. The road was steep and perilous and closed to all who erred in their allegiance. Many would lose their way, a few would win praise and many others would swell the crowd of obscure and anonymous heroes who are the stuff of history.

Conclusion

In 1955, at the age of 57, Jean Borotra made a come-back in the French team against Sweden. Partnering the nineteen-year-old J.N. Grinda in the doubles, he dominated the match and provided his country's only victory. 'Jean Borotra's triumphant and moving reappearance before the astonished King of Sweden and a few thousands of his subjects did not fail to excite a new upsurge of admiration for the extraordinary "musketeer". His tremendous new exploit in Stockholm is an exceptional performance to add to the innumerable, legendary feats of the "Bounding Basque".'[29] However his prestige was more than simple recognition of a prowess which seemed invulnerable to the passage of time. His authority rested in the rediscovered legitimacy of the principles he had always defended. As a believer in an educational model, which attributed an essential role to sport in the process of socialisation, he contributed in 1960 to the work of the High Commission for Sport.[30] He presided over the committee responsible for defining the issues and objectives of an authentic sports policy. In January 1965, in a long interview in *Le Monde*, he outlined the spirit and general philosophy of their final report.[31] The fundamental postulate of the new doctrine was the integration of sport into the educational system which therefore would have to be profoundly transformed. 'The development of sport implies in the final analysis an authentic revolution in our educational methods for the good both of man and society'.

In its aims, but also in its principles, this plan for renewal was in complete harmony with the projects Borotra worked out at the Commission for Sport in 1940 and was based upon exactly the same value system.[32] The champion did not impose his point of view and indeed did not have to. The distinguished contributors to the *Essai de Doctrine* and their collaborators all spoke the same language. They shared a common culture whose values and references belong to a different time frame from that of the upheavals of political historiography. Such a cultural configuration generates its own symbols of heroism and greatness and Jean Borotra's status, exploits and commitments earned him an undispisputed place among these ideal figures. He gave expression to the essential truth which unconsciously binds them all together: 'The supreme honour is to play for France'. Surveying his exceptional career, it is of course possible to honour the man by writing an old-style biography in which the hero becomes at once the herald of faith and chivalry, a mirror of virtue and a representative of what is best in France. These life histories cannot be called history; they rather contribute to the process of heroic myth-making. However, provided he avoids the temptation of being no more than an apologist, the biographer who sticks to facts can still open up other horizons.[33] 'Biography gives the historian the feeling of life as men actually lived it';[34] it enables him to understand the mentality and the historical dimension of an era through exceptional individual destinies. According to Anatole France, who cherished narrative and felt an equally violent aversion for structural studies ('those cold *post mortems*', as he called them), the two approaches were as mutually exclusive as 'the rose and the potato'. The comparison is not without charm. Yet the historian must come to terms with both of these ways of understanding his subject whilst acknowledging that frequently it is the glorious fragrance of the rose alone which can excite interest in the soil from which it springs.

NOTES

The author wishes to acknowledge and express his gratitude for the interest, support and assistance of his translator, Vittorio Ballardini, Maître de conférences, University of Nantes.

1. Guy de Maupassant, *Gil Blas*, 6 June 1887.
2. Gentien, 'Aventures d'un joueur de tennis', in *Les Sports Modernes*, 6 July 1908.
3. Editorial by Fernand Bidault in *Les Sports Modernes*, May 1908.
4. Alexandre Dumas, *Les Trois Mousquetaires* (page ref. etc. not available).
5. Pierre Guillou, first President of the French Lawn Tennis Federation.
6. J. Borotra, 3 hour interview at his home, Tuesday 17 March 1992.
7. Jean Samazeuilh, French singles and doubles champion, president of the Philosophical Studies Group at the University of Bordeaux, writer and critic on the *Miroir des sports* and the *Petite Gironde*.
8. *Excelsior*, June 1929.
9. J.Borotra, interview.
10. Paul Veyne, *Comment on écrit l'Histoire* (Paris: Seuil, 1978), p.137.
11. E. Desmolins, *L'Ecole des roches de l'éducation nouvelle* (Paris, 1902).
12. G. Lamirand was General Manager of the Iron and Steel works at Pompey, in Lorraine. He was the driving force behind the Association of Young Catholic Workers and set up apprenticeship and guidance centres as well as training schools for executives. He became managing director of Renault after the armistice and presided over the destinies of the General Secretariat for Young People in 1940. His views were close to whose of Dunoyer de Segonzac and the school at Uriage. At the end of 1942, the Laval faction had him dismissed.
13. Jean Borotra, interview.
14. Henri Dubief, *Le déclin de la troisième république 1929–38* (Paris: Seuil, 1976).
15. *Gringoire*, July 1929, Editorial by Joseph Peyre.
16. P.Veyne, op.cit., pp.126 and 127.
17. J. Borotra, 'L'éducation générale et les sports', in H. Mavit, *Revue d'Histoire de la deuxième guerre mondiale*, 5, 6 (October 1964).
18. 'The same importance is about to be accorded to chest measurement as to breadth of mind', wrote R. Vercel. And *Le Temps*, expressing the official view of the Committee of Ironmasters, underlined the point: 'Let's not forget intelligence; a cult of brute force is undesirable and no amount of stirring athletics contests will supply the moral and intellectual restoration the country needs'.
19. J. Borotra, 'L'éducation générale et les sports', lecture at the Ecole Libre des Sciences Politiques, March 1942.
20. J. Borotra, op.cit., pp.22 and 23.
21. From April 1942 onwards, the pro-Nazi tendency which took over made it clear that 'the period of innocence ended once and for all with the first National Revolution; the task now

is to bring about a European National Socialist Revolution'.

22. Archives of the German H.Q. in Paris quoted by W.D. Halls, *Les jeunes et la politique de Vichy* (Paris: Syros), pp.212 ff.

23. *Cahiers d'Uriage*, 30 (April 1942).

24. Among the members of the Secretariat for Young People was Louis Garonne, a pure product of the *Ecole des Roches* of which he was to become headmaster after the liberation. He was also the brother of the future cardinal. Hated by the partisans for collaboration with the Germans, Garonnne was criticised both for his Popular Front leanings and for belonging to a school which was in favour of an English-type education for 'young, upper-class snobs'. As for those who were connected with Uriage, there is an endless list of great names: Dunoyer de Segonzac, Hubert Beuve-Mery (subsequently editor of *Le Monde*), Paul-Henri Chombart de Lauwe, Joffre Dumadezier, Claude Roy, Paul Claudel, Jean-Marcel Jeannemey. 'It was a medieval microcosm', wrote Jean-Marie Domenach, the future editor of *Esprit*, 'a salubrious environment, devoid of the pretension and chicanery which are the bane of intellectual coteries, a place where the mind and true military discipline could find common ground'.

25. Speech by General Weygand in Africa, 29 April 1941 before a crowd of 15,000.

26. Jean Borotra, op.cit., p.23.

27. In their turn, on 20 April 1942, the Germans appointed a 'neuer Sportsführer' with the task of supervising sport in France. National archives, German papers, A.J. 40,557.

28. W.D. Halls, *Les jeunes et la politique de Vichy* (Paris: Syros, 1988) and Pierre Giolitto, *Histoire de la jeunesse sous Vichy* (Paris: Perrin, 1991).

29. *Tennis de France*, 1992. Texts republished to mark the 30th anniversary of the magazine.

30. Haut Comité des Sports, *Essai de doctrine du sport*, 1965.

31. *Le Monde*, 17, 18, 19 January 1965.

32. When considering the relationship between sport and politics one should abandon the antiquated notion that the former is either admirable or detestable according to the political context. Thus, in a democracy, sport is considered to be an excellent means of socialisation whereas in a totalitarian regime it suddenly becomes a formidable instrument of indoctrination and coercion. In other words, sport is essentially pure but can be perverted by use. It would no doubt be more sensible to examine the political nature of sport itself, the curious way it affects public life while pursuing objectives of its own. Max Weber's sociology provides the key in the way that it seeks to explain how legality evolves out of brute force, how obedience becomes a duty and how for subjectively necessary reasons individuals recognise the legitimacy of a ruling power. However, these problems have first to be properly posed before they can be answered.

33. These accounts always begin by recalling some initial event which transforms a life into a destiny. The biographies of Jean Borotra are no exception: 'A little eight year old, strapped up tight in a black frock coat hastily put together the previous night, headed his father's funeral procession, as was required by Basque tradition ... His mother had simply told him as she held him close to her: Jean, you've seen what's happened, you're the head of the family now; I'm counting on you ... Sometimes only a few hours are needed to change a destiny. The child's had been set once and for all on a path that his mother has carefully traced for him.' Marie-Hélène Roukhadzé, *Revue Olympique*, 1987.

34. Bernard Guénée, *Entre l'église et l'Etat: quatre vies de prélats français à la fin du moyen âge* (Paris: Gallimard, 1987).

Symbol of National Resurrection:
Max Schmeling, German Sports Idol

SIEGFRIED GEHRMANN

According to a poll conducted a few years ago by the 'Institute for Empirical Psychology' in Cologne to determine the German Sports Personality of the Century, he ranked fifth behind contemporary stars like the outstanding swimmer Michael Gross, the tennis hero Boris Becker, the double Olympic champion in high jump Ulrike Meyfarth and the soccer 'Emperor' Franz Beckenbauer, even though he reached the pinnacle of his sporting career fifty years before the poll was taken. In a telegram on his seventieth birthday the then President of Germany, Walter Scheel, named him 'Germany's Number 1 Sportsman for Life'.[1] The name of this man is Max Schmeling – World Heavyweight Boxing Champion from 1930 to 1932.

What is the explanation for the unique popularity of a sportsman whose prime has long since passed, whose great success only a small percentage of the living population experienced and who represented a sport that in Germany is now a mere shadow of its former self? Before attempting to answer this question, a few remarks about Max Schmeling's biography and his career as a boxer are in order.

Background and Career

Max Schmeling was born on 28 September 1905 in Klein-Luckow, a small town in Pomerania only a few kilometres west of Stettin. His father was a seaman and his mother worked part-time as a postal employee. On account of his father's work the family moved to Hamburg before the First World War. After finishing school, Max Schmeling began an apprenticeship with an advertising agency. Inspired by a film of the world heavyweight championship fight between the Frenchman Georges Carpentier and the American Jack Dempsey in Jersey City in the United States on 2 July 1921 in front of 80,000 spectators, Max Schmeling decided to become a boxer and after two years as an amateur he turned professional. He was soon very successful. On 24 August 1926 he knocked out the German light heavyweight title holder Max Dieckmann in Berlin. In the following months Schmeling won another nine fights before he fought Fernand Delarge on 19

June 1927 in the newly built 'Dortmunder Westfalenhalle' for the European title. Schmeling won the fight on a technical knockout and successfully defended his European light heavyweight title on 6 January 1928, against the Italian champion Michele Bonaglia. Shortly after this fight Schmeling moved up to the heavyweight division and won the German title on points against the reigning title holder, Franz Diener, on 4 April 1928.

On 24 November 1928 Schmeling had his first fight on American soil. This took place in Madison Square Garden, then the largest indoor stadium in the world, against the American Joe Monte, the 'Bull from Boston'. Schmeling knocked him out in the eighth round. In the crowd was the most important figure in American boxing in the 1920s, Tex Rickard. The convincing manner in which Schmeling made his first appearance in the ring in America and the fact that he acquired as his manager Joe Jacobs, an American of Hungarian Jewish ethnic origins and a knowledgeable exponent of the American boxing scene, provided the basis for his rapid rise from this time on. In quick order and in convincing fashion he dispatched Joe Sykra, Johnny Risco, Pietro Corri and Paolino Uczudun – all in 1929. The press judged the match against Johnny Risco from Cleveland 'one of the most dramatic heavyweight fights in the history of boxing'.[2] This contest, in which Schmeling forced Risco to throw in the towel in the ninth round, made the German famous overnight throughout the American sporting world. In the following year Max Schmeling reached the culmination of his career; his dreams were fulfilled with a fight for the world heavyweight title.

On 26 July 1928 the reigning heavyweight champion of the world, Gene Tunney, knocked out the New Zealander Heeney in the eleventh round. On the evening of the same day immediately after the match, Tunney gave up his title without re-entering the ring. The title remained vacant. The New York Boxing Commission decided that Max Schmeling and a Lithuanian American named Jack Sharkey were eligible to contest the title. Schmeling's first fight with Sharkey took place on 12 June 1930 in New York's Yankee Stadium in front of 80,000 spectators. It ended in scandal. In the fourth round Sharkey delivered a low blow that put Schmeling out of commission and was immediately disqualified. Max Schmeling was declared the winner and thus became the new 'World Champion of All Divisions'.

It was, of course, a crown without glory. Max Schmeling himself was at first rather depressed. For some time he refused to accept the title, which he had won through a disqualification. Only when his manager and especially his coach urged and then implored him did he change his mind. In Germany there was no rejoicing. Even in extreme nationalist circles the winning of the title did not stir up any enthusiasm. When Schmeling was invited to an event in the Sport Palace in Berlin and was introduced to the spectators as the 'World Champion', there was loud whistling and booing. In the satirical revues of late Weimar they would sing songs about 'how to become a world champion from a hit below the belt'.

Max Schmeling held the title for about two years before losing it to Sharkey in the return match on 21 June 1932 as a result of a blatantly bad decision. Sharkey won on points in fifteen rounds, although virtually all the experts at the ringside thought that Schmeling had finished well ahead on points. If Max Schmeling's tenure of the world title from 1930 to 1932 was technically the high point of his career, his real and enduring fame came four years later. It was not until then that Schmeling became the most popular athlete in Germany.

Jack Sharkey's fortunate victory over Schmeling had brought him no luck. He lost the title only one year later to the Italian Primo Carnera, who in turn gave it up after a year to Max Baer, an Austrian-American Jew. But Baer too could not hold his title for long, losing it to the New Yorker, James Braddock. The quick succession of title holders made it all too clear that these years had not brought a dominant athlete to the throne of the heavyweight division. The sympathy of the American sports world accordingly turned to younger, up-and-coming boxers, especially to one who, like Max Schmeling, came from nowhere and had earned a reputation as a fighter of almost superhuman qualities. This was, of course, Joseph Louis Barrow, whom the world came to know as Joe Louis.

Born on 14 May 1914 and thus nine years younger than Max Schmeling, Joe Louis was the seventh of eight children of a poor share-cropper family from Alabama deep in the south, where his great-grandparents had worked as slaves.[3] Louis had begun boxing only in 1933 but even as an amateur his great talent was apparent. In June 1934, he turned professional. In his first year he won twelve fights. In New York, the capital of American boxing, he made his debut at Yankee Stadium in June 1935 against Primo Carnera in front of a live audience of 62,000. The Italian, who the year before had held the heavyweight title, was knocked out by Louis in the sixth round. Much the same happened in quick succession to King Levinsky, Max Baer, Paolino Uczudun. and Charley Retzlaff, all highly ranked boxers. Caswell Adams of the *New York Herald Tribune*, one of the most important sports reporters at the time, described Louis as follows: 'Louis...can punch with terrific power. He can move with lightning speed. He can feint a foe out of position. And his timing on the defense is so perfect that blows usually miss him and never land squarely...He is as cold as ice and when he moves, he does so as would a tiger or lion.'[4] The last sentence became a *leitmotiv* repeated in press reports whenever Joe Louis and his personality were characterized. For example, Paul Gallico of the *New York Daily News*, who had observed Louis long and carefully, reported:

> I felt myself strongly ridden by the impression that here was a mean
> man, a truly savage person, a man on whom civilization rested no
> more securely than a shawl thrown over one's shoulders. That, in
> short, here was perhaps for the first time in many generations the
> perfect prizefighter. I had the feeling that I was in the room with a wild
> animal...I see in this colored man something so cold, so hard, so cruel
> that I wonder as to his bravery. Courage in the animal is desperation....
> It acquits itself over pain and panic.[5]

Crude racial stereotyping was the stuff of sporting journalism even in
quality newspapers.

On the evening of 19 June 1936 in Yankee Stadium Max Schmeling
challenged Joe Louis to a scheduled fifteen-round bout. The winner was to
fight Braddock for his title. The odds were 8 to 1 in favour of Louis. In his
Erinnerungen ('Memoirs') Max Schmeling describes in detail the course of
the bout; he recalled the crucial twelfth round as follows:

> Three times in just a few seconds my right hand lands solidly, and I
> fire each punch as though it were a pistol shot. With all the precision
> that I still possess, directly at the target with all my strength. Louis'
> left-hand jabs, by this time only a defensive weapon, merely wave in
> my face. Again I throw a right cross. Louis sags against me in a
> clinch. Donovan, the referee, peels him off me. I attack again, force
> him onto the ropes and smash a right to his chin. At that moment his
> arms fall limp. Joe Louis is finished and, stunned, he finally presents
> his head to me as I had hoped he would for twelve rounds. This is the
> moment of truth. For finally I do not need to punch over his left arm
> but can deliver the punch from 'inside' and thus freely release all of
> my power. I put everything I have into the punch. It turns Louis
> completely around. Bereft of sense he looks at me out of eyes that no
> longer see anything. Then he pivots around and falls to his knees
> against the ropes. His arms reach behind him. Donovan sends me to a
> neutral corner and begins to count. Louis tries to struggle up the ropes.
> For one or two seconds he holds himself still, his face oddly vacant.
> Then his head droops, the shoulders slide along the ropes, and his
> body, as if suddenly betrayed by his will, collapses. Then he lies
> stretched out on the canvas. Desperately Louis seems to try once again
> to regain his feet. He actually raises his shoulder-blades a few
> centimeters, then collapses once more. Joe Louis rolls over on to his
> face and stretched out, moves no more. As my heart leaps out of my
> throat, I see the rhythmic fall of Donovan's hand: seven – eight – nine!

Then he spreads his arms wide apart: Joe Louis has been knocked out![6]

On the following day an American newspaper wrote that 'coming generations will tell their children: One day the continents split apart. One day the pyramids collapsed. One day Max Schmeling defeated Joe Louis'.[7]

With this victory Max Schmeling reached the high point of his athletic career. Nevertheless he was never allowed the title fight with the champion Braddock that he had earned by beating Louis. Without his knowledge, and in violation of agreements with Braddock, Braddock's manager, Joe Gould, and Louis' manager, Mike Jacobs, agreed upon a title bout that took place on 22 June 1937 in Chicago. Louis became world champion when he knocked Braddock out in the eighth round.[8]

The reason for Schmeling's exclusion was political. In 1933 Hitler had seized power in Germany. Two years later the so-called Nuremberg Race Laws were passed which severely discriminated against those of Jewish descent. On the other hand at this time Jews played an important part in American boxing: the managers of Louis and Braddock, for instance, were both Jews. It would not be surprising if these men considered coming to an arrangement that would benefit themselves and hinder the chances of a country governed by an inhuman and anti-Semitic political system of claiming the world heavyweight championship.[9] After all, the Berlin Olympics of the previous year had provoked a fierce debate within the United States about sporting contacts with those perceived as representatives of the Nazis.

However, after winning the title, Joe Louis himself insisted on offering Schmeling the chance to fight him once again. He could not feel like a real champion until he had beaten the German. The match took place on 22 June 1938 in Yankee Stadium in the most difficult psychological conditions, which clearly disturbed Schmeling. Hitler had begun the expansionist phase of his foreign policy in the winter and spring of 1938. In March 1938 the Third Reich annexed Austria. Then the German propaganda machine fixed its sights on Czechoslovakia. At the same time the Nazi regime intensified its repression of Jews. These developments were followed with increasing alarm, especially amongst Jewish and Eastern European elements in the United States. Consequently nearly all of the American public turned against Schmeling, especially because in large sections of the American press he was closely linked with Nazism and presented as a symbol of Nazi racist ideology. He was depicted as a representative of the Aryan master race for whom it was important to demonstrate in the forthcoming fight its superiority over the racially inferior Negro. Although Schmeling vehemently contested this image, a wave of protest and hatred greeted his arrival in America[10] and he was deeply disturbed by it. He was demoralized before the fight even began and had little chance against the vengeful Louis, who overwhelmed him in the first round with such a furious rain of blows that he was counted out after just over two minutes. As a result of this defeat, he fell into disgrace, was disowned by the Nazi regime which at first had courted him. He only fought a few more times before hanging up his gloves. His last bout at the age of forty-three against Richard Vogt from Hamburg was in October 1948.

To account for Max Schmeling's unique popularity in Germany, it is necessary to remember the truism that in most cases an athlete's public acclaim depends chiefly on his or her performance. But in Schmeling's case this cannot be the only explanation. There are in the history of German sport many examples of athletes who have achieved outstanding results measured by world standards without reaching anything like his popularity. In fact there are not a few who during their prime were household names but who are scarcely remembered today. In the case of Schmeling there appear to be two factors besides his athletic performance that need examination: first, his own personality, which contemporaries repeatedly describe as charismatic and which had nothing to do with athletic ability;[11] secondly, and this is central to the historian, the psyche of a society the most important experiences of which were two world wars and the most brutal of dictatorships.

The Spirit of the Times: Boxing and the Struggle for Survival

At the end of the First World War Germans developed, after a period of unparalleled tension and denial, a zest for life and search for pleasure that went beyond anything hitherto experienced. This phenomenon expressed itself partly in a virtual explosion of sporting activity. Willy Meisl, one of the most renowned sports writers of the time, described this movement in these words: 'The war was over and peace had broken out ... Many people had learned how transitory life is; they felt that life was there to be lived. Subconscious drives ruled them; they had returned from the land of the dead and sought life; they were open to adventure, for the old way offered them no chance ...The body was in ... sport and all its ramifications were the future ... .'[12] Besides soccer and the Six-Day Race, it was boxing which fascinated the people. It aroused interest in sport amongst the masses and became the dominant topic in the sports pages of the daily newspapers. Significantly, its attraction was not limited to the lower classes. Artists and sculptors like George Grosz, Rudolf Belling, Ernesto de Fiori and Renée Sintenis began to choose their subjects from the world of boxing. In 1921, for example, the well-known Berlin art dealer Alfred Flechtheim founded the periodical *Der Querschnitt* ('The Cross-Section'), a cosmopolitan magazine designed chiefly for an educated public and equally capable of writing both about the October Revolution and Modern Art and about the aesthetics of the body. Its subtitle proclaimed it to be the 'Magazine of Art, Literature, and Boxing'. One of its most enthusiastic readers, Bertolt Brecht, started in collaboration with the German heavyweight champion, Paul Samson-Koerner, *Die menschliche Kampfmaschine* ('The Human Fighting Machine'),[13] and in his opera *Aufstieg und Fall der Stadt Mahagonny* ('The Rise and Decline of the Town of Mahagonny') occur the lines:

> First, don't forget, comes eating.
> Second, comes the love act.
> Third, don't forget, boxing.
> Fourth, drink as much as you can.[14]

The general enthusiasm for boxing that gripped Germany after the First World War was perhaps connected to a powerful individualistic feeling that was gradually developing in reaction to the experience of daily life as remote, institutionalised, incomprehensible, run through bureaucracies and organizations, which increasingly were felt to be complex, abstract and 'non-physical'. Joyce Carol Oates expressed this notion as follows: 'There as in no other public arena does the individual as a unique physical being assert himself; there, for a dramatic if fleeting period of time, the great world with its moral and political complexities, its terrifying impersonality, ceases to exist. Men fighting one another with only their fists and their cunning are all contemporaries, all brothers, belonging to no historical time'.[15]

This rather speculative but attractive interpretation can be augmented by another that is no less speculative but all the more remarkable for being uttered by Max Schmeling himself. In his *Erinnerungen* he records his conversation about the attraction boxing exercised over artists and intellectuals with his acquaintance, the actor Fritz Kortner, an enthusiastic boxing fan:

> 'It's the time,' he said. 'What happens in the ring reflects life. So unmerciful, so angry the way you go at each other, that is how we all struggle for our own existence.' He sat across from me, his chin resting on his fist, beseeching me in his inimitably high-pitched and scratchy voice. 'You see, Max,' he said, 'we can present such a scene on the stage. But for us it's only theatre. After I as Richard III kill dozens of people and the curtain falls, we all get up and politely make our bows to the audience. And the people applaud. But for you the

matter is really one of life and death. When one of you is floored, it can really be the end. Your blood isn't make-up. That's what's so exciting about boxing: nowhere else is the lust for fame and success so palpable, so deadly earnest! Boxing is really not a sport. It's a battle for life compressed into twelve rounds.' Kortner had become increasingly worked up. His face, as always fascinatingly homely, bore the marks of his perplexity. His final remarks, although addressed to me, seemed merely spoken out loud. There was no doubt that he had meant to make clear to himself and not to me why boxing enthralled him. Towards the end, he scoffed: 'Derwish calls life a boxing match. You should read Lessing, Max!'[16]

Of course, we may question how representative of a larger part of German society are the feelings of a highly sensitive artist, especially one so obviously influenced by social Darwinism. There are, unfortunately, no empirically sound investigations of the history of German attitudes that could help us here. On the other hand, if we assume that the cultural elite of a society possess a certain sensitivity for that which characterizes its people – admittedly a contentious assumption – then such notions as those of Kortner must have been fairly widespread. In so far as boxing obviously became for many a metaphor of human existence and the survival instinct, a boxer like Max Schmeling symbolized one who had fought and conquered. He was a hero, to quote Joyce Carol Oates once again, in the 'drama of life in the flesh'.[17]

The Social Climber

Closely connected with this point of view was another one that allows us to see how this story resonates in terms of the prevailing mentality. Max Schmeling earned his first big purse as a boxer for his bout with Hein Domgoergen on 8 November 1927, for which he received 20,000 German marks. For his fight with Johnny Risco on 1 February 1929 he received $25,000 or about 70,000 marks, against Basken Paolino Uczudun six months later about 300,000 marks and for his first title bout with Sharkey about a million marks. Max Schmeling was generally regarded by the end of the 1920s as a wealthy man, who never threw his money around but did not hide it either. Pictures showing him in an expensive sports car, beside a thoroughbred race horse or in front of his rural mansion just outside Berlin, appeared regularly in the press. He had not only earned a respectable fortune as a boxer but had also established himself in a social environment that was then classified as 'Berlin society'. This included artists, physicians, actors, journalists, writers, racing drivers and scholars from various fields.

They were not necessarily the rich and powerful of the period, but they were people, as Schmeling himself remembers, 'about whom one talked'.[18] Above all, they dominated the headlines of the society pages. Schmeling was able to establish relationships with not a few of these individuals, among them (in addition to Fritz Kortner) the no less well-known representatives of the German theatre world, Emil Jannings and Ernst Deutsch, the celebrated opera singer Michael Bohnen, the sculptor and later Nazi beneficiary, Josef Thorak, the film stars Hans Albers, Willy Fritsch and Olga Tschechowa, and the idol of millions, the racing driver, Bernd Rosemeyer.[19] In these circles Schmeling also met his wife-to-be, the movie star Anny Ondra, who at the time was at the peak of her fame. They celebrated their wedding on 6 July 1933: it was a major media event and in the news for several weeks.

In recording that in the late 1920s Max Schmeling became an envied subject not only in the sports papers but also in the society columns, the fact that this largely took place during the Depression, which was especially severe in Germany, should not be forgotten. The number of the unemployed rose to about thirty per cent in some areas, and many people led grim lives bordering on stark poverty.[20] All the more reason why Max Schmeling fed people's fantasies, especially those of the young, for here was someone who had risen from nothing and in a few years had through the strength of his own fists succeeded in acquiring wealth, prestige and acceptance. His career touched a chord in the collective psyche; this is what in the United States came to be called the 'American Dream' and which F. Scott Fitzgerald's eponymous hero, in *The Great Gatsby* embodies. Schmeling's rise to fame became a symbol of countless longings for a more exciting, comfortable and better life.

This psychological disposition, in so far as it has been studied as a means of explaining Schmeling's popularity in Germany, was by no means confined to Germany in the 1920s and 1930s. When we examine the social history of professional boxing in other European countries, as well as that of the United States, differing shades of what is a very similar picture emerge. We need only think of the biographies of Georges Carpentier, Tommy Farr, Tommy Milligan, Jack Dempsey and Gene Tunney. In Max Schmeling's case, however, there are several additional elements peculiar to Germany which are of crucial importance.

The National Hero

Germany had lost the first Great War of this century and in the Peace Treaty of Versailles was subjected by the victors to severe reparations. Even more difficult than the financial burden was the decision of the Western powers to require Germany to admit its responsibility for the outbreak of the war. The paragraph defining this, the so-called 'war guilt' clause (Article 2.1 of the Versailles Treaty), created a deep feeling of national humiliation and resentment which, as is well known, was so disastrously exploited a decade later by Adolf Hitler. A nation such as Germany, whose pride and sense of values had been so seriously injured, was not surprisingly mesmerized by a boxer like Schmeling who had triumphed so spectacularly in international competitions. His athletic success against opponents from countries which had earlier been Germany's enemies must have functioned as some kind of collective psychic compensation for the national humiliation of Versailles.

Max Schmeling became for many the symbol of national resurrection, immeasurably more concrete, palpable and thus psychologically more convincing than, for example, German industrial successes in comparison to their international competitors. Similarly the success of the German soccer team at the World Cup Championhips in 1954 in Switzerland, whose players are still today seen by some as the 'Heroes of Bern', provided a positive post-war image of German achievement. There are many examples of how Max Schmeling's international success contributed to this sense of achievement. The following are only a few from his early career.

When Schmeling defeated the Belgian Fernand Delarge in the Westfalenhalle in Dortmund on 19 June 1927 in the fourteenth round to win the European Light Heavyweight Title, one newspaper wrote:

SCHMELING EUROPEAN CHAMPION

Hanke's [the referee] voice screamed through the tumult of the large hall. Shouts of joy echoed through Germany's most popular boxing arena. Like a typhoon, a tidal wave, storms of frenzied applause swept through the site of the earth-shattering battle, taking everything with it; the elemental weight of the enthusiasm gripped the mass in its might: the enthusiasm turned to ecstasy: Schmeling! Schmeling! The Champion of Europe. In it the enthusiasm of thousands. Schmeling, the first German European Champion, embodies from now on Germany's dominant position in boxing ... Enthusiastically, the band struck up the national anthem, and it was sung lustily by thousands, Deutschland, Deutschland Über alles! Accompanied by the sounds of this hymn, the champion of Europe was carried through the arena. With tears in their eyes, enraptured by the transcendence of the moment, the masses dispersed...[21]

If in the wake of the general catastrophe of defeat in war Schmeling thus became a kind of national hero who enabled many Germans to regain their lost pride, the triumph over Joe Louis in 1936 may be viewed similarly, although by this time the political situation had been transformed. National honour was again perceived to be at stake but the terms of the debate had been radically changed in the intervening period.

Courage and Decency

On 30 January 1933 Adolf Hitler was named Chancellor of the German Nation. Max Schmeling was one of the very few athletes in Germany with whom Hitler sought contact soon after he assumed power, and Schmeling openly admits in his *Erinnerungen* how flattered he felt.[22] His first visit to Hitler took place at the end of April 1933 in the State chambers, where the new dictator received him with elaborate courtesy. The events leading to this meeting are extraordinary. Since his fights in America in 1928 Max Schmeling's manager had been Joe Jacobs, a Hungarian-American Jew, who had become a close friend. The Nazi regime, specifically the Reich's sports director, Hans von Tschammer und Osten, categorically demanded that Schmeling dissolve his partnership with the 'sub-human' Jacobs. Schmeling refused and did something which in retrospect appears foolish and self-destructive. He appealed to Hitler personally and requested in an audience in the State Chambers to be allowed to continue his alliance with Jacobs. Only now, when one considers the terrible hatred of the Jews, the ferocity of their persecution at Hitler's command and the danger Germans risked by conducting business with or even being friendly towards Jews, can one appreciate the extraordinary courage Schmeling displayed in his interview with Hitler. Not only did he jeopardize his own athletic career but also his own personal safety. Hitler showed no inclination even to discuss the question with Schmeling and abruptly ended the conversation before it had really begun.[23]

For Schmeling, who nevertheless maintained his relationship with Jacobs, there were no direct negative consequences for this transgression. After the beginning of the Second World War, he was drafted – although thirty-five years old – and saw combat in the spring of 1941 in the air-land operation in Crete which exacted heavy casualties. Although there is no direct evidence, according to Schmeling a number of circumstances suggest that his military service can be traced to Hitler's own directive and was perhaps a belated revenge.[24] Schmeling's allegiance to Jacobs in the autumn of 1934 was at the time noticed by only a few contemporaries. Nevertheless, Kurt Tucholsky, one of the most well-known writers of the Weimar Republic, wrote in his *Briefe aus dem Schweigen* ('Letters from Silence') from his exile in Sweden to his Swiss girlfriend Hedwig Müller: 'Mr. Secbecker [an acquaintance of Tucholsky's] told me that Schmeling had refused to fire his Jewish manager. Which really was decent of him. He obviously can think only one way.'[25]

The Joe Jacobs affair became known to a wider public in Germany only after the war. This is true of other similar cases in which Schmeling was involved. He made, for example, efforts on behalf of the Jewish former wife of the sculptor Thorak and successfully intervened with Joseph Goebbels for her shortly after the introduction of the Nuremberg Race Laws in the autumn of 1935 to prevent her arrest by the Gestapo.[26] Another example of behaviour that could be construed in Nazi terms as critical or nonconformist concerned Schmeling's role in the operation in Crete, in which he was wounded. Schmeling gave an interview to an American journalist from an army hospital in Athens. In this interview, which was broadcast by the Transoceanic Agency and which drew worldwide attention, he vehemently criticised Nazi propaganda against the methods of combat of the British troops. In addition, Schmeling emphasized in this interview that he thought the eventual entry of the United States of America into the war would be a great calamity. America, he claimed, was his second home. Because of this behaviour Schmeling was threatened initially with criminal charges before a court tribunal, and then with a court martial. Fortunately this was suspended.[27]

By making reference to such events I do not wish to present Schmeling as part of an underground resistance movement fighting against the Nazis. He was basically much too apolitical for such a stance. But it should be clear that Schmeling as a sportsman was anything but a symbol of the Nazi regime. After the war he seemed to many Germans a man for whom certain principles were more important than his own career ambitions and concerns about his own welfare. He became for them a kind of witness for a better Germany in a time of darkness. Max Schmeling's popularity, based in the beginning on his extraordinary athletic success and expressed in a society especially predisposed to celebrate it, thus acquired a strongly moralistic substance. He was an ordinary decent man caught up like so many others in great and terrible events beyond his control. Outside his achievements in the ring, he was not a hero in the normal sense of one risking his life for his country or his beliefs. Yet he did show moral courage and tried to do what he thought was right. He was not just a boxer who wanted to make money; his material success did not mean he threw away his sense of common humanity; in an occupation hardly reknowned for its standards of personal conduct, especially in the United States, he had emerged uncorrupted and had lived a life of ordinary decency and occasional courage to which many 'good' Germans aspired even though they had no choice but to participate in a regime which may briefly have seemed patriotic and progressive at the outset but soon showed its true colours of racial hatred and totalitarian oppression. Perhaps it is for this reason rather than simply for his boxing feats – exceptional though they were – that his fame does not appear to be fading. He was a sportsman with a conscience who refused to bask in the nationalist rhetoric and racial superiority of the Nazis without ever claiming to have done anything spectacular to oppose it. He was an admirable ordinary man who wanted the good things of life but not at any price; a man with whom the new democratic and increasingly affluent citizens of postwar Germany could identify.

NOTES

1. Hans-Joachim Noack, 'Kraft und Naivität. Härte und Herz', in *Der Spiegel*, 39 (1985), 208.
2. Max Schmeling, *Erinnerungen* (Frankfurt a.M., 1977), p.130.
3. On this point see Chris Mead, *Champion: Joe Louis, Black Hero in White America* (New York, 1985), pp.7 ff.
4. Ibid., p.44.
5. Ibid., pp.67 ff.
6. Schmeling, p.353.
7. Matthias Forster, *Max Schmeling: Sieger im Ring, Sieger im Leben* (Munich, 1987), p.67.
8. Chris Mead, *Champion*, pp.108 ff.
9. Ibid., pp.99 ff.
10. Schmeling, pp.121 ff.
11. Matthias Forster, ibid., p.24. Schmeling himself also writes in his *Erinnerungen* (p.58) that 'Anyone who appears before the public, irrespective of the platform on which he stands, must possess something intangible, a certain radiance, that attracts the public and draws them towards him. This does not have to depend upon talent or ability: it depends upon the individuals themselves. I must have had something of this radiance long before I became a ring attraction because I was winning. This interest was in addition to my abilities. It was never alone centred on the boxer.'
12. Willy Meisl, *Der Sport am Scheidewege* (Heidelberg, 1928), pp.21 ff.
13. Jost Hermand and Frank Trommler, *Die Kultur der Weimarer Republik* (Munich, 1978), p.149.
14. Bertolt Brecht, *The Complete Works*, Vol.III, ed. Name (Berlin, 1964), p.249. Translation is my own.
15. Joyce Carol Oates, *On Boxing* (London, 1987), pp.114–15.
16. Schmeling, pp.100 ff.
17. Oates, *On Boxing*, p.115.
18. Schmeling, p.84.
19. Ibid., pp.10 ff.
20. Horst Moeller, *Weimar: Die unvollendete Demokratie* (Munich, 1985), pp.2–9.
21. Quoted by Karl Mintenbeck, *Es begann 1848: Der Ruhrgebietssport im Spiegel der Presse* (Essen, 1988), p.139.
22. Schmeling, pp.262 ff.
23. Ibid., pp.296 ff.
24. Ibid., pp.445 ff.
25. Mary Gerold-Tucholsky and Gustav Huonker (eds.), *Briefe aus dem Schweigen. Briefe an Nuuna* (Hamburg, 1977), no page numbering.
26. Schmeling, pp.408 ff.
27. Ibid., pp.460 ff.

The Immigrant as Hero: Kopa, Mekloufi and French Football

PIERRE LANFRANCHI and ALFRED WAHL

How can an immigrant be a hero? Is greatness on the field of play the sole requirement? Or does the player have to adopt the culture of the host nation to be accepted by it? There have been a number of instances in recent years of sportsmen and women with ethnic or national origins outside of France, who have become French sporting heroes; but was this possible in previous generations? French football, in particular, had a long tradition of having a substantial number of immigrant players, from Yugoslav students to Polish miners and those who came from French-speaking North Africa. This article examines the contrasting careers of two of the most famous French footballers of the post-war era, their expectations of themselves and public expectations of them: first, Raymond Kopa of Reims, Real Madrid and France, born in France of Polish parents, who saw himself as purely French, both sharing and exemplifying many of the social aspirations of his generation; and, secondly, Rachid Mekloufi, the Algerian-born captain of Saint Etienne, who came to France to play football but remained deeply committed to Algeria personally and politically.

Raymond Kopa: The Meaning of the Myth

Raymond Kopa was the greatest and the most popular French footballer of the 1950s, a status which brought with it social roles which he performed both simultaneously and successively. The star player of Reims, the French champions, later winner of the European Cup with Real Madrid, and finally hero of the French team in the 1958 World Cup in Sweden, he was the idol of several generations of young people. His style of playing provoked a controversy which transcended football and was linked with wider changes in French society in the 1950s. Throughout this period, Kopa symbolised not only the possibilities of social mobility but the successful and full integration of the immigrant. After a brief period in the limelight in the role of rebellious hero, he was soon reconciled to being a source of social stability and cohesion.[1]

The Dream of a Sporting Career

Raymond Kopa was born in 1931. He was picked for the youth team of the Northern League in 1948, and ranked second overall in the competitions traditionally organized at the Colombes Stadium prior to the French Cup Final. When he was eighteen, S.C.O. d'Angers, a second division club, offered him a contract.[2] He moved to Reims during the 1951–52 season and rapidly came to prominence as a result of selection for the France 'B' team. The next season, in October 1952, as a member of the French national team that beat Germany he suddenly became a star. An English journalist coined the term the 'Napoleon' of football after his performance in a match against Spain in June 1955. The following year he played for Reims when they lost in the final of the European Cup against Real Madrid; he then joined that great Real Madrid side himself and won three successive European cups with them. In the mean time he had also taken his place in the French national side, contributing greatly to their superb run in the World Cup in Sweden where they lost in the semi-final to a great Brazilian team, who were the eventual winners. Fontaine, who had a Spanish mother, set a new record of thirteen goals in the tournament, most of them supplied by Kopa. The two players later formed a famous club partnership at Reims who won the French championship in 1960 and 1962.

Throughout the 1950s Kopa was the hero especially of the young in the big city suburbs and in the countryside who dreamed of becoming professionals and being idolised by the crowds. In every team of boys at that time there would be a 'Kopa', earning the nickname for his dribbling skills and technique. For Kopa was known supremely for his skills; he played a particular kind of game – 'beautiful', 'spectacular', 'brilliant' were the kind of adjectives used about him; and it was for this that he was renowned in France.[3]

A Controversial Star as a Player

His style of play started a great debate in the sporting press. In effect, Kopa became the symbol of a graceful way of playing football. His was the example to follow as far as the staff of *Miroir Sprint* and *Le Miroir du Football* of François Thebaud were concerned; these were the sporting papers attached to the Communist press grouping. They stressed the beauty of his game in innumerable accounts, each more rhapsodic than the last, evoking the 'dance', the 'magic' and the 'sorcery' of their hero.[4]

On the other hand, the group of journalists who ran *But et Club* and *France Football* were less impressed. They were former players like Lucien Gamblin and Gabriel Hanot; the latter, an adviser on tactics to the football authorities, was especially concerned with effectiveness and international success. To avoid open conflict with a public already seduced by Kopa, they were obliged to applaud his exploits when his attractive dribbling game and short passing 'in the Reims style' brought success to the team. But if the team lost they did not hesitate to denounce the 'limitations' of his game and his 'contempt' for defence. Gabriel Hanot talked of his 'romantic approach', meaning that he was not really serious about winning and old-fashioned in relation to new ideas of 'effectiveness'. Georges Boulogne, the coach and tactician, who came to prominence in the early 1960s, shared this point of view.[5]

This debate was on the one hand clearly rooted in the game itself. From one point of view there was the beauty of the game, the pleasure of playing and the joy of the spectators; football was to be seen as a leisure activity to be enjoyed without becoming too fanatical about it. On the other hand, there was the view that winning was the most important thing and that all means, including physical commitment and fitness, should be mobilised, even if this detracted from the pleasure of the spectacle. However, it was clear that the debate also went beyond football and was linked to the wider and differing political and social values of left and right in the 1950s. For the journalists from the Communist camp, football had to remain playful, a kind of relaxation and an idealised expression of social harmony; a festival for the players and for the crowd . They were harsh in their criticisms of those they accused of wanting to turn the pitch into a kind of factory where the players were expected to work hard and be subject to harsh discipline in order to win. The upholders of what they called 'modern' football, however, believed the game had to adopt the dominant values of contemporary economic life: rigour, hard work and discipline. They were in harmony with the wider legislation being enacted as France was transformed and modernised at a hectic economic pace. In this 'New France' older ways of doing things were under attack. Without his realising it or wishing it, Kopa was caught up in a wider debate about the fundamental changes taking place in France and its future.

The Star Who Symbolised Social Mobility

Raymond Kopa had been born in Noeux-les-Mines in the mining area of northern France, to immigrant parents born in Poland. His family name was Kopaszewski. His father and his elder brother were both miners but Kopa himself dreamed of becoming an electrician. This modest ambition failed and he too went briefly to the mines. Later the press would write of Kopa the 'poor pit-boy' when it wanted to promote him as a model of social mobility in a society where talent could flourish, the so-called 'New France'.

There are two versions of why Kopa became a miner instead of an apprentice electrician. Both are significant. The first claims that going down the mine was simply a matter of economic necessity as the family needed another income. But in his 1972 autobiography Kopa himself gives another version. He blamed the attitudes of those around him, their lack of knowledge and contacts.[6] Whatever the true version, both explanations were used to stress just how far he had come in terms of social advancement. Kopa's own view fitted in rather better with the new sociological orthodoxy that it was not so much absolute poverty which held back individual mobility as social and cultural deprivation.

Kopa often underlined his satisfaction at having 'made it' in material terms. Money was the first step on the ladder of social advancement from humble beginnings. His villa at Angers was the concrete expression of his success. Of course, Kopa's social promotion has to be seen in the context of what someone starting from the bottom could hope to achieve in the 1950s. This was of a different and more modest order to the vast incomes and assets offered to less gifted players only twenty years later.

The Myth of the Well-Integrated Immigrant

Raymond Kopa never tried to keep in touch with his Polish roots. The son of an immigrant but born in France, he never tired of stressing that he was a Frenchman. He even claimed that he could hardly speak Polish although his parents had arrived in France in 1919 aged fifteen and still spoke to each other in Polish at home.[7] At the outset his origins hindered Kopa: he was unable to get a place as an apprentice electrician partly because the Poles were seen as destined only for the mines. Furthermore, he had been unable to play in the French youth team because he was not French. However, at the age of twenty-one he took out French citizenship and cheerfully did his military service. Numerous press photos of Kopa in his military uniform testify to this strong desire to be French. He was a more than willing partner in the publicity[8] and endlessly and rather ostentatiously reiterated his pride in being French, of representing his country, of 'defending the French colours to the limits of his powers'. His whole story was designed to show how well-integrated he was and, like many new French citizens, how happy to be so well accepted.

The Promoter of Social Harmony

There is no doubt that Kopa was an aristocrat of the football world. His presence on the field and his performance were lordly. His natural class marked him out as an exceptional being and put him among the sporting elite. And yet his biographers and the press never forgot to supply the parallel image of Kopa the artisan, who worked at his game. For it was important that Kopa's career should illustrate the hard path by which those born at the bottom might ascend the social ladder. It was not appropriate that a humble footballer should simply inherit natural gifts as the son of a rich family might do, seeming to play around and still coming out top of an elite graduate school (*'grande école'*). On the contrary, Kopa had to appear to sweat for his laurels; his success had to be seen to be the product of hard labour, unfailing self-denial and constant discipline. The very difficulties of his childhood had given Kopa the means to surmount them: 'If I had been born into a wealthy family, there would probably never have been a Raymond Kopa. Without the mine, I'd have been a good player. Nothing more. But there was the mine. My name was Kopaszewski and to get out I had nothing but football.'[9]

Kopa was happy to play the part. When he finished his playing career in 1967, he frequently addressed himself to lower class youth in moralising terms. The young were having it too easy. He deplored the fact that improved facilities no longer provided the challenges necessary for character-building. Thus he became a significant social actor. In maintaining that hard work alone could bring social success, Kopa appeared as a force for order and harmony. His own career was the proof of what hard work could do and was used to promote acceptance of the wider social system.

A Rebellious Hero

Nevertheless his career was not entirely without political incident. He was no mere stooge of the Establishment. In 1963 Kopa abruptly involved himself in the denunciation of the code regulating the contracts of professional players. He gave an interview to the mass circulation *France Dimanche* denouncing the fact that 'today, in the middle of the twentieth century, the professional footballer is the only man who can be bought and sold without anyone even asking his opinion'.[10] These regulations in effect tied players to a club until they were thirty-five, in violation of the general labour laws of the country. When the left-wing sporting papers announced their support for Kopa, rival magazines more to the right immediately took the contrary view. His popularity meant that he could not be criticised too fiercely; rather more subtle and indirect lines of attack had to be found.

First of all *France Football* wrote '...the only truth that Raymond Kopa has to offer is on the pitch, the best gift he can give us is his play'. In other words, play up and shut up. The same magazine accused Kopa of being a recent convert to militant trade unionism. Discussing the question of disqualification, *France Football* presented him as a man incapable of understanding the complex problems involved in the structure of professional football. For *Football Magazine*, Kopa was simply badly advised, surrounded by dubious characters, even manipulated. Kopa could only be shown the respect he deserved if he was kept under control and appropriately advised.[11]

Kopa never really understood the role which the two opposing camps in the sporting press wanted him to play. He showed his gratitude to the Communist-inclined sporting press by giving them favours without understanding or wanting to understand what it was about his way of playing that accorded so well with their wider conception of society. He was far too keen to stick exactly to the image that the right-wing press had of him to see how they exploited this image to spread the message of social conformity. Moreover, the ideal of the separation of sport and politics was so deeply entrenched that neither the left- nor the right- wing press could be too open about their manipulation of his image without incurring the wrath of their readers. It was the very fact that his life was for the most part not explicitly politicised that made the social myth and the message of conformity it carried all the more potent.

Mekloufi: A French Footballer in the Algerian War

When, in April 1958, Rachid Mekloufi joined nine other professional players of Algerian origin to help form a football team for the Algerian national liberation movement, the FLN team, he abandoned the French national team preparing for the World Cup Finals in Sweden and instantly became an Algerian national symbol. A few months earlier he had been part of a French team which won the world military football competition in Buenos Aires on the French national day, 14 July 1957. As a member of that team he had been portrayed as a model of the fraternal and successful integration of the indigenous Arabic population and the large settler community in a French Algeria, the legitimacy of which the political authorities were striving to establish on the eve of the Franco-Algerian War. Ten years later, in May 1968, as captain of Saint Etienne, he received the French Cup from the hands of General de Gaulle, who congratulated the players with the historic words 'La France, c'est vous'.

Roger Chartier has noted that 'understanding sport in terms of a variety of different historical configurations leads to acceptance of a fundamental link with politics and denial of the autonomy of sporting activities'.[12] As a representative of the professional player in France and a symbol of revolution in Algeria, Mekloufi embodies the contradiction and the conflict between sport and politics. As an Algerian he played football, which was, after all, despite being widely played in the Islamic community, a colonial sport, the game of the occupier. He was seen as too attached to this aspect of European culture, and to succeed in the sport he had to prove himself in France, at Saint Etienne. His usefulness as a symbol of Algeria was only fully apparent when he was chosen to play for France in international matches and his departure in April 1958, as Jean Meynaud remarked, only took on its full meaning when seen in the context of the struggle of others equally well-integrated to obtain formal recognition of the fact of Algerian nationality.[13]

Although a hero of the struggle for liberation and of the FLN, in fact Mekloufi spent his war peacefully on the football fields and in the hotels of Tunis without touching a weapon or setting foot on Algerian soil. He was too valuable a symbolic commodity to risk in action. Once the war ended and Algeria became independent in 1962, unlike his other FLN team members, he briskly resumed his professional career and returned to France. Hence his popularity in Algeria derives more from mythology and popular imagination than from the experience of seeing him play in his native land and the adulation of the crowds on the terraces of Algerian football grounds.

But, just as the reality of the war in Algeria was fading in the national mind, the exploits of Mekloufi kept the memory of the conflict alive:[14] for some he was a prodigal son, for others the embodiment of the spirit of the Algerian revolution. He was criticised in France for his political commitment and in Algeria, which had set out on the socialist path, for his professionalism. He finally returned to Algeria in 1970 and became coach to the national team. In this role his professional approach and his allegedly European way of running the national team brought him into frequent conflict with the political system. For the last twenty years the African press have presented him as competent and popular but incapable of adapting to the reality of sport in Algeria with its compromises, changes of course and improvisation.

The Political Symbol

Mekloufi's case poses the problem of the interpretation of a sportsman as a symbol in two different societies and from two diametrically opposed points of view. The sheer sense of pleasure bound up with the passionate sense of identification which football creates helped form the myth of Mekloufi and the FLN team. Yet ideological accounts tend to present the sport as dominated by politics, as if the stadium were no more than a site for the struggle between the dominators and the dominated.[15] In colonial society, especially in Africa, there was a marked increase in the popularity of football after the Second World War,[16] which has been interpreted in terms of a wider political mobilisation.[17]

If it is seen as a legacy of cultural imperialism, the Algerian passion for football can only be legitimised if it becomes part of a struggle against colonialism using colonial methods.[18] In fact, from the summer of 1954 onwards, the football stadium assumed a significant role in FLN strategy. During the final phase of the World Cup in Switzerland in 1954 a summit conference brought together the main political figures from Cairo, Algiers and Paris – Boudiaf, Ben Boulaid, Didouche and Ben Bella and the decision to resort to armed struggle was taken.[19] On 26 May 1957, on the occasion of the French Cup Final, Ali Chekkal, former President of the Algerian Assembly, was assassinated by Mohammed Ben Sadok, a member of the FLN.[20] The victim had been a firm supporter of the indissoluble link between France and Algeria, and two of the best of the Toulouse players at the game, Said Brahimi and Ahmed Bouchouk, were, like Mekloufi, members of the FLN.[21] This subsequently inspired a novel by Rachid Boudjedra in which he describes Ben Sadok as a political activist, who was uninterested in football.[22]

Algerian writing stressed the political role of the FLN team: 'sport in the service of liberty';[23] Mekloufi was simply 'the footballer of the Revolution'.[24] Similarly, in France politicisation of football continued and football is now seen as an antidote to racism and the National Front: 'the French team is a team against Le Pen just as all the French teams were, filled with the likes of Kopa and Budinski, Ben Barek and Platini, Ujlaki and Mekloufi'.[25]

A few months before the Algerian players left France for Tunis, pro-Castro insurgents in Cuba had kidnapped Fangio just before a Grand Prix in Havana, and released him a few hours later – an action which the Argentinean driver refused to condemn.[26] For this group of revolutionaries a sporting event was unacceptable if it contributed to the stability of a dictatorial regime. Similarly the FLN stated: 'As patriots seeking the liberation of their country above all else, our footballers have given the youth of Algeria a example of courage, rectitude and unselfishness'.[27]

En route for Tunis the FLN players were received in Switzerland by Ferrhat Abbas and applauded by the Tunisian President Habib Bourguiba upon their arrival with the words 'I wish you great success and Algeria her liberty as quickly as possible.'[28] But they had to put their political commitment to the test on the field in front of the crowds. They had to 'honour the true spirit of football – and be attacking, constructive and spectacular'.[29] In the words of Franz Fanon: 'the colonial peoples should win but they should do so without barbarity'.[30]

As ambassadors of the FLN, Mekloufi and his team-mates appeared in fourteen countries between 1958 and 1962: Tunisia, Morocco, Libya, Iraq,

Jordan, the Soviet Union, Poland, Czechoslovakia, Hungary, Romania, Bulgaria, Yugoslavia, China and North Vietnam, prefiguring the alliances of the future Algerian Republic itself.[31] Their style and success seemed a message of hope and renewal. For the left-wing French sports press, notably the monthly *Miroir du Football,* Mekloufi and his comrades had a politically engaged playing style. It also praised Kerroum, a player with Association Sportive de Troyes, only a few days before he rejoined the FLN team at Tunis: he was 'intelligent, thoughtful and simple, a creator despite the weaknesses of the colonial training system , not to be understood just in terms of his technical skill but as a representative of the combatants in the struggle for liberation'.[32]

Scoring an average of four goals a game and winning many of their games, the FLN team embodied the inescapable momentum towards victory of the liberation movement itself.[33] Overturning right-wing stereotypes, the *Miroir du Football* wrote in December 1960 that 'the Algerian players gave their Tunisian friends considerable help in understanding the collective side of the game'.[34] This 'Algerian model' inspired others, notably a Palestinian team also based in Tunis, who have played regularly in Algeria. However, this team has not been successful enough to promote the image of Palestine as a modern and victorious nation and consequently has never been a strong political symbol.[35]

Once independence was achieved, Mekloufi migrated once more back to France. He was unable to follow his career in a new country where professionalism in sport was banned. He was, in the phrase of Abdelmalek Said, part of a second wave of emigrants pushed back to France by their ambiguous status in Algeria.[36] Once again the logic of sport and of politics were opposed. Official recognition of Algeria and the end of his playing suspension encouraged him to play competitively again, despite threats from the OAS.[37] Although he showed his commitment by participating in annual reunions of the FLN team for gala matches against their old rivals until the mid-1970s, in other respects he returned more or less to being an ordinary professional player.[38]

The Sporting Symbol

For four years I became an absent, anonymous footballer, playing matches that were too easy and following a training regime that was not tough enough. I had lost the taste for effort, the necessary fight. However, I had also learned a good deal watching others; the Hungarians whose creativity and inventiveness were constantly renewed; the Yugoslavs, artistic but still fighters. For four years I

roamed around the world. In China and in Vietnam I learned
something too, their joy in playing, their simplicity of approach,
qualities we tend to neglect.[39]

This piece of self-criticism and reflection came in an interview given to
Football Magazine, part of the *L'Equipe* group, which had so strongly
criticised him during his absence from France for bringing politics into
football, and marked his rehabilitation as a sportsman in France.[40]
Meanwhile football in Algeria became increasingly fraught with difficulty.
After his departure from Algeria, the Minister for Sport and Youth, Sadek-
Bartel, decided in 1964 to forbid spectators from watching championship
matches because of incidents between spectators on the terraces.[41] Football
grounds, in fact, remained favoured places for political conflict.[42]

The underlying logic of the sporting hero was constructed in terms of
two axioms, both of which Mekloufi's career had called into question. The
first concerned the independence of the world of sport from the social, the
political and the economic; the second suggested that the worth of a
sportsman was determined at different stages of his career in terms of team
selection or payment, over which he had no control.

Mekloufi could be seen therefore as a symbol of the autonomy of sport
and distanced from wider discrimination against indigenous Algerians. He
was born in Setif in 1937 and in 1954 his qualities as a footballer brought
him to the notice of scouts from Saint Etienne who watched him play for
Union Franco-Musalmanne de Sétif in 1954. Politics did not come into it.
The example of the Moroccan, Ben Barek, star of Marseille and of Atletico
Madrid, was already there to prove that sport had its own rules. In the case
of Algeria, football formed a privileged space where the two communities
mixed. According to the evidence of some 'pieds noirs' (French settlers),
'football really was a common bond between the two communities'.[43] Were
not Albert Camus, the goalkeeper for the young Racing Universitaire
d'Alger and Ahmed Ben Bella, who had played professionally for
Olympique Marseille, the most eloquent proof of the autonomy of sport?

However, until 1956 Algerian teams were not entitled to enter the
French cup competition or the professional championship and when the
French team came to Algeria it was only to play against local teams; an
official representative match was never played in Algeria. After Mekloufi
left France, a match between Real Madrid, one of the best ambassadors of
a Spain still isolated on the international scene, and Reims, the most
prestigious club in France, was organised at Oran.[44] This was done to
comfort a 'football public which had been more concerned about the
disappearance of Mustapha Zitouni than Ferrhat Abbas and was still in
shock over the departure of ten Algerian players'.[45] Mekloufi felt he owed

his status as a star not to politics but to the game and especially to his trainer, Jean Snella. 'When I was just seventeen, he changed the course of my life and my career. But when I was twenty-six he was there again, in Geneva, to give me a second chance as a professional footballer'.[46] He took full advantage of this and charmed the crowds and his fellow players. His team-mate at Saint Etienne, Bernard Bosquier, noted that 'everything he did was bright and of a childlike simplicity; he had a genius for taking on the defense on one side of the pitch and seemingly without looking shifting the play to the other. This was what Jean Snella called his dummy runs'.[47]

Here was a player who in the late 1960s crticised the Algerian authorities for refusing to allow talented young players to sign professionally in France and who said that his happiest moment as a player had been winning the world army championship with the French team in 1957; even adding that he still thought fondly of the French team: 'When they're beaten, I feel fed up.'[48] However, he also criticised French coaches, who on the pretext of helping Algerian football, stopped talented young players from expressing themselves.

It was over his sporting integrity that Mekloufi had been most criticised in France: 'one could well imagine that the players concerned, Zitouni and Mekloufi in particular, who were internationals and certain to be selected for [the World Cup] in Sweden submitted reluctantly to the political pressure placed upon them. Others joined their exiled comrades in Tunis. For more than four years they lived out the disappointed existence of revolutionary footballers. The career of Zitouni ended there whilst Mekloufi saw his chance for greatness melt away.'[49] And yet he was also criticised in Algeria after 1962: 'Neither indispensable nor negligible, recourse to players in exile to be beneficial should be part of well-defined plan and not just a response to the demands of the masses or for the purposes of expedience.'[50] Mekloufi remarked in 1990, when he had become a luminary of Algerian football, rising to the Presidency of the Federation and living in the smart, expensive suburb of Hydra, 'You know, in my own country I take steps that don't always please those who decide things. It may be logical to the majority but illogical to the authorities, and it's always been that way.'[51]

During the 1970s the Algerian team, trained by a Romanian, suffered defeat after defeat without making use of the services of Dahleb, who like Mekloufi had opted for professionalism; some commentators saw in this a baleful illustration of the disappointed hopes of the revolution.[52] Two years before Mekloufi had been dismissed for wanting to inspire the team along French lines. Too impregnated with professional sporting methods and attitudes associated with those who had emigrated, he never succeeded in winning over the Algerian power elite after his final return from France, whilst in France he is remembered as an excellent player too involved in politics for the good of his career and the interests of French football. Too professional and Europeanized to be a true hero in Algeria, his career was too interrupted and politicised to satisfy the French.

Kopa and Mekloufi could hardly have followed more different paths. Kopa sought to be French, not just to be assimilated into France but to be fully integrated. His life seemed to fulfil the Republican ideals of moral and material progress within a tradition and framework that defined nationality in cultural rather than ethnic terms; French democracy in principle provided for a meritocracy based upon the Declaration of the Rights of Man. Kopa availed himself fully of the possibilities France offered him. In doing so he personified not just the new immigrant's longing for success and acceptance but drive for material improvement and social mobility that typified so many of the working class in a period of rapid economic growth – the 'Long Boom' of the late 1950s and 1960s. But Kopa was born in France and alienated from his roots. Not so Mekloufi. He grew up in Algeria and gave up his chance to play in the 1958 World Cup for France because of his loyalty to his country, and perhaps fear of ostracism if he did not heed the call of the FLN. Kopa was admired by many ordinary Frenchmen for making money: Mekloufi was worshipped by the Algerian masses for refusing colonial gold. Kopa was the greater player and the more enduring sporting hero, Mekloufi the more potent and powerful symbol. Kopa remains a mythic figure, still seen and quoted in the game; Mekloufi's status seems less secure: he is still a great figure, but one whose fame depended too much on changing political fashions and too little on his remarkable natural talent as a player.

NOTES

The section on Kopa was written by Alfred Wahl and that on Mekloufi by Pierre Lanfranchi; the article was translated by Richard Holt.

1. For a survey of French football see A. Wahl, *Les archives du football: sport et société en France 1880–1980* (Paris: Gallimard, 1989); for the professional context of Kopa's career see A. Wahl and P. Lanfranchi, *Les footballeurs professionels des années trente* (Hachette Paris, 1995); R. Kopa, *Mes matches et ma vie* (Paris, 1958) is an early autobiography that was followed later by R. Kopa and P.Katz, *Mon Football* (Paris, 1972); see also B. Verret, *Raymond Kopa d'hier et d'aujourd'hui* (Paris, 1980).
2. For details of his early career see A. Wahl, 'Raymond Kopa une vedette du football', *Sport Histoire*, 2 (1988), 84–6.
3. Kopa as a player is discussed in P.Delaunay, J. de Ryswick, J. Cornu and D. Vermand, *100 ans de football en France* (Paris, 1986); see also J. Ph. Rethacker, 'Raymond Kopa, in *Nos champions* (Paris, 1955).
4. *Sport Histoire*, 2 (1988), 87.
5. Ibid.
6. R. Kopa and P. Katz, *Mon football*.
7. For the wider context of immigration into French football, see Wahl and Lanfranchi, *Les footballeurs professionels*, pp.129–38.

8. *Sport Histoire*, 2 (1988), 91 for a photo of Kopa arriving at the barracks.
9. Wahl and Lanfranchi, *Les footballeurs professionels*, p.136.
10. See *France Dimanche*, the May issues, 1963.
11. Press reaction is examined more fully in *Sport Histoire*, 2 (1988), 94–6.
12. R. Chartier, comment on 'Sport, Religion and Violence', *Esprit*, special number on 'the new age of sport' (April 1987), 69.
13. J. Meynaud, *Sport et Politique* (Paris: Payot, 1966), p.29.
14. B. Stora, *La gangrène et l'oubli: la mémoire de la guerre d'Algérie* (Paris: La Découverte, 1991), p.252.
15. There is a large Anglo-Saxon literature on colonial sport, especially cricket, notably B. Stoddart, 'Sport, cultural imperialism and colonial response in the British Empire', *Comparative Studies in Society and History*, 30, 4 (1988); also J.A. Mangan and W.J. Baker (eds.), *Sport in Africa: Essays in Social History* (New York, 1987).
16. As early as 1934 there were more officially registered players in Algeria than in the Paris region (13,494 against 13,448) but facilities were unequally distributed (110 equipped stadiums in Paris against only 20 in Algeria), Meeting of the Fédération Française de Football reported in *Les sports du Sud Est*, 21 and 26 July 1934.
17. B. Stora, 'Algérie, années coloniales: quand le sport devient un facteur de mobilisation politique', *Jeu et Sport en Méditerranée*, Actes du Colloque de Carthage, 7–9 Nov. 1989 (published in Tunis, ed. Alif, 1991), pp.143–53.
18. This area has seen some of the most interesting work on the spread of sport. The formal equalising of chances permits an assertion of identity, for example, D.J. Roden, 'Baseball and the Quest for National Dignity in Meiji Japan', *American Historical Review* (1980), 229–45; also, Tony Mason, 'Football on the Maidan: Cultural Imperialism in Calcutta', *International Journal of the History of Sport*, 7, 1 (1990), 85–96.
19. C.H. Favrod, 'La Suisse des négociations secrètes', in J-P Rioux, *La guerre d' Algérie et les français* (Paris, Fayard, 1990), p.397.
20. M. Amar, *Nés pour courir: sport, pouvoirs et rebellions 1944–58* (Grenoble, P.U., 1987).
21. *Le Monde*, 28 May 1957.
22. R. Boudjedra, *Le vainqueur de coupe* (Paris: Denoel, 1981).
23. F. Chehat, '1958–1962: La grande saga de l'Equipe du FLN', *Actualité de l'immigration*, 97, 8–15 July 1987, 129–31.
24. F. Mahjoub, *Le football africain* (Paris: Jeune Afrique livres, 1988), p.185.
25 P. Demerin, Seville, in *Autrement*, 80 (May 1986), 122.
26. Amar, *Nés pour courir*.
27. FLN Communiqué, *Le Monde*, 17 April 1958.
28. *Le Monde*, 22 April 1958.
29. F. Mahjoub, '30,000 Algérois ont choisi le football', *Miroir du Football*, 229, 21 November 1974.
30. F. Fanon, *Sociologie d'une révolution* (Paris: Maspero, 1960), p.10.
31. F. Chehat, '1958–1962'.
32. F. Thebaud, *Le temps du 'Miroir': une autre idée du football et du journalisme* (Paris: Albatros, 1982) traces the history and political involvement of the *Miroir du Football*.
33. The FLN team won 43 of its 57 matches scoring 244 goals, Chehat, op.cit.
34. *Miroir du Football*, 11 November 1960: 'the inadequate education I received and the fact I was never taught a skill left me only able to be a shopkeeper after my career was over'.
35. *El Pais Magazine*, 2 February 1992.
36. A. Said, 'Les trois ages de l'émigration algérienne en France', *Actes de la recherche en sciences sociales*, 15 (June 1977), 59–79, which notes that emigrants aged between 20 and 35 made up 60 per cent in 1954.
37. M. Granger and B. Poullet, *La grande histoire de l'ASSE* (Le Coteau: Horvath, 1985), pp.97–8; in an interview in November 1991 Mekloufi minimised this danger without denying it.
38. FIFA suspended the FLN players and banned any of their members from playing with them. On the demand of the French Football Federation the Moroccan Football Federation was excluded from FIFA for its contacts with the Algerians and the French expressed their

disappointment when Morocco was readmitted in 1959 (FIFA archives letters of 12 Dec. 1958 and 14 May 1959). To avoid the risk of suspension teams playing the FLN did so informally but often including their best players. Algeria was admitted to FIFA in the autumn of 1962.

39. Interview of Mekloufi in *Football Magazine*, 89 (June 1967).
40. *L'Equipe* 15 April 1958; E. Seidler, *Le sport et la presse* (Paris, 1969), provides good evidence of official attitudes.
41. *Le Monde*, 28 May 1964.
42. Y. Fates, 'Jeunesse, sports et politiques', *Peuples méditerranéens*, 52–3 (1990), 57–72.
43. Rioux, *La guerre d'Algérie et les français*, p.528.
44. C. Fernandez-Santander, *El futebol durante la guerra civil Franquismo* (Madrid: San Martin, 1991), p.154.
45. Editorial by André Fontaine in *Le Monde*, 17 April 1958.
46. Rachid Mekloufi interview, *Miroir Sprint*, 23 October 1965.
47. B. Bosquier (with J. Thibert), *Vive le Football!* (Paris: Calmann-Levy, 1973), 103–5.
48. *Miroir Sprint*, 23 October 1965.
49. J. Thibert and J. Rethacker, *La fabuleuse histoire du football* (Paris: ODIL, 1962), pp.434–6.
50. F. Mahjoub, *Le football africain*, 30; for a similar case see R. Holt, 'King across the Border: Dennis Law and Scottish Football', in G. Jarvie and G. Walker, *Scottish Sport and the Making of the Nation* (Leicester University Press, 1994), pp.58–74.
51. Interview in *Afrique Football*, 24 January 1990.
52. F. Mahjoub, *Miroir du Football*, 229, 21 November 1974.

Italian Cycling and the Creation of a Catholic Hero: The Bartali Myth

STEFANO PIVATO

The barriers between East and West have collapsed in recent years and the former ideological confrontations of the Cold War era are disappearing so quickly that it is already becoming difficult to imagine how strong they once were. In some ways the most recent past can be the most remote. In a world now dominated by political pragmatism and the free market, the 1940s and 1950s – years of the opposing ideologies of capitalism and communism, of the American and Soviet systems, and in Italy of the Christian Democrat Catholic Right and the Italian Communist Party (PCI) – seem to belong to another age. These old alignments are now disintegrating in Italy, especially on the Right as the Christian Democrat network of patronage and corruption is exposed. Nor is the PCI, once the largest Communist Party outside the Soviet block, the force it was. All in all the early Cold War era seems further away than the relatively short period of time that has actually elapsed since figures like Peppone and Don Camillo, the anti-clerical mayor and the anti-Communist priest, amused a generation of cinemagoers and were household names. Not so long ago these crude literary and cinematic stereotypes were credible, a metaphor of Italy in the 1940s and 1950s – the post-fascist clerical Italy of Pius XII, of Togliatti, the leader of the Left, and of Gino Bartali, the great Catholic racing cyclist and Fausto Coppi, his 'Communist' rival.[1]

This article seeks to explain how a sport came to be sharply ideologically split; to understand how two great sportsmen, who more or less retained cordial personal relations throughout, were adopted and projected in the press and on the screen as representatives of opposed traditions. There can, perhaps, be no more striking example of how sport can be 'constructed' along ideological lines determined by the traditions and circumstances of the nation-state than the story of Bartali and Coppi. To understand this extraordinary politicization of these two heroes after the Second World War one must go back to the Fascist era when Bartali first emerged as a champion of Catholicism. For it was Bartali, the older of the two, whose career was first embedded in the political discourse of Italy. Coppi came later and his opposed image as 'Communist' (he was never politically active) was a response from the Left to the systematic exploitation of the the pious Bartali by the Right. Hence the bulk of our analysis will focus on the careful creation of Bartali as a model Catholic first under Mussolini, when the Church wished to distinguish itself in terms of popular culture from the Fascist model; then later during the post-war reconstruction of Italy, when the Church and the Communists were locked in a stuggle for power culminating in the elections of April 1948 and the beginning of the forty-year Christian Democrat domination of Italian public life.[2]

Whilst the reputation of these two great cycling champions was bound up in the politics of the period, their impact on millions of Italians cannot be understood without some idea of the brilliance and magnetism of their performances; for these were no ordinary victors of ordinary races; they were in their different ways two of the greatest riders of all time, endowed with amazing reserves of strength, courage and determination. Bartali, born in 1914, won the Giro d'Italia in 1936 and then the Tour de France in 1938. The war intervened and it was not until 1946 that he resumed his racing career – an exceptionally long interruption in so physically demanding a sport – and went on to win the Giro d'Italia that year. Remarkably this was only the beginning of a second flowering of a career that included winning the Tour of Lombardy, the Milan San Remo four times, the Giro d'Italia three times and the Tour de France again in 1948. Bartali seemed to defy time, to refuse to age like other mortals.

Behind Bartali in the 1946 Giro came Fausto Coppi, who was five years younger than Bartali. Thus began the rivalry that became the most popular element of Italian sporting mythology after the war. At this point Gino Bartali was nearly 32 – quite old for an athlete of this kind – and the victory of the 'old' Bartali over the 'young' Coppi became an essential mythic element in the great races that were to come. Bartali alone could put up a struggle against the athletic superiority and freshness of Coppi, the 'Campionissimo', the 'champion of champions'. After winning the Tour in 1946, Gino Bartali won the Milan-San Remo in 1947 aged 33 and came second behind Coppi in the Tour of Italy. In 1948 he won his second Tour de France at the age of 34 in a race that the sports journalist Emilio de Martino of the Gazzetta dello Sport called with typical understatement 'the greatest sporting enterprise of all time'![3] The following year, however, indisputably belonged to Fausto Coppi. In a season that will be remembered in Italy as long as bicycles are raced, he won both the Giro and the Tour – two races of similar length and demanding terrain – in a feat that was widely held to be beyond the physical and psychological resources of any single rider.[4] But with Coppi and Bartali it was not just the fact of winning but the manner of victory that set them apart. As riders they had much in common; neither liked sprinting and both were masters in the mountains, risking all in long, lonely breaks from the main pack, driving themselves to the limit in the Alps and Pyrenees. A lone rider pulling away from the field, forcing himself up seemingly impossible gradients, descending at breakneck speeds through compelling and vast landscapes – this really was the stuff of sporting heroism. The Tour builds up slowly to the climax of the Alps. Here Bartali and Coppi had some of their finest moments. The Alpe d'Huez, the most imposing of all, climbs to nearly 8,000 feet, 'a steep ladder of hairpins rises to the most imposing sight of all, the Casse déserte, a ledge of road cut across a vast incline of small rocks like an arrested landslide. From this rubble jagged pinnacles of brown rock protrude, and on the side of one of these is a plaque to the memory of Fausto Coppi. Subscribed by readers of L'Equipe (for he was more than an Italian hero), it bears a bronze relief of the Campionissimo's head looking back across the route of his great solo ride in 1951'.[5]

In Coppi's triumphal year of 1949, Bartali came in second in both the Tour de France and the Tour of Italy. The next year he won the Milan-San Remo for the fourth time. Finally in 1952, at the age of 38, he wore again the tricolour jersey of the Champion of Italy. Like Coppi he was a great solo rider, just as brave if less dramatic, but in his longevity in what was the most physically demanding of sports even more remarkable. Out of these elements the Italian Catholic press fashioned a new myth of 'eternal Christian youth'. To understand the origins of this distinctive set of sporting and ideological oppositions, one has to go back before Coppi to the 1930s and the activities of the Catholic propagandists.

How did Bartali come to be seen as the 'perfect Christian athlete'?[6] This image came into being after his first professional victories in 1936. One of the leading sports journalists of the period, Carlo Bergoglio, revealed to the public the deep Catholic faith of the rider. After interviewing Bartali during the Tour of Italy for the Gazzetta del Popolo, he wrote that the Tuscan cyclist was a 'God-fearing man who wore the insignia of Catholic Action and went to mass every Sunday'.[7] Carlo Trebucco, who, like Begoglio, was a Catholic journalist from Turin, Piedmont, which was a stronghold of Catholic activism, observed: 'Bartali is not only a serious young man, he is pure of heart ... his deep faith, his serenity, make this racing cyclist a magnificent Christian athlete. Catholic Action should be proud to have him as an example to others, a light shining in the world which is all the more beautiful for being the only one.'[8]

This article marked the beginning of a widespread propaganda campaign in the Catholic press, which at times almost amounted to canonising Bartali. In addition to Bergolio and Trabucco, there were other Catholic journalsits like Antonio Cojazzi, Dino Bertoliti and Bartolo Paschetta, who stressed in their various ways his 'steely faith', his dramatic and 'angelic' appearance, and his regular participation 'at meetings of Catholic Youth'. At the same time the Catholic press forged a new vocabulary , which for over twenty years described the achievements of Bartali as those of a 'magnificent Christian athlete', 'an archangel of the mountains', the 'pious Bartali', 'the winged hero', 'Gino the mystic', 'the divine climber'.[9]

Behind this remarkable campaign lay the skilful hand of Luigi Gedda, who had been a Catholic youth leader in Piedmont and became President of the Italian Catholic Youth movement in 1934. Gedda, who was closely associated with the creation of the Bartali myth both in the Fascist period and in the Christian Democrat years after the War, was an enthusiast for the new forms of popular culture. He had written a book, *Lo Sport*, in 1931.[10] He became deeply involved in Catholic youth propaganda from 1932 onwards, seeking to use popular magazines and the cinema to promote the Church. Bartolo Paschetta was close to Gedda and acted as a press agent for him, obtaining the maximum favourable publicity for the Catholic Youth movement. But why did the national president of this body try to mobilise journalists around the figure of Bartali? Why did Gedda chose a champion sportsman as a role model for the Catholic youth?

Here an understanding of the political context of popular culture in the 1930s is essential. Gedda came from the political wing of the Italian Catholic sports movement, which had come into being in the early twentieth century as the Church moved away from mass gymnastic displays and moral education through sport to embrace the Anglo-Saxon and even protestant sports like football for more directly political ends. Cycling, which orignated in Britain and France, also proved popular. Activist political Catholics set up proper 'clubs' rather than 'circles' with names like Robor, Fortitudo, Juventus, Audax Vogor, and Vis Nova, which challenged the 'liberal' state-supported clubs, especially in the strongly anti-clerical areas like Romagna and Tuscany. These clubs prospered. But when Mussolini came to power in 1922 new problems arose. The Fascists set up a mass leisure and sport movement, the Dopolavoro, which aimed to bring the youth of Italy into a new nationalist concensus organized around the leisure activity of the corporate state. They resented the entrenched power of the Church in this area and in 1927 the Church agreed to close down its own Catholic sports clubs. However, these continued to be active informally and again, in an agreement of 2 September 1931, the Fascist state required the Catholics to limit themselves to purely recreational and religious activities; competitive sport was not permitted in Catholic youth clubs in order to encourage mass attendance at the state clubs. For a man like Gedda this was a blow despite the measure of ideological sympathy there was between the Church and the Fascist state. Denied the possibility of promoting Catholic sport through direct participation, the chance to exploit the new importance of mass spectator sport for Catholic propaganda was clearly attractive.

Mussolini was extremely keen to use sport to promote a virile chauvinist image of Italy abroad. This was precisely the period when a new element was introduced into the collective psychology of the Italian public: the cult of the sports star. During the 1930s a whole new set of names entered the popular imagination: Nuvolari, Meazza, Guerra, Giradengo, Carnera, Varzi among many others. The 1930s were above all the golden age of football; its group solidarity and stress on grass roots organisation along with its huge potential for spectator mobilisation behind the national team gave it a favoured place in the sports policy of the Fascist regime. Between 1930 and 1938 Italian football won two World Cups and one Olympic title. Bologna, 'the team that shook the world', who won the Paris Exhibition Tournament in 1937, 'won a hard battle using the virile style and irresistible attacks that characterize Fascist atheltes', according to Leatti, the Secretary of the Partito Nazionale Fascista. 'They present themselves before the crowds of the whole world,' he enthused, 'in the image of their nation: young, valiant, combative everywhere, at every moment, in every action.'[11] The national team, known by their national colours as the 'Azzuri', were personally congratulated and urged on by Mussolini. Historians of Fascism have demonstrated the role of these great sporting moments and personalities in creating acceptance of the regime.[12]

Hence the creation of a 'Champion of the Faith' has not only to be set in the context of new forms of popular culture but also of Italian Fascist propaganda. Although the Catholic Church had made a Concordat with the regime and approved of its anti-socialist policies, Catholic and Fascist popular culture were by no means identical. In particular, the Church was critical of the swaggering, macho image popular in the Fascist youth movement and cult of the body, personified in the posturing of Mussolini with his mistresses. Although there was no question of making open attacks on the Fascist state, it was possible to promote an alternative vision of manhood along more traditional Catholic lines. For this the Church needed someone with whom the youth of Italy could identitfy. The young Gino Bartali was the answer to a Catholic prayer, especially after he won the Tour de France in 1938.

Here was a man around whom they could build a myth which would stress the differences between the sensual and militaristic Fascist image of man and the Christian ideal. By praising Bartali they could by implication criticise the excesses of Fascist propaganda without directly challenging the Fascist state. Cycling was a sport approved by the Church unlike for example, boxing, a favourite with the Fascists. Gedda had remarked that 'there was no difference between a boxer breaking a skull and an aborigone from Queensland doing the same thing with a boomerang – except that the aborigine is more elegant and doesn't use his hands'.[13] Cycling was quite different; it combined the attractions of technology and speed thus identifying the Church with technical progress whilst embodying the idea of struggle which appealed strongly to the Jesuit element in Catholicism. Winning was not simply a question of defeating others: it was a metaphor for living the long night of the soul, fighting to live the good life, struggling with oneself against tempatation and winning the ultimate prize.

Bartali's life as a good Catholic man was ideal for the purpose. His victory in the Tour de France was presented as a triumph of three cardinal Catholic virtues: chastity, stoicism and charity. His strict morality stood out in sharp contrast to the double standards of the Fascists, who accepted the idea of young men as promiscuous – proving their virility and increasing the numbers of young Italians in the process, whilst expecting women to be virtuous wives and mothers at home. Bartali's stoicism, his ability to bear suffering without complaint, his acceptance of pain and fatigue, were all essential Christian virtues with obvious parallels in the life of Christ. Most striking as an implied criticism of Facism, however, was the idea of Bartali's charity, his generosity and kindness to others and in particular, his refusal of violence, his Christian courage to turn the other cheek in contrast with Fascist glorification of aggression and arrogance. An incident in the 1938 Tour de France was cited to illustrate Bartali's goodness and spirituality. The Belgian rider, Vervaeke, had tried to bring him down and as the champion's team-mates were ready to attack the aggressor, Gino intervened with the words 'Leave him , God will punish him.'[14]

The Fascist press, of course, also made a great fuss of Bartali. An Italian winning the Tour de France in the same year that Italy retained the World Cup in Paris was a sporting triumph almost beyond the dreams of Mussolini. But the honeymoon with Bartali did not last long. When Bartali argued about the terms of his contract to defend his title the following year, the Fascists accused him of putting money before country – an accusation that the Communists would also make against him after the war. The real problem, however, was that 'il fraticello' (the 'little brother' was a popular monastic nickname for the new Catholic hero) turned out to be too genuinely religious for their purposes. He was not prepared to identify himself entirely with the pagan aspects of the regime. In September 1938 an instruction went out to the Fascist newspapers only to report Bartali's successes as a cyclist and not his role and beliefs as a citizen.[15] Bartali's strict principles saved him from becoming a full blown Fascist hero and from the inevitable hostility that followed when the regime collapsed.

After the fall of Mussolini, Gedda, who had been put in charge of the Catholic Film Insitute in 1942, wrote to the interim regime of Badoglio on

11 August 1943, offering the support and cooperation of the Catholic Church in putting post-Fascist organisational structures of sport in place.[16] Out of the chaos of defeat and the revolt against Fascism, the Catholic Church and the Communist party emerged as the key players in the period of reconstruction that followed from 1944 to 1948. In 1946, the year in which Italian sport began again after the forced interruption of the war, Bartali won the Tour of Italy. He was able to re-emerge as a sporting hero more or less untouched by direct association with the former regime and rapidly became almost a cult figure for the emerging Christian Democratic movement – the de Gasperi of cycling – praised by and pictured with the President, Einuadi, with de Gasperi and a the young pretender and future godfather of Italian Catholic politics, Mario Andreotti.

From this point of view, the new rivalry with Coppi did not diminish Bartali's popularity even though the younger rider's exceptional performances outstripped his own. On the contrary, he continued to exert a strong and lasting influence on the Catholic masses in whose mind he was exactly what the clerical press presented him as: 'a sportsman to admire and a Catholic to imitate'. For all those in awe of the endurance and sporting longevity of the Tuscan rider, the Catholic press had a ready response. Gino's vitality sprang from 'the religious basis of his life which made his moral and physical development run like clockwork'. Just as the Jesuits preached, Catholicism was not just a way to heaven; 'a Christian life led in a Christian fashion is the ideal way to achieve earthly success'. If Bartali began as a quiet nonconformist as far as the macho Fascist sporting model was concerned, in the post-war years when the political context was transformed, he became the Catholic and anti-Communist model for Italian man, a symbol of Christian Democrat conformity.

This public image was fostered by the key forces of political authority. Most remarkably, Bartali was taken up by the Holy See in what was a unique compliment to a sporting personality. Pious XII referred publicly to him as the 'example' for the men of the Catholic Action movement. In September 1947, in front of a vast crowd in St. Peter's Square, he praised Bartali in glowing terms: 'now is the time for action...now the time to put ourselves to the test; the hard struggle of which St. Paul spoke is now upon us: this is a time of intense effort. A few moments are enough to decide our fate. Look at Gino Bartali, a member of Catholic Action; he has won the coveted winner's jersey several times. And so you too must run in this greater race, to win an even more noble palm: *sic currite ut comprehendatis* (First Corinthians 9.24).[17] The meaning was unmistakeable in the run up to the decisive elections of 1948: Catholics had to make sure they were on their mettle, ready to struggle for the faith against the menace of Communism just as Bartali battled his way to victory.

In the days following this speech Bartali himself launched a series of appeals to the population to vote for the Christian Democrats. If Bartali's success as a cyclist lent itself naturally to the role of Catholic propagandist, there was no chance of his rival. Coppi, doing the same; for the Campionissimo found himself taken up as a symbol by those who had had quite enough of what they saw as Bartali's reactionary clerical platitudes and devised a counter myth: the myth of Coppi the Communist.

This was a particularly complex issue because it became so transformed and twisted in the process of becoming part of popular culture. The history of the rivalry between Coppi and Gino Bartali, which was orally transmitted by whispers and asides as well as in the press, is very hard to determine. This is partly because great sporting achievement is in itself so open to polishing and mythologising and partly because of its wider social and political ramifications. It is clear that Coppi's elevation to the role of a Communist icon took place *after* the most intense period of sporting rivalry with Bartali had passed. In particular, the notorious affair of the 'white lady' – a married woman with whom Coppi conducted a semi-public and widely reported affair – alienated Catholic opinion and pushed Coppi further into the ranks of the Left. But the 'white lady' scandal took place in the early 1950s after the heroic duels of the late 1940s when the dogged Gino tried to keep up with the Campionissimo at the height of his powers.[18] In an Italy still based on moral values strongly rooted in Catholicism, the romantic liaison of Coppi was seen as flouting public morality. This pushed Coppi and Bartali further apart and located Coppi in the popular imagination with a certain section of anti-clerical and secular opinion where more permissive standards prevailed. Until the 'white lady', Coppi had been presented in the Catholic press not as anticlerical or Communist but simply as a dedicated athlete.

What, then, is the origin of the popular perception of Coppi as Communist? The year 1948 was crucial, the year of the elections and Bartali's triumph in the Tour. The Catholic press was triumphalist, claiming both victory in the elections and Bartali's *maillot jaune* – the first post-war Italian victory and sign of international rehabilitation – as victories for the Church. Not since Italy had won the World Cup ten years before and Bartali his first Tour de France had there been comparable success. Bartali's victory in the world's greatest cycle race not only ended a ten-year gap in sporting achievement, but also rekindled a national pride that had been torn to shreds in the war. It allowed the Italians to reclaim a patriotism that had been appropriated and prostituted by Fascism. Bartali won in Paris where only a few months earlier the international peace negociations had damaged Italian self-esteem. If the Italian press presented Bartali as the 'peacemaker' between France and Italy, his victory in some quarters was seen as revenge for this recent diplomatic humiliation.

A specific incident gave Bartali's triumph added significance. The attempted assassination of the Communist leader Palmiro Togliati took place at precisely the moment Bartali made his decisive move to win the Tour with the eyes of Italy upon him. On the same day that a nationalist fanatic gravely wounded the Communist leader, Gino Bartali won an unforgettable Bastille Day stage from Cannes to Briançon. The next day he repeated his lonely exploit arriving first at Aix-les-Bains and taking the yellow jersey. The news that Bartali had taken the *maillot jaune* resounded around all of Italy at the same time as reports on the state of Togliatti's health and the unrest in the streets provoked by the attempt on his life. It is obviously difficult in the light of the mythic role of the victory in the popular mind to estimate its actual part in containing revolutionary sentiment on the streets. What is more certain is that Catholic opinion came to believe Bartali's achievement was a kind of miracle which had diverted the public from disorder. The journal of the Catholic Youth Movement, for example, thought that 'the victory in the Tour and the social and political repercussions that followed were the result of the true qualities of an authentic product of Catholic youth ... for Gino .. was no mere creation of electoral propaganda pressed into service at the last minute'.[19] If the general strike had been 'won' and 'insurrection' had been kept within bounds through the turn of a pedal, the credit went to Bartali and his fantastic victory. Catholic Italy had an 'exceptional amabassador' and a 'saviour of the country'. Anti-clerical opinion, which was clearly irritated by this exhaltation of Bartali, took up the cause of Coppi and hence completed the politicisation of support for the two champions.[20]

The explanation of the perceived political alignement of Bartali and Coppi, therefore, lies in the peculiar psychological climate of the post-war years and the symbolic oppositions nurtured in the popular mind. In an era dominated by cultural antagonism and the Cold War, by the Manichaen and irreconcilable opposition of the American and the Soviet systems, of western Catholics and eastern-orientated Communists, Bartali and his admirers took their stand and this had the effect of pushing the admirers of Coppi to form a rival coalition. As Catholicism won the political battle, defeated anti-clericals and Communists saw Coppi's victories over Bartali as a symbolic compensation, a triumph of 'youth' over 'age', 'change' over 'tradition', 'progress' over supersitition. This process, of which there is ample evidence, can only be understood if Bartali is seen as the ideal type of an almost medieval *societatas christiana* – a social model that was still current in Catholic circles. The Pope himself helped foster and exploit the Bartali myth as the basis of a new moral and political order. It was not Bartali the cyclist or even Bartali himself that supporters of Coppi despised but Bartali as 'God's cyclist' – the name given to him by clerical propagandists.

At a personal level Bartali and Coppi had never been enemies. Bartali was a great athlete whom Coppi admired and Bartali respected Coppi. Bartali, the great champion, desperately fighting to stay with Coppi, driving himself to stay in touch with the 'champion of champions', was a supreme moment in the sport of cycling which caught the public imagination rather as the Ancquetil-Poulidor pairing would do in France a decade later. There is a famous image of the two on the Tour, off on their own in the mountains in the heat of the day, passing a water bottle between them. The press campaign and the political labelling, however, pushed the men apart. The wider process by which Bartali was turned into a Catholic hero and the role played by the media and by the politics of religion turned a great sporting confrontation into something more. It began under Fascism as the Church responded in kind to the manipulation of sport by Mussolini and carried on after his downfall in the face of the new challenge of Communism. The accident of having a perfectly ordinary if rather pious Catholic man as cycling hero just too good to miss and the Catholic hierarchy from the Pope down, urged on by new populists like Gedda, took their chance. Without a Catholic Bartali, there would have been no Communist Coppi.

NOTES

This article was translated from a short French version of a much longer introductory essay to the author's *Sia lodato Bartali* (see note 2 below). It was necessary to expand the French summary significantly by incorporating and synthesising elements of the longer work. I am most grateful to Michael Stabenow for assisting in translating from the Italian. The author gave me a free hand to rewrite quite extensively, although the core of the piece stays close to the original French text which appeared in J. Adoino and J-M Brohm (eds.), *Anthropologie du Sport: perspectives critiques* (Paris: AFRISE, 1991), pp.66–71.

Richard Holt

1. For a general overview of Italian social relations after the Second World War as context for the Coppi–Bartali rivalry see Paul Ginsborg, *Storia d'Italia dal dopoguerra a oggi: società e politica 1943–1988* (Turin: Einaudi, 1989); Silvio Lanaro, *Storia dell'Italia republicana: dalla fine della guerra agli anni novanta* (Venice: Marsilio, 1992); for the symbolic fiures of Peppone and Don Camillo see Gian France Miro Gori, *Insegna col cinema: guida al film storico* (Rome: Studium, 1990), pp.173–87.

2. S. Pivato, *Sia lodato Bartali: ideologia, cultura e miti dello sport cattolico (1936–1948)* (Rome: Lavoro, 1985) gives a full account of the Bartali–Coppi phenomenon including extensive selections from the press reports of the time.

3. Emilio de Martino, Apoteosi, *La Gazzetta dello Sport*, 26 July 1948.

4. There is an extensive bibliogrpahy of Fausto Coppi; in particular see Gianni Brera, *Coppi et il diavolo* (Milan: Rizzoli, 1981).

5. G. Nicholson, *The Great Bike Race* (London: Magnum ed., 1978), p.109.

6. See lengthy introductory essay to Pivato, *Sia lodato Bartali* from which much of this present

article is drawn; on the wider cycling context see S. Pivato, 'The Bicycle as political symbol: Italy 1885–1955', *International Journal of the History of Sport*, 7,2 (Sept. 1990), 173–87.

7. 'Il Giro fermo a Montecatini. Impressioni di Carlin', in *Gazzetta del Popolo*, 20 May 1936.
8. C. Trabucco, 'Gino Bartali di Azione cattolica', *Gioventù nova*, 14 June 1936.
9. See Pivato, *Sia Lodato Bartali*, passim; also J-P Ollivier, *Gino Bartali: Gino le pieux* (Paris, 1983).
10. L. Gedda, *Lo Sport* (Milan, 1931).
11. P. Lanfranchi, 'Bologna: The Team that Shook the World', *International Journal of the History of Sport*, 8,2 (Sept. 1991), p.336.
12. For an initial approach see F. Fabrizio, *Sport e fascismo: la politica sportiva del regime 1924 –1936* (Florence: Guaraldi, 1976); see also S. Pivato, 'Sport et rapports internationaux: le cas du fascisme italien', in A. Wahl and P.Arnaud, *Sports et Relations Internationales: actes du colloque Metz-Verdun 23–25 September 1993* (Metz, 1994), pp.65–72.
13. L. Gedda, *Lo Sport*, p.28.
14. 'Un grande atleta', *Pro Familia*, 7 August 1938, p.480.
15. F. Flora, *Stampa dell'era fascista. Le note di servizio* (Rome: Mondadori, 1945), p.79.
16. Pivato, *Sia lodato Bartali*, p.19.
17. Discorso di S.S. Pio XII agli uomini di Azione Cattolica, in *La Civiltà Cattolica*, III, 1947, p.553.
18. On the events surrounding the 'white lady' see substantial discussion by Gianni Brera in *Coppi e il diavolo*.
19. Dino Bortolotti, Bartali ha battuto di Vittorio, *Gioventù* , 1 August 1948.
20. For a more comprehensive review of the reaction to Bartali's victory in the Tour de France in 1948, see Pivato, *Sia lodato Bartali*, pp.98–101.

A Culture of Urban Cosmopolitanism: Uridil and Sindelar as Viennese Coffee-House Heroes

ROMAN HORAK and WOLFGANG MADERTHANER

In 1936 a book entitled *In Conversation with Sportsmen: light-hearted sports interviews* was published in Vienna.[1] The book, by a journalist named Rudolf Kastl, is a collection of twenty-five articles based on talks with some very well-known sportsmen, but also with less popular ones. On leafing through this quite amusing volume one is struck by the leading role of football; one-third of all the articles are devoted to the game. The book starts with the portraits of three football stars of the 1930s (Sindelar, Sesta and Franzl) followed by anecdotes about young suburban football talents, the troubles of referees and women's football. The prominence of football in this volume is not without reason. In the early 1920s football had become not only a mass sport but also an important part of Viennese popular culture. A newspaper article of 1924 headlined 'Europe's football capital – Vienna leads again', claims, 'Vienna is the football capital of the European continent ... Where else can you see at least 40,000–50,000 spectators gathering Sunday after Sunday at all the sports stadiums, rain or shine? Where else is a majority of the population so interested in the results of games that in the evening you can hear almost every other person talking about the results of the league matches and the clubs' prospects for the coming games?'[2] The introduction of a two division professional championship in 1924 – the first of its kind on the continent – both responded to and reinforced this trend.

Austrian football was a peculiarly Viennese phenomenon.[3] It was geographically confined to the capital, which was also its productive foundation. The opponents of the Viennese clubs did not come from other Austrian towns but from Berlin, Prague, Bologna or Budapest. Big-city self-confidence and a sort of Central European internationalism created a context that also left room for local bonds and club loyalty. This culture of urban cosmopolitanism was characterized by the institution of the coffee house as the meeting place for all football fans, and by the idea of locality rooted in the differing identities of the Viennese suburbs, where most of the clubs were based and from which virtually all the important players were

drawn.[4] Such was the case with Uridil and Sindelar, two of the coffee-house
heroes of Viennese inter-war football, whose careers form the subject of this
article. However, before looking more closely at their lives, the special
world of the café and of the suburbs of Vienna, where their fame was first
and most fiercely celebrated, requires some explanation.

The Coffee House

By the end of the Habsburg Empire, the coffee house flourished in the big
cities as an important cultural institution. It was a kind of 'public salon'
where men and women of all classes congregated, but which was
particularly frequented by the Bohemian, literary circles that brought the
coffee house its special fame.

William Johnston has characterised the typical coffee house as follows:
'The coffee house afforded much besides conversation. Most persons relied
upon their café to furnish daily papers, which could be bought only at
widely scattered kiosks. For some of the "regulars" or *Stammgäste*, the
coffee house provided a place to receive mail and laundry or to change
clothes. Games of cards and chess abounded. It was customary to hold
election campaign meetings at a café or restaurant, where the voters could
eat and drink before listening to the candidate.'[5] During the football boom
of the 1920s, a special institution came into existence – the football club
café.

The first 'Professional Football Championship' kicked off in Vienna on
21 September 1924. As the father of Austrian professional football, Hugo
Meisl, was to note in an article of 1926, the introduction of professional
football, though courageous, was essentially no more than the legalization
of 'the practice of "compensating" the players for their expenses, which had
already begun during the war years'.[6]

The introduction of professional football in Vienna grew from a process
of democratisation that it was to accelerate and reinforce, but also to
transform. Starting in the immediate post-war period, football had become
a 'mass entertainment'. This new interest was manifested not just in rising
gates but also in all the attendant phenomena, ranging from the rise of sports
reporting to the new star status accorded to the 'tank' Uridil for several
years from 1922.

Football had, then, become something that transcended the narrow
boundaries of sport *per se*. It had become a social phenomenon. This, of
course, is nothing special in itself and by no means peculiar to Vienna. In
Britain, the cradle of football, various social meanings – local, regional and
'working-class' affiliations – had been embedded in it at a very early stage.
However, in Britain the redefinition of the sport from elite to popular was

relatively unambiguous; the situation in Vienna was considerably more
complex. The simple equation that football equalled proletarian that is more
or less correct for the United Kingdom did not quite apply to Vienna in the
1920s and 1930s. True, workers played for the various first division clubs,
and the majority of the fans who travelled to 'their team's' fixtures weekend
after weekend were not drawn from the upper classes. But there was more
involved than this; something else was going on, too.[7]

The club café was the place where the concerns of the respective club
were discussed by fans, players and officials, where celebrations were held
and also where bitter defeats were best got over, with everybody sharing the
consciousness of past and future greatness. Though it experienced its
heyday during the First Republic, the institution continued to exist after the
Second World War. In an account dated 1948, we find the following
distribution of supporters according to coffee house: Austria fans met in the
Café Parsifal in the city centre, and Rapid supporters in the Café Holub on
the Hütteldorferstrasse. The Café Resch in Meidling was the rendezvous for
the Wacker fans and the followers of Simmering gathered in the café owned
by the former Simmering player, Hans Horvath. The account concludes:
'Certainly every club has its café, though all cannot be listed here. Each
"football fanatic" knows where he can meet his idols, and each fan's wife
knows it too, but this knowledge does not bring her any joy.'[8]

The perfect example of the Viennese coffee house as a meeting place for
football fans was the Ring Café. Originally the club café of the anglophile
elite cricket community, it soon became the central meeting point for the
Viennese football scene. As a place where foreign tours, transfers, etc were
discussed, where everybody could put in a word at the round table, it was a
'kind of revolutionary parliament of the friends and fanatics of football...;
one-sided club interests could not prevail because just about every Viennese
club was present'.[9] The Ring Café, however, is not only of interest and
importance as a particular social environment. It also represents the classic
combination of football with certain elements of Viennese cultural
modernism.

The coffee house in its Viennese manifestation – the home of art, music,
literary debate and philosophical speculation – fed off its own legends and
reputation. Though it was a place of the moment, it was this myth-making
dimension, this ideal of immortality, that the coffee house was perfectly
equipped to nurture and promote. In its everyday aspect the coffee house
was a world of quick 'one liners', witty remarks on seemingly insignificant
subjects. But alongside this there was a mythologising of its discourse and
thus of itself in the shape of the countless articles for newspapers and
magazines that flowed from coffee house conversation. It is no real surprise
that the coffee house took up football as well. For many of the well-known

coffee-house writers, the 'wonder team' of the early 1930s, and especially its captain Matthias Sindelar, were the subject and *raison d'être* of so many of their literary reflections. In terms of the process by which heroes are created as mythic figures from the stuff of their sporting performances, Vienna clearly had an important and distinctive place.

The Suburbs

Football became a mass phenomenon in Vienna in the immediate post-First World War period. Before the war, the matches had been attended by only a few hundred spectators, most of them relatives and close friends of the players and even a confrontation with the subsequent 'arch-enemy' Hungary hardly attracted a gate of more than 10,000.[10] Yet from the early 1920s onwards the constantly expanding football grounds were often unable to accommodate the crowds who poured in. Apparently, a new type of spectator had come upon the scene. The suburban working-class population, who had become a great deal more self-confident and vocal during the post-1918 revolutionary crisis not only became a decisive factor in political life but also conquered the realm of leisure and new social spheres, establishing a sort of 'counter' culture, openly antagonistic to the values of an older, more refined Viennese way of life. Their crude, noisy and often aggressive behaviour at football grounds deeply disturbed their respectable contemporaries and was attributed to the disastrous impact of the war on public manners. An anxious comment in the *Neues Wiener Journal* of December 1922 ran as follows: 'Since then, crowd trouble has not only become more frequent but has also increased in intensity, the larger the group of football fans has grown, and wider the sections of the population attracted by this sport have become. They grab stones and wooden posts, and if the front-line troops from the Fuchsen- or Drachenfeld (notoriously rough neighbourhoods on the outskirts of Vienna) are present, they even fight with knives.'[11]

Vienna's interwar suburbs differed significantly from the outskirts of any other large European city in two respects. In the first place, two central conceptual levels of definition are associated with them. In a socio-geographical sense, they were those quarters situated outside the town proper, the centre of the city. Being more or less grey areas where urban and agrarian culture merged into each other, they embodied the successive integration of the countryside into the urban structure. On the other hand, the concept of the suburb also denoted particular styles of life and mentalities. These distinctive cultural, political and aesthetic attitudes in many ways sprang from and reflected the transitional character so typical of the suburb as a whole where an essentially rural consciousness and style of behaviour were caught up in rapid processes of industrialisation and urbanisation.[12] This was a fundamentally different kind of 'suburb' from the largely middle-class residential areas opened up by rail commuting in Britain.

From the last third of the nineteenth century, the industrial exploitation of these 'suburbs' had been virtually unrestricted. The development pattern in these areas typically involved the interspersing of industrial and residential buildings. In between them there were extensive open spaces in neither agricultural nor industrial use. These were no-man's-lands; anarchic places beyond the control of adults or the authorities, places were gangs could form and meet, the site of youthful suburban revolt.[13] Being appropriated for a social use, these localities became a focus for sub-cultural learning and leisure. It was here that football grew and it was from the suburbs that the majority of the spectators and protagonists came. The main sports grounds were therefore sited on the outskirts of the city. It was in the suburbs where the future football professionals learned their skills by kicking balls around the waste ground, the most successful of them working their way up to social prestige and relative prosperity. Two of them, in their day, rose to early fame and acquired the status of popular heroes, even legends: Pepi 'the Tank' Uridil and the 'papierene' Matthias Sindelar, light as paper and translated here as the 'Wafer'.

Josef Uridil

I developed a special liking for football at an early age, and when I was ten I started playing with a soccer ball. It was a pleasure for me, but it also involved unspeakable suffering, because after every football match, delightful as it was, I was rewarded with a sound thrashing. But this did nothing to prevent me from playing again as a 'Hasnerstrassler' against the 'Brocken' (hunks) from the Koppstrasse the very next day. [14]

Before publishing his life story in 1924, from which the above extract is taken, Josef Uridil had earlier told the story of his beginnings as a football player in a commemorative volume published in 1919, on the occasion of the 20th anniversary of his club, S.K. Rapid. He then looked ahead, full of hope:

I am now 23 years old, and I trust that my 81 kilograms will be in action for the green-white colours for another eight years. I close with the wish that everyone may be as lucky in his professional career as I have been. Even if sometimes my mother is still waiting behind the door with a rolling pin or some other aggressive instrument, the club motto goes from strength to strength: 'hurrah for the green-and-white colours, the champions of Vienna'.[15]

In the immediate post-First World War period Uridil was already a well-known and popular football player, but at that time Vienna had many of them. There was nothing to suggest that within a few years he would become a legendary football star and a popular hero.

If the sources can be relied upon, this phenomenon began in 1922. In that year, the song 'Heute spielt der Uridil' came out, its co-author being the well-known singer-songwriter, Hermann Leopoldi. One kind of popular culture was celebrating another; from the theatrical and café world a song expressed the new thrill of the stars of the stadium. The song, a lively foxtrot, more precisely defined in the score as a 'football-walk' became one of the biggest hits of the 1920s. A photograph, taken in autumn 1923, showed a band made up of Rapid fans, welcoming the team to the pitch with the 'Uridil song' when they played league derbies against their arch rivals, Wiener Amateursportverein.

The lyrics, celebrating Uridil as an unstoppable forward, made him a familiar figure even amongst those who did not belong to the ever-increasing army of football fans. Uridil's popularity grew and grew, and therefore it is no wonder that the new mass medium of cinema began to take an interest in him. In the film *Pflicht und Ehre* (Duty and Honour), which sadly has been lost, he played himself, as a footballer of the people who helps an impoverished but upright aristocrat to retrieve his lost livelihood through gainful employment. At the same time, a novel of the same title, by the producer Alfred Deutsch-German (evidently a pen name) was published. The film's premiere on 1 February 1924 coincided with a musical entitled 'Seid umschlungen Billionen' (Let me embrace you, billions), in which the football star, in his green-and-white colours, presented a music-hall song every evening. Uridil had become fashionable. Wherever he was, he met with acclaim. His name was on boxes of chocolates and bottles of fruit-juice, spirits, soaps, underwear, wines, spirits, sportswear and many other items of everyday use. A well-known sculptor made a Uridil bust which was unveiled at a special exhibition and artists vied for the honour of painting his portrait.[16]

Who was the footballer who caused such a stir? Born on 24 December 1895, the son of a small master tailor in the working-class suburb of Ottakring, he learned the trade of stonemason during the first years of his football career. The available source material indicates that he chose this trade because it enabled him to play football after work stopped at 5.30 p.m. After playing for a few smaller clubs, he joined Rapid shortly before the outbreak of the First World War I. It was no coincidence that it was with Rapid he was to rise to fame.

Rapid Wien was *the* club of the suburbs. Local bonds, club loyalty and solid, almost conservative management – at least between the wars – made Rapid a remarkable football club. To play for this club was something to be proud of. Hans Krankl, a recent Rapid manager not blessed with great success, would still hark back to the great traditions of the club: for a 'a real Rapid player' has to be imbued with the famous 'Rapid spirit'. As early as 1927, an article in the *Illustriertes Sportblatt* said of the Rapid team: 'They have yet to let their supporters down, because they never give up and fight to the final whistle. Rapid have their roots in the local population, and never neglect their home territory. The Green-Whites are a suburban club in the best sense of the term.'[17]

This characterisation of Rapid was well founded. The Club was established in the autumn of 1898 as the 'Erster Wiener Arbeiter-Fussballklub' (First Vienna Workers' Football Club). According to the statutes, the purpose of the club was 'to introduce sport loving comrades of the working class to football, which has become so popular in Vienna'. Coming at the time of the rise of the labour movement, this commendable aim was not wholly uncontroversial. Although the new club had no close ties with the Social Democratic movement – the latter was not particularly happy about the emerging spectator sport of football, and sought to promote hiking, cycling and swimming – the mere mention of the term 'the working classes' was sufficient to arouse the worst fears of the authorities. The Club was compelled to change its name, and set out to make Viennese football history under the new name of 'Sport-club Rapid'. However, it never lost its proletarian flavour, which became the trademark that would accompany it throughout the following decades.[18]

There is no doubt that Josef Uridil was the first representative of the 'Rapid-spirit'. Like Krankl, his most recent successor, he was a goalscorer. His career tally is said to have been a thousand goals. But it was not so much the number as his manner of scoring them that made him first popular and then famous. A contemporary put it as follows:

> Others scored goals before him, but not one of them had his enormous momentum, the irresistible force with which he powered across the football field. Woe betide the opponent who dared to cross the path of this racing machine. He was knocked over, almost crushed and decomposed into his chemical constituents. His rivals quivered when the small but sturdy Uridil launched one of his devastating attacks.
>
> In most cases, the business ended with Uridil and three or four of his opponents lying on the ground and the ball in the other side's net. [19]

That was it in a nutshell. This was the footballer from the suburbs, the personification of their rougher side and style. This was what made him a popular hero. Uridil, appropriately nicknamed the 'tank', scored goals; he was a matchwinner, often netting after solo runs. To the suburban crowds that were increasingly filling the football stadiums, he was one of their own.

It should also be remembered that this was the period shortly after the First World War. There was widespread discussion of the brutalisation caused by the war. What was the explanation of the football riots? If crowd violence was one element of the new popular culture, perhaps Uridil's emergence as a football star was another; both were products of the turbulent, dynamic aggressive culture of suburban Vienna. Uridil's ferocious image was a very early form of image creation, before mass media began to be used for such purposes, and this is why it was on the whole restricted to Vienna.

Uridil kept his feet on the ground; he was an 'honest fellow', 'a man of the people'. He was able to handle it quite well. At first he resisted his new role a little, but then he quickly came to terms with it and learned to turn his popularity to financial advantage. But he was careful and, probably following the advice of his Club, did not accept every offer. When he grew tired of the hullabaloo and being courted by celebrities, he commented with a mixture of resignation and defiance: 'Others can make anything they want of me – except call me a bad footballer'.[20] And a footballer he remained, staying with his club, Rapid – apart form a brief interlude – until 1928. In that year he left Austria, first going to Bratislava as a manager, then to Bari and finally to the Netherlands. In 1934 he managed the Romanian World Cup team in Italy. He worked in Yugoslavia, Switzerland and Germany before reluctantly but with his usual obedience serving in the German Wehrmacht. He returned to his beloved Rapid after 25 years and won the championship with them in 1954. Unlike his profoudly different successor, Matthias Sindelar, his fame in world football has faded. The 'tank' remains a figure of the early 1920s, who remained a hero of the suburbs of Vienna but ultimately of the suburbs alone.

The 'Wafer': Matthias Sindelar

According to the Viennese coffee-house writer Friedrich Torberg, Uridil was the only player with a claim to be regarded as the equal of Vienna's football king of the 1930s, Matthias Sindelar. 'Yet they can only be compared as regards popularity; in terms of technique, invention, skill, in short, in terms of culture, they differed from each other as a tank from a wafer.'[21]

This opinion, delivered with hindsight but also with the exact knowledge

of a football fan of the time, pinpoints the difference in the kind of view
taken of the two players by contemporaries and by later generations. Like
Uridil, Sindelar was a true son of the suburbs. Both were from Bohemian-
Moravian immigrant families. Both were popular heroes in the true sense of
the word. Yet Sindelar was and remains more than this. He became a subject
of the literature of the time which, like the art, music, philosophy and
business life of interwar Vienna, had made its home in the coffee houses.[22]
Sindelar was the strategist of the so-called Austrian 'wonder team' of the
early 1930s; he was internationally accepted as probably the world's best
centre-forward and was admired, almost loved, by every Viennese who
knew him. This effectively meant the entire population, for Sindelar's fame
went far beyond football as he became a figure of the literary imagination,
a metaphor and a symbol of the Viennese character.

In fact, Sindelar personified as nobody else the art of Viennese football
during the 1930s – a style characterised by sophisticated technique,
intelligent movement off the ball, accurate passing on the ground, and last
but not least, avoidance of physical contact. Sindelar, nicknamed 'der
Papierene' by his fans because of his manner of playing and his slight
physique, elevated football to a fine art. His was an aesthetic approach. He
seemed to read the game in the same way that actors would interpret their
roles; he wrote sketches, parables and short stories on the pitch just as the
celebrities of Viennese coffee-house literature put them on paper. And they
were to see themselves and their view of art in his 'play' – a word which
here goes beyond the familiar connotations of physical effort and
amusement to conjure up a sense of spontaneity and of drama, of style and
creativity.

Torberg relates that one of his friends, an enthusiast for theatre and
football, once told him that he wanted to watch the Mitropa Cup final
between Austria and Bologna because he was interested to see how Sindelar
would interpret his role as a centre-forward this time. 'He was endowed
with such an unbelievable wealth of variations and ideas that one could
never really be sure which manner of play was to be expected. He had no
system, to say nothing of a set pattern. He just had – allow me to use the
expression – genius.'[23] This opinion was shared by *The Times* on the
occasion of a visit by the Austrian team in 1932, whilst in Vienna itself
Sindelar had the reputation of a creative genius in the truest and highest
sense, as Hans Weigel later put it.[24]

In a magisterial obituary written from exile in Paris, Alfred Polgar, the
celebrated theatre critic, wrote of Sindelar:

He would play football as a grandmaster plays chess: with a broad
mental conception, calculating moves and countermoves in advance,

always choosing the most promising of all possibilities. He was an unequalled trapper of the ball and stager of surprise counter-attacks, inexhaustibly devising tactical feints which were followed by the true attacking move that his deception had made irresistable, the opponent having been cunningly fooled by a flash of skill. In a way, he had brains in his legs, and many remarkable and unexpected things occurred to them while they were running. Sindelar's shot hit the back of the net like the perfect punch-line, the ending that made it possible to understand and appreciate the perfect composition of the story, the crowning of which it represented.[25]

It is no accident that Polgar uses the metaphor of the chess-player, or that people would talk of 'lawn billiards' in connection with Sindelar. The Viennese coffee house had also produced Austria's strongest chess-player, Carl Schlechter, who challenged for the world championship in 1910. Viennese Bohemian and artistic circles recognised and appreciated Sindelar as one of their own, the more so as he was not merely a striker but rather a strategist who could also score decisive goals. Still more, he was the playmaker of Austria, a city club noted for its associations with the liberal Jewish bourgeoisie, typical of that strain of Viennese football associated with Bohemian life and coffee-house culture. Against the physical style of play of the immediate post-war period represented by the 'Tank', Sindelar opposed skill and intelligence – the embodiment and reflection of the sophisticated culture so typical of prewar times.

Matthias Sindelar grew up in grinding poverty in Favoriten, on the outskirts of Vienna. His father, like ten thousands of others, was a Moravian immigrant who found employment in the Vienna brickworks. After the latter's death on the Italian front, his mother had to work as a washerwoman to feed her four children. Sindelar's childhood was in many respects that of a typical street urchin. It was here that the slightly built Sindelar grew into a star of the street.

There is another side of street football which is easy to overlook but crucial to the culture of the game. Football between the curb and the lamppost, in the alleys and squares was against the law. The children who played it lived in permanent, latent conflict with the police, caretakers, park-keepers and other guardians of public spaces. In the process, they evolved an antagonistic relationship to figures of state and private authority and learned to hold their own against them with guile, agility and quick-wittedness. Above all, they learned that, as children of the propertyless classes, they must constantly fight for their claim to 'elbowroom' in the literal and metaphorical sense. It was just such experiences that, consciously or unconsciously, were transposed into their later style of play, constituting the special form and inner content of the high school of Viennese football. This was an approach to the game that was to gain worldwide recognition in the Thirties as the 'Vienna school', and which virtually became synonymous with Matthias Sindelar. Its origins lay in the daily hunger and absolute poverty of the immediate postwar period.[26]

The street urchins, who spent most of their days beyond the reach of direct parental control, in the back streets and vacant lots, were not merely a favourite target for reforming middle-class liberal or Social Democratic youth workers because of their unruly antics, wandering and alleged deprivation. They also frequently attracted the attentions of so called 'talent scouts'. Sindelar was signed straight off the street by a local club, Hertha from the Favoriten district itself. Hertha was a first division club that had long brought together Vienna's most gifted young players in its youth team and provided a virtually inexhaustible reservoir of talent for the big clubs, especially the more middle class city clubs like the Wiener Amateursportverein (the future Austria), which Sindelar joined in 1924 together with three fellow Hertha players.[27]

Here, after initial difficulties, he followed in the footsteps of the Hungarian Alfred Schaffer, one of the world's best players at that time. The legendary manager, Hugo Meisl, long resisted calls to pick Sindelar as centre-forward in the national team. When he yielded to pressure from the sports journalists at the Ring-Café in 1931, Sindelar led the team to a series of astonishing successes and his fame assumed unparalleled proportions. He knew how to exploit this popularity, advertising wrist watches and dairy products, and even eventually acting in a full-length feature film. The film was based on a review called 'Roxy and her Wonder Team', for which Alfred Grünwald and Hans Weigel wrote the script and Paul Abraham the score.

At heart, however, he remained true to his profession, his background and his city. He turned down lucrative offers from abroad, including one from Manchester United. While completely apolitical in public, in his private life he made no secret of his Social Democratic leanings. As the unquestioned captain of a national team which was effectively a purely Viennese squad, composed solely of players from the city's clubs, he embodied the same conflict that marked the small country that had recently arisen from the ruins of the Habsburg Empire. He symbolised the split between the capital and the provinces – between a 'Red Vienna' noted throughout world for its municipal socialism and the Catholic, monarchist and reactionary countryside. He thus captained the team of a country afflicted by deep social and political divisions which had not yet even started on the path of nation building. Precisely for this reason, he became a figure with whom most Viennese could identify; a man who saw the Viennese model and its specific cultural (and political) structures as a shining example and as a model for a future all-Austrian identity.[28]

Less than a generation of players earlier, Josef Uridil had not even begun to encounter such issues. His status as a popular idol stemmed solely from his affiliations with a particular local, social environment, whose fighting spirit and virtues he perfectly embodied on the field. In this context, competition between national teams was of secondary importance. The wartime alliances persisted on the pitch until the mid-twenties as the victorious Allied powers excluded Central European football from international competition. This meant that initially close international football relations could only develop with immediate neighbours and neutral countries such as Sweden or Switzerland. There were frequent fixtures between Austrian, Czech and Hungarian teams, and at club level there were often games with German teams.

In many ways, the Mitropa Cup, which was first staged as a formal competition in 1927, cemented this situation of lively but geographically limited sporting activity concentrated in Central Europe. From the first, Viennese professional football (which was organised in two leagues with 12 teams each) had faced severe financial problems. The clubs therefore attempted to secure their annual budgets by means of foreign tours, international friendly tournaments and so forth in the close season. By 1926 when a match between Vienna and Slavia Prague – then at the height of their success – attracted a mere 3,000 spectators to the Hohe Warte stadium, it was clear that the structure of the international game was in need of fundamental reorganisation. Thereafter, the General Secretary of the Vienna Football Association and manager of the Austrian national team, Hugo Meisl, devised a scheme for a competition 'in which the top Central European teams will participate, and which must have a valuable trophy'.[29] The Mitropa Cup took place until 1939 but Austrian participation ceased after 1937 and the Anschluss. Initially, top clubs from Austria, Czechoslovakia, Hungary and Yugoslavia competed but from 1929 onwards Italy took the place of Yugoslavia. This occurred at the precise point in time when Mussolini and his foreign minister, Grandi, were paying greater attention to Central Europe and concluded bilateral agreements with Austria and Hungary that broke the diplomatic isolation of the two Danube states. However, the true contribution of the Mitropa Cup lay in the final crystallisation of a specifically Central European playing style with the accent on ball and tactical skills, which was to challenge the British dominance of football. For in Prague, Budapest and Vienna, football soon reached an exceptionally high level.

On 16 May 1931, Scotland, who had traditionally shown continentals how to play the game, were seen off with a 5–0 defeat in an exhilarating match at the Hohe Warte. Even the *Arbeiter-Zeitung*, which was normally so cool towards 'bourgeois' professional sport, enthused: 'If there was an elegaic note in watching the decline of the ideal that the Scots represented for us, even yesterday, it was all the more refreshing to witness a triumph that sprang from true artistry. Eleven footballers, eleven professionals – certainly, there are more important sides to life, yet this was ultimately a tribute to Viennese aesthetic sense, imagination and passion.'[30] The 'Wonder Team' was born and it had found its inspiration in the classic attacking footballer, Matthias Sindelar.

In the following year and a half, this team was unbeaten in eighteen representative matches, with a tally of fifteen wins and three draws. The most important seven games, against the best teams in Europe, brought five wins and a quite extraordinary total of goals scored. Whenever the press discussed the Wonder Team, the well-rehearsed, marvellously polished moves of that inspirational forward line were recalled – and Austrians recall them still. There is talk of unpredictable feints and tricks, of sudden changes of direction that no defence could anticipate and that each player in an attacking move was capable of instigating. There is the memory of a supreme inventiveness and superb athletic intelligence, but also that strong team spirit that came from a the solidarity of a shared youth of street football and suffering in the suburbs.[31]

Yet the Wonder Team would probably not have been such a uniquely Austrian, or to be more precise, uniquely Viennese phenomenon, if its greatest triumph had not been a defeat. At this time England, still 'splendid in isolation' in football terms, were regarded as unbeatable at home – a non-British team had in fact never beaten them on their own territory. As the best continental side the Austrians were deemed worthy to play in a 'challenge match' at Stamford Bridge on 7 December 1932. All Vienna was in the grip of football madness. Crowds gathered on the Heldenplatz, where three large loudspeakers had been set up, to listen to live commentary by Willi Schmieger and Balduin Naumann. Even the Parliamentary Finance Committee adjourned its sitting for the duration of the match.

The Viennese had a highly nervous start. The normally unflappable Hiden, a keeper known for his ability to read the game and an agility that sometimes verged on the acrobatic, made unaccountable mistakes. By the 27th minute England led by two Sampson goals. The Austrian team only gradually found its rhythm, but for the last half-hour it relegated England to the role of spectators. Yet England defended stubbornly and the equalizer and winning goal would not come. The British press unanimously conceded that the better team had lost. The *Daily Mail* described the Austrian attack as 'a revelation', and spotted 'players of genius', ranking Sindelar, Smistik, Nausch and Vogel among 'the greatest players in the world'. *The Times* went into raptures about the 'passing skills' and 'speed' of the Austrians, accorded the 'moral victory' to the Wonder Team and argued that the era of English dominance of world football had now probably drawn to a close.[32]

After this game the Wonder Team disintegrated. Against all the expectations, the 1934 World Cup in Italy was not won but ended with a fourth place. Strictly speaking, this unique flowering, which has never been equalled before or since, lasted for no more than the 1931 and 1932 seasons.

Death and Myth-making

When Sindelar and his mistress, a half-Jewish ex-prostitute of Italian extraction, were found dead on the morning of 23 January 1939, wild rumours spread rapidly. After only two days of inquiries the police reported poisonous fumes as the cause of death. However, the Public Prosecutor's Department, which had not yet entirely lost its independence, continued its investigations into the possible murder of Matthias Sindelar for another six months until the proceedings were suppressed by the Nazis.

On closer inspection, the exact circumstances of Sindelar's death become rather less important than the cultural interpretation of them. 'Those whom the Gods love die young', especially in Vienna; genius flowers early and those upon whom it is visited often die early and under mysterious circumstances. It is these premature deaths that stimulate the creation of myths and legends by future generations, elevating the deceased to the rank of immortal and unimpeachable heroes.

Myth-making and attempts to hijack his memory started immediately after Sindelar's death. The Nazis, who probably feared that his popularity would cause a backlash against them, had no qualms about styling him the 'best known soldier of Viennese football' and giving him a state funeral, which was attended by 15,000 people. It is a characteristic of all such posthumous typecasting and claiming of reputations that the victim is in no position to answer back.

'Sindi' certainly had no time for fascism, particularly its Prussian form. He expressed his heartfelt dislike of it in his own way.[33] Before the unification of the German and Austrian football associations, a 'reconciliation game' between the 'Ostmark' team and an all-German line-up was staged on 3 April 1938. Though he had increasingly withdrawn from the national team in the past few years, Sindelar allowed himself to be picked as centre forward – and put on one last, great performance. He insisted on red and white jerseys for the Austrian team, and for the last time played brilliantly, almost humiliating the Germans.

It was rumoured that there had been an order that the Austrians were not to score. In all events, as the newspapers reported with one voice, Sindelar missed countless hundred-percent chances in such an elegant and skilful manner that the humiliation of the 'Reich Germans' could scarcely have been more apparent, and every one of the 60,000 crowd – mostly composed of loyal Nazi Party members – must have seen who was in charge on the pitch. This went on until the second half, when he could no longer contain himself, and scored from a rebound, with a delicate, curving shot. When his best friend, 'Schasti' Sesta lobbed the goalkeeper with a 45-meter free kick, for the final 2–0 result, Sindelar ran in front of the directors' box, which was packed with Nazi potentates, and danced with joy. Even the *Neue Freie Presse*, which had already been forced to toe the line, could not resist the general euphoria, and after paying tortuous deference to the new order of German sport according to National Socialist principles, turned to an extensive eulogy of the 'triumph of the Vienna School of football'.[34] There followed invitations to the 'Reich training sessions', that is, selections for the Reich football squad. Sindelar paid them no heed. His dancing days were over.

In August 1938 this true professional, who had always kept his future financial security in mind, became the owner of a popular café in Favoriten's Laxenburgerstrasse. This was an 'aryanised' business. Like so many other thousands of Viennese, Sindelar had taken advantage of the situation. Nevertheless, he paid the Jewish ex-proprietor, whom he knew well, a sum approximating to the true value of the property. This was the considerable amount of 20,000 reichsmarks, RM 15,000 of which were immediately deposited with a notary public and the remainder to be paid in half-yearly instalments as his will makes clear.[35] He also went through the political motions that appeared to be required for survival. A number of Nazi bosses were invited to the opening of the café. In interviews, he spoke optimistically of the future of football in the 'Ostmark', arguing that the undernourished children were at last being properly fed. But that was the end of it. When his sisters wished to continue running the coffee house after his death, the NSDAP Vienna Gauleitung replied to the effect that Sindelar had been known to be 'very pro-Jewish', and his relatives were unlikely to think differently. The management of the coffee-house had taken a 'fairly negative' attitude to Party collections, and Party posters had been put up either very reluctantly or not at all.[36]

The Viennese café literary world, now in exile, also laid claim to Sindelar in its own special way, and did much to create the legend, by a making a fact of a possibility that official investigations certainly did not exclude. In his famous and frequently quoted 'Ballad on the Death of a Footballer', Friedrich Torberg leaves no doubt that the centre forward committed suicide because he no longer wished to live during a period of barbarism to which Viennese football fell victim together with so much else – and in which in football as in life, the Vienna School had no place. In an emotional obituary, Alfred Polgar wrote: 'The good Sindelar followed the city, whose child and pride he was, to its death. He was so inextricably entwined with it that he had to die when it did. All the evidence points to suicide prompted by loyalty to his homeland. For to live and play football in the downtrodden, broken, tormented city meant deceiving Vienna with a repulsive spectre of itself. .... But how can one play football like that? And live, when a life without football is nothing?'[37]

The attempts to usurp Sindelar's memory and to create a myth, from diametrically opposed and irreconcilable positions, thus started immediately after his death. That by the Nazis was bound to fail. They soon banned the annual memorial meetings at the graveside, organized by friends and admirers, on the grounds that such manifestations of grief were 'not in keeping with the times' in view of the mass death on the battlefields. By contrast, the coffee-house writers' version was capable of being transmuted into history because it actually contained a kernel of truth, portraying Sindelar as an 'artist' in whom the classic Viennese virtues of lightness and grace, humour and erratic genius were combined. In so doing, it contributed to the search for a civic, regional, and in a wider sense national identity directed against bureaucratic 'Prussian' dirigism and centralisation.

For all his marvellous force and prolific gaolscoring 'the tank' could never match the illusive magic of 'the wafer', the paper 'dancer' who made football into an art form, embedded in the cultural consciousness not just of the impoverished 'suburbs' but of the more sophisticated 'city'. In this sense Uridil remained literally and metaphorically a peripheral figure while Sindelar's forging of a style that combined grace and goals, artistic form over brute content, took him to the heart of the city itself. His death, whatever its true cause may have been, made him a martyr as well as an idol; a symbol not just of the artistic potentialities of football and of the way a boy could rise from the gutter, but of the wider humanity which that street culture and its politics enshrined; not a fascist populism of racial hatred and chauvinism but a strong, communal solidarity stemming from a shared moral sense of social justice and the generous sociability it nurtured. Whether Sindelar's actual life really lived up to its posthumous appropriation by those Viennese who suffered under Nazism is not really the point. His genius as a player made this myth-making possible – a myth of martyrdom, of a beautiful player who died because of what had happened to the city and the game he loved; a myth that has profoundly marked the subsequent history of Austrian football and popular culture.

NOTES

This article is based on the results of a research project dealing with the history of Viennese football in the interwar period financed by the 'Kulturamt der Stadt Wien'. The authors would like to thank SR Dr Christian Ehalt for support, assistance and criticism.

1. R. Kastl, *Sportler sprechen zu uns. Heitere Sport-Interviews* (V Vienna, 1936).
2. *Neues Wiener Journal*, 15 November 1924.
3. R. Horak, 'Austrification as Modernisation: Change and Viennese Football Culture', in R. Guillanotti and J. Williams, *Game without Frontiers: Football, Identity and Modernity* (Aldershot, 1994).
4. R. Horak and W. Maderthaner, 'Vom Fussballspielen in Wien: Uberlegungen zu einem popularkulturellen Phanomen der Zwischenkriegszeit', in P. Muhr, P. Feyeravend, Cornelia Wegeler (eds.), *Philosophie, Psychoanalyse, Emigration: Festschrift fur Kurt Rudolf Fischerm* (Vienna, 1992), pp.99–118.
5. W.M. Johnston, *The Austrian Mind: An Intellectual and Social History* (Berkeley, 1972).
6. H. Meisl, 'Der Professionalismus', in *Der Professional: zentral organ der Union der Berufsspieler und Trainer ...sterreichs*, 1 (1926).
7. R. Horak, 'Football Culture in Vienna: Some Remarks on History and Sociology', *Innovation in Social Science Research*, 5, 4 (1992, 1990).
8. *Welt am Montag*, 13 December 1948.
9. *Welt am Montag*, 22 March 1948.
10. Karl H. Schwind, *Geschichten aus einem Fussballjahrhundert* (Vienna, 1994), p.25.
11. *Neues Wiener Journal*, 10 December 1922.
12. Horak and Maderthaner, *Vom Fusballspielen in Wien*, p.107.
13. See H. Berg and G. Meissl, 'Florisdorf 1894–1904–1954–1994', *Wiener Geschichtsblätter*, Beiheft 3 (1994).
14. '20 Jahre S.K. Rapid Wien: Wien 1919', in H. Fonje and H. Lang, *Das ist Rapid! Der Weg der grün-weissen Meistermannschaft* (Vienna, 1952), p.48.
15. Ibid.
16. J. Uridil, *Was ich bin und was ich wurde: die Lebensgeschichte des berühmten Fussballspielers von ihm selbst erzählt* (Leipzig/Vienna, 1924).
17. *Illustriertes Sportblatt* , 8 October 1927.
18. *Arbeiter Sportzeitung*, 16 Nov. 1921.
19. W. Schmieger cited in K. Schauppmier, *Heute spielt Uridil* (Regensburg, 1956), pp.62–3.
20. Uridil, *Was ich bin und was ich wurde*, p.186.
21. F. Torberg, *Kaffeehaus war überall* (Munich, 1982), p.247
22. W. Maderthaner, 'Ein Dokument wienerischen Schönheitsinns: Matthias Sindelar und das Wunderteam', *Beitrage zur historischen Sozialkunde*, 3 (1992), pp.87–91.
23. F. Torberg, *Die Erben der Tante Jolesch* (Munich, 1978), p.161.
24. *Neues ...Osterreich*, 23 April 1950.
25. *Pariser Tageszeitung*, 25 January 1939.
26. W. Maderthaner, 'Der 'papierene Tänzer: Matthias Sindelar, ein Wiener Fussballmythos', in R. Horak and W. Reiter (eds.), *Die Kanten des runden Leders: beiträge zur europäischen Fussballkultur* (Vienna, 1991), p.205.
27. Franz Blaha, *Sindelar* (Vienna, 1946), p.17.
28. W. Maderthaner, 'Osterreich in den Beinen und im Kopf', *Osterreichische Zeitschrift fur Geschichtswissenschaft*, 1 (1995).
29. J. Gero, 'Mitropa-Zentropa: der erste kapitel der authentischen entstehungsgeschichte der beiden konkurrenzen', in *...Osterreichischen Fussballblatt*, 8.
30. *Arbeiterzeitung*, 17 May 1931.
31. W. Maderthaner, *Ein Dokument wienerischen Schönheitssinns*, p.88.
32. A. Steiner, *Reisetagebuch im Fussballfieber: das Londoner Wunderspiel* (Vienna, 1932), p.9.
33. Horak and Maderthaner, *Vom Fussballspielen in Wien*, p.99.
34. *Neue Freie Presse*, 4 April 1938.
35. Estate of Matthias Sindelar, Favoriten Local Museum, Vienna.
36. Ibid.
37. *Pariser Tageszeitung*, 25 Janaury 1939.

Courage against Cupidity: Carpentier–Dempsey: Symbols of Cultural Confrontation

ANDRE RAUCH

The Dempsey–Carpentier Fight

On 2 July 1921 in Jersey City, USA the immense bowl of the arena hummed with expectation while the boxers waited in their cabins two metres square;[1] two tables were pushed together to make an improvised massage table and next to it were a chair and a heater. This was all the boxers had been provided with in a match which was to bring its organisers the biggest returns in the history of boxing.[2] 'Tex' Rickard had certainly constructed a marvellous arena thanks to which the ticket receipts amounted to more than a million and a half dollars. A new business era in the history of boxing was beginning.

The most testing part of a fight is not the fight itself. During the fight, what matters most to the fighter is how he is seen. The fear of humiliation is greater than that of physical suffering or injury. For Carpentier, with the image of Dempsey fixed in his head, the fight really began in that tiny changing room,[3] where the hum of the world outside and the expectant noise of the vast crowd was plainly audible above some last words of advice from Deschamps, his manager, and the final slaps Gus Wilson gave to his already sweating body.[4]

Removed from the domain of the public law, the circus that was Jersey City was now a privileged place where an American could enjoy beating a famous foreigner. How delightful it was to have a feeling of superiority for once over a country still so admired for its history and culture. The roots of the United States might be in Europe but it was a time of national assertion, almost the Fourth of July, and Dempsey was the child of white America. The large receipts in Jersey City revealed a growing sense of nationalism in the United States during and after the war.[5] Strengthened by a new and common culture, the crowd were united in their expectations of *their* champion. To understand why the receipts were so high, it is necessary to recognise that the mentality of the crowd was in the end more important than the identity of the opponent himself.[6]

The fight began. By the third round Carpentier's punches were finding their target with great accuracy but he could do little to prevent the relentless pounding from the American. Breaks in the fight brought only momentary relief from the shower of punches to the Frenchman's body and face. As he absorbed this punishment, he was the personification of the indomitable 'big-hearted fighter'.[7] Dempsey knew he had nothing more to fear from his opponent and, determined to finish Carpentier in the fourth, he stepped up the pace. Having savoured the Frenchman's suffering, the public was now to be treated to his quick execution. Waiting for the big punch that would finish him off generated high emotion in the arena. To miss the knockout blow would almost be like wasting the entrance fee. Complete concentration was called for. This desire to see the victim crash to the floor created an atmosphere that Carpentier knew well: only on this occasion he was the victim. But, as a national symbol, he must find a way to end the fight with honour. The public nature of his defeat, captured by the world's press, created in Carpentier the sensation that all of France were fighting with him. If he was to go down, he had to go down fighting. After a left-right one-two to the jaw followed by a flurry of blows to the body, he hit the canvas. On referee Hany Ertle's count of nine, he somehow scrambled up one last time, like a cat that surprises a tormentor by scratching his face; another one-two to the chin and a hook to the stomach finished him off. More from lack of strength than from loss of consciousness, he did not get up again.[8]

Carpentier's suffering has been enough to make him a worthy contender, a symbol of what the championship meant. The next day, the *Chicago Tribune* wrote: 'There is no dishonour for Carpentier to have lost in this way. One left punch that Dempsey aimed at the body hit Carpentier just below the heart. It is hard to know why this fearsome blow did not knock his heart out of his body.' The American public had come to see a body broken. The courage of Carpentier meant that ironically what they saw was collapse from fatigue. Dempsey had succeeded in exhausting him but had not broken him. Such public praise made what would otherwise have seemed horrific, admirable.

Jersey City in the Faubourg Montmartre

Paris, at 8 p.m. on Saturday 2 July, the balconies packed with people. All eyes were turned to the skies where flares would proclaim the outcome of the fight between the Frenchman Georges Carpentier and the American heavyweight Jack Dempsey to decide the World Championship. Red: Carpentier is the winner; Green: Dempsey is the winner; Yellow: a Draw. This is how the result was to be shown on the balcony of the *Sporting* newspaper, 16 boulevard Montmartre. At Le Bourget, the *Petit Parisien* and the *Petit Journal* would release flares from planes in the sky, red for a Carpentier victory and white for Dempsey. Aeroplanes from Villacoublay would do the same. The French *Compagnie Générale de Télégraphie* (wireless) had installed a special link to the office of the sports paper *l'Auto* and to Radio-France. The result would be known almost immediately. Within a matter of seconds the outcome would be announced to the public. Posters, bill-boards and speakers would describe the fight round by round to the crowd gathered in Faubourg Montmartre. *Le Matin* would broadcast a report by loudspeaker. On the boulevards, in the Place de la Concorde, on the rue Royale, the results would be shown round by round on banners. Cafés and restaurants had contacted telegraph agencies to keep their clientele informed. In theatres, music halls and cinemas, the result would be announced by loudspeaker or on the screen.[9]

The world championship that began at 3.17 p.m. was over by 3.30 and 16 seconds American time (8.30 and 16 seconds p.m. French time). By 8.31 and 57 seconds the result reached France. The speed of communications surpassed even the most optimistic expectations. At 8.32 p.m. the loud-speaker in Place de la Concorde announced the event. 'It really seems like we are in touch with what is going on over there three thousand miles away and it's a special feeling.' Then there was confusion. An American announced in English that Carpentier had lost. Emotion mounted as the wait continued. A Frenchman declared that the result was not official. In English and then in French the first details were displayed on a screen. While the crowd waited a picture of the French President and one of Marshal Foch were shown. This was enough to subdue the crowd. Then came the third announcement: 'Carpentier was knocked down in the first round'. This information was greeted with stunned silence. Then, a new turn of events. The front of the crowd heard applause from inside the building. The loudspeaker announced 'Carpentier has won in the fourth round'. Finally the speaker corrected himself and announced Dempsey's victory. A streak of white flares illuminated the sky and the result was confirmed.[10] Yet what followed the American Dempsey's victory was not so much dejection as delight. France might have lost the fight but had another kind of triumph to celebrate for it was the invention of a Frenchman, Branly, that made the broadcast technically possible.[11]

The effect of waiting for the result heightened the public mood of exhilaration at the efforts made to broadcast the information. The speed of the transmission was as important in its way as the result and the action of the fight. According to *Le Temps*, 'Here in this Parisian square we are witnessing an event which has thrilled 90,000 spectators in Jersey City. We have the immediate echo of their voice. We know what they know virtually as soon as they know it themselves – with only a few minutes in between.

This is profoundly significant.'[12] Speed was seen as good in itself in a world where slowness was equated with backwardness. The Carpentier–Dempsey fight revealed two sides of France: the one of technical modernity, the other technical tradition.

The older French world was suspicious of Parisian frivolity and American extravagance, which was so far removed from the general culture of the French elite. But in the streets of Paris the Carpentier–Dempsey match brought the public the pleasure of instant news. The crowds could follow events almost as they happened without having to wait in ignorance and bemoan the present state of affairs or attack the idea of progress. The news became a kind of airborne event.

The streets around the Place de la Concorde, Palais Royal and the Faubourg Montmartre made up a kind of enlarged arena, amplifying the atmosphere and increasing the excitement of being there catching the news as it arrived. The fight was not just a matter of two physically well-trained men, pumped up with aggression, weighed and put in a ring together. Through the media the event dramatised a deep and instant conflict of identity. The organisers underlined this psychological dimension of the event. The image of Dempsey portrayed by the media created a mood of public hostility. Their passions had been channelled against the 'other', the sportsman as foreigner.[13]

The Patriotic Subject

After the war boxing matches triggered emotions through which citizens of a nation-state could express themselves. The war had subjected French soldiers to the fear of annihilation. In the trenches, life was at times instinctively brutal; men were confronted with their most basic and sinister drives. At the front, social order sometimes ceased to exist. Men had to be able to give full release to their emotions just in order to be able to go on. In addition, to endure life in the trenches a soldier had to have his insensitive side.

At the same time, the feeling of fraternity which arose from sharing extreme danger, and the memory of solidarity in the face of the enemy were more positive and beneficial products of the Great War. Almost every week, the radio would broadcast the views of those who had served with Carpentier, and proclaim his virtues as a soldier. The contest became openly enmeshed in patriotic discourse and the mythology of war. 'Let the Americans be sure of one thing, Carpentier is going to America to fight with all his heart just as the French Tommy ['poilus'] did at Verdun.' Vindication of the French war effort and the spirit of their troops became part of the build-up to the fight in the French press.

In French towns and villages the sight of wounded soldiers had become part of everyday life. Boxers had their own martyrs to France, a roll of honour that included Henri Piet (April 1915), Battling Lacroix (May 1915), Eugène Trickri (July 1915), Gaston Clément (August 1914), Jules Dubourg (October 1918), Robert Loesch (February 1917), Maurice Castérès (May 1916), Max Ludo (December 1914), Henri Barklett (October 1918) as well as the manager and promoter Emile Maltrot. The list of the wounded was also public knowledge: Hogan was blinded in one eye, Adolphe had his arm amputated, Poesy lost a leg, Criqui injured his jaw and so on. This list of names made memory of the unprecedented slaughter stick in the mind. The proof of patriotism was to hand and so was the evidence of a solidarity that had to be sustained in peace as it had been forged in war. The French soldiers who fought at Verdun are especially good examples of this rhetoric of remembrance. The French post-war press based much of their coverage of boxing on the charitable support it gave to the suffering and the wounded. After so much deadly conflict, the violence of boxing did not stir the same passions as before the war. A match became a serious occasion rather than a mere evening of pleasure. There had to be a solemn opening ceremony in the ring to dedicate the match in the minds of the boxing public to the war victims. This was a symbol of national unity and achievement, and a tribute to the war heroes. Focussing upon the idea of national unity helped to reconcile the mood of national mourning with the more ordinary need for entertainment.

On 10 March 1920 at the Paris Circus, a gala was held in honour of those boxers wounded in the war and of Louis Pontieux, who had just had his arm amputated. The evening was organised with the help of the President of the Fédération Française de Boxe, P.Rousseau, assisted by Herring, Roth and Decoin. The participation of English, Belgian and French boxers was announced. The Continental Sporting Club cancelled its usual evening at Wagram in order to participate.[14] The first and second rows as well as the boxes were reserved for people who had made charitable contributions. The boxers and the managers asked to pay their own entrance fee so that no complementary tickets were given out. The number of judges from the Fédération was so large that there had to be a rota for the referees. As a further gesture, the gloves were donated by *France-Sport* of 29–31 rue Bonaparte in Paris. There was also formal government recognition: 'Mr. Maginot will preside over the meeting. He is a famous disabled serviceman and a keen sportsman too.'[15] The band of the 83rd Infantry Regiment provided the musical accompaniment to this solemn occasion.

The nation took this event to its heart. During what was a memorable evening, the boxing ring represented a place of public homage to the example and sacrifice of the dead and injured, of concern and relevance to the whole country. When, after years of warfare, more than one thousand people organised an event which featured physically aggressive combat, the ceremony itself had to combine a sense of deep public mourning with the festive enjoyment of human violence.

Signs of Glory

The fight between Carpentier and Dempsey was unlike anything to be found on the smaller Parisian scene. It took place in an immense outdoor arena which held 80,000 spectators who had arrived by train, car and boat. It was a huge affair for the press and the top promoters whose names were on everybody's lips. The Englishman Charles Cochran, himself a former boxer who had managed the world tour of George Hackenschmidt before the war, was the promoter of the match between Carpentier and Dempsey and negotiated a deal with William Brady in the United States, where the rules were less strict than in Europe.

However, the greatest promoter of such shows and certainly the most influential, was the American Tex Rickard.[16] He was known to have been a cowboy in Texas, hence his nickname Tex. He was the first to offer very high purses, for example a hundred thousand dollars and a percentage of the cinema rights for the Jeffries–Johnson fight at Reno in July 1910. News of this astronomical sum for promoting a sporting event caused controversy. The promotion of the fight deepened a sense of resentment because of the disparity between the length of the fight and the size of the purse and the disparity with average earnings. Such massive differences not only captured the public imagination, but also fuelled a sense of frustration. 'Enormous offers were made last time to Deschamps from all corners of the New World and it was evident that because of the purse offered and the added exchange value of a contract in dollars, Europe could kiss good-bye to the big match. For above all else, Deschamps was a businessman.'[17] This expression of everything in cash values was a decisive shift in post-war boxing. The purpose of conflict was enlarged from a simple agenda of vengeance – revenge for a defeat or a slight – to include speculation by financial profiteers on the outcome.

These vast amounts of money certainly increased interest in the Carpentier–Dempsey fight. Over a period of weeks and months, the money at stake continued to spiral upwards before the amazed public gaze. As early as July 1919, a big London promoter offered 625,000 francs for a match between Dempsey and the winner of the Beckett–Carpentier fight with 375,000 francs to the winner.[18] A few weeks later, Jack Callaghan offered 875,000; the Director of French 'Wonderland' boxing hall, Decoin, immediately set about arranging for the fight to take place at the Pershing

stadium in Paris. Bidding rose again when Kearns in Chicago declared he
had received an offer of $185,000 from Cochran to stage the fight in
London. 'The two offers, if correct, will be around 1,850,000 and 1,500,000
francs each'.[19] The choice of which city would host the fight was a matter
of national pride, aggravated by the growing power of the American dollar
– symbol of the appearance of the New World on the global stage.
Negotiations for the fight became newsworthy in their own right and
interest was such that Cochran confirmed he had Deschamp's signature for
a venue to be in London. In Paris, Théo Vienne, Léon Sée and Decoin
declared that they also had official promises.[20] Three days later the sporting
newspaper *L'Auto* announced that Rickard 'had offered Carpentier
$150,000 plus travelling expenses to face Dempsey in America, at the
exchange rate at that time, 1,738, 500 francs'.[21]

In short, the commercial spectacle to be held at Jersey City was as
different from the national charity evening as it was possible to imagine.
The commemorative event for the veterans was part of a process of
solidarity and mourning rather than a vehicle for chauvinism and
commercialisation. Carpentier's decision to fight in the States put the issue
of the money at one remove from the European scene but nevertheless
illustrated the cleavages within post-war France between those who could
and could not come to terms with the new rampant commercialism led from
the United States.

American Depravities

The public image of Dempsey was one of arrogance. Rumour fuelled
outrage at his allegedly unpatriotic behaviour in avoiding fighting in the
war. *L'Auto* reprinted American headlines such as that from the *Denver
Local Post*: 'American justice brands Dempsey for avoiding the war'.[22]
American journalists met Dempsey's close relations and other reliable
witnesses to fill out their murderous copy. 'Muckraking' was the new
journalistic style. An investigation had been made, the date of the trial had
been announced.[23] The French press padded their pre-match features with
this American material, which provoked a reaction in France. Talking about
Dempsey as a 'shirker' became part of talking about him as a boxer and part
of the pleasure of general discussion of the sport. Justice had to be seen to
be done. The alternatives seemed straightforward. Either the justice system
of the United States did its duty and removed Dempsey from boxing, or this
man, who had to be 'hoisted into the ring' against Tex Willard in Toledo,
had to fight. Dempsey was depicted not simply as a deserter but as a
coward.

The role of the press and the telegraph was increasingly significant in the demand for Dempsey's disqualification on the 12 May 1920. A press statement from New York announced that Jack Dempsey would appear before the Court of Justice in San Francisco on the 6 June to answer to the accusation of avoidance of military service. French public opinion was outraged. With the memory of the French 'Tommy' and the trenches so fresh, the fight at Jersey City belongs as much to the history of a generation as to the history of boxing itself.

Furthermore, what was perceived as contempt for traditional values in American civilisation implied an arrogance which required a European response. On 5 June the French press announced that the marriage of Jack Dempsey has just been annulled by the New York Court of Justice. It was rumoured that the annulment violated the divorce laws of the State of Utah. In contrast, Carpentier's reassuring image was of a man deeply attached to the virtues of rural and of middle-class France, of a man who stands by his commitments. Thus he became the defender of family values. Public opinion was mobilised both against Dempsey's apparent perjury and the penetration of foreign customs into France. Stigmatising Dempsey became a part of a wider resistance to the brutalising forces of the New World; and so a boxing match allowed the press to make headlines about the collapse of traditional values. In a post-war climate of cultural anxiety, the need to affirm the cohesion of the group and of French values had become focused around something as simple as a title fight.

A cable from New York on 15 June stated that the Dempsey trial in San Francisco had ended in the acquittal of the champion, the judges disregarding 'the testimony for the prosecution given by his divorced wife'.[24] This did nothing to redeem Dempsey's image in the French press. In short, if a court could be relied upon to give a fair judgment, then a Frenchman must see that justice was done in the ring. After the horrors of war and the Versailles settlement, the idea of enforcing justice had become a persistent theme of democratic life and people were united in thinking the guilty should be shamed and punished in public.

There was outrage over the vast sums in dollars pocketed by the champion for fights while soldiers were fighting in the war for their own survival and for that of their nation. Jack Kearns understood the trap his fighter was in: 'I met Dempsey while he worked as a riveter in a naval dockyard in Philadelphia. He demonstrated his patriotism by taking part in a number of boxing matches for the benefit of charitable societies working for the war effort and helped to raise over $100,000.'[25] There seemed to be something sinful about continuing to box while the world was at war. Boxing for money seemed immoral when men were dying for their country, but it could be redeemed according to Kearns if the money was properly used.

After the publication of the verdict of the San Fransico court, a second image was quickly created in the press. From being a greedy shirker Dempsey turned into a simple-minded brute, trapped by his wife, who did not even know his own strength. In an interview with Max Linder, he is supposed to have declared, 'People say I'm too rough with my sparring partners and in fact, apart from Bill Tate, I often have had to change them. Well, honestly, I don't do it on purpose.'[26] The banality of the statement is strangely at odds with the massive press coverage it received. Here was the brute force of nature, hardly even aware of its own power; an image well calculated to contrast with Georges Carpentier's intelligent, refined boxing: he was 'an intellectual of the ring whose astute boxing brain controls physical reflexes that serve him perfectly'.[27] This was a truly French image and one that would be recognised outside boxing in artistic milieux and cultivated circles. His was an intelligent admirable violence locked in combat with an egotistical, unsocial brute.

Next the negative Dempsey stereotype was elaborated from a new source close to the boxer himself. The sparring partners of the 'Giant from Utah' – Jim Darcy, Leo Houck, Jeff Clarke, Marti Burke, Chuck Wigins and the middleweight Eddie Ohara – were reported to have walked out of his camp saying they had not been properly paid for all the blows they had received. Dempsey now had a reputation for greed. The child of a big family, born into toil and misery, he was now obsessed with money to the extent of denying the hardship of his own kind and his origins. He was despicable and his indifference to others abominable. Dempsey was a champion but he was vile – the image of the 'bastard'.[28] The stark contrast between the characters of the two contestants served to tarnish the entire identity of Dempsey and make him seem contemptible.

This French confrontation with America had not developed overnight. In April 1920 Carpentier had toured about 60 cities in the United States and Canada. An 'American Dream' of its kind, Carpentier and his manager had travelled in a special train, a real suite with bathrooms, diningroom, kitchen, living-room – 'I wouldn't have been surprised if there had been a wireless since it is available on some luxury American trains allowing one to telegraph ahead whilst travelling at fifty miles an hour.'[29] This display of wealth had its dangers; Carpentier's great popularity might be affected if he started to appear as someone from another social world; hence the constant reassurance of the journalists. As he embarked on the Savoy at Le Havre on 13 March 1920, his love for his country was stressed: 'Carpentier is happy to spend three months in America but he will be even happier when he returns to France. These were the words of the European champion when I left him and Deschamps.'[30] The statement was turned into a kind of statement of faith in France and in the things which make living in France worthwhile; it showed the champion had not got above himself; his fame had not gone to his head. Carpentier made a point of appreciating the virtues of home, of simple surroundings, of old friends; that was what was real, worthwile and to which he would return.[31]

The way Carpentier presented himself and was presented was important, for he was talking to an ageing France whose youth had not returned from the war; he was confirming the validity of old values; he was the stereotype of the 'good guy'; straightforward, sensible, modest, realistic, devoted, resolute and responsible. He no longer inhabited the world of the miner but he was at pains not to deny it. He had experienced the feelings of ordinary folk and forgetting this would make him unworthy in the eyes of people although wealth and fame had in reality removed him from ordinary life.

Conclusion

Dempsey was taller, weighed 7 or 8 kilos more and his reach was about twenty centimetres longer than Carpentier's. He had 45 knock-out victories, Carpentier had 30. Dempsey had only ever been knocked out once, had stamina; a frightening punch, could win by a knock-out in the first round or go on fighting until the last round. He was extremely resistant in a clinch, was a 'taker', a 'puncher' and a 'searcher'. In a country where the top fifty heavyweights were better than all but the very best in Europe, Dempsey was head and shoulders above the rest. His fighting style – the position of his body and feet and his frontal attack – emphasized his fierce determination. He could beat Carpentier with a straight blow to the chin or by wearing him down.

The bookies were not in doubt. They offered odds of 3, 4 or even 5 against Carpentier. Expectations of the result were based on the different physical capacities of the fighters. Those who hoped for a French victory had to trust in some surprise turn of events or in the sheer genius of their man. In reaction to this one-sided view of the contest, the French press criticized their American counterparts for trying to demoralize Carpentier and pointed out that Dempsey had been out on the town celebrating his birthday just a few days before the fight. Two opposing images of what great boxing means are summed up in the way America dwelled on the idea of strength combined with weight and staying power, whilst the French were more concerned with skill.

The Americans wanted a straightforward knock-out. Dempsey talked not just about his successes but about the hardness of his punching. 'A boxer', he said, 'can only succeed because of his fists. Experts talk about strong, legs, courage and staying power. But put all that to one side, it is his fists that really make a boxer. First I twirled a broomstick for hours, then I squeezed objects in the palm of my hand...then I took a huge sack filled with a hundred kilos of wet sand and punched it without stopping for a quarter of an hour.'[32] Dempsey conceived of training according to a principle of the resistance of solids, wood, stone, and the bones being the points of reference. Two different ways of describing pain and estimating the limits of suffering were evident. For the Americans the strong fighter would always be superior in the end to the more technically accomplished performer; there would always be a moment when the fact of being able to absorb more punishment and to pressure the opponent would tell. Dempsey was the harder hitter; he had the advantage because he could do more damage and Carpentier had not been trained to endure such a battering and come back.

Analysis of the press coverage reveals three themes. First there was the threat posed by Dempsey's weight, his height and the power of his fists. Set against that Carpentier seemed faster, more technically talented and his one-two had an undeniable kind of magic. Put in a nutshell, the logic of mass and force was opposed to that of subtelty and skill – a solid against a fluid. The second dimension of the coverage concerned Dempsey as a champion and his motivation. The title itself was not important to him. What mattered was defending it against the highest bidder. Dempsey's obsession with the size of the purse damaged him as much as it helped Carpentier: Dempsey was selfish and lacked integrity, Carpentier was a man of honour. Cupidity was set against courage. Finally, there was the third theme: here the showman side of Dempsey came to the fore; he invited the public to his training sessions; he was self-assured in front of spectators. Carpentier, on the other hand, was secretive, training in a closed camp behind barbed wire; those around Carpetier wanted to keep an element of surprise and to play up his charm and novelty; this made Dempsey look the more experienced of the two, an old hand against a newcomer.

An unbearable suspense built up around the ring. The fight had to end in a knock-out to release the tension and allow catharsis. On the day itself, the jokes, the insults and the barrage of accusations were banished by the heroism of the performers, the excitement of the vast crowd and the presence of the film cameras perched high above the scene and the press corps themselves like an army waiting for the battle.

The Carpentier–Dempsey fight was not the property of its organiser nor of the crowd who came to fill the great arena of Jersey City. The aggressive atmosphere of the day was not just the product of the tens of thousands of spectators on that hot afternoon. This unprecedented mass of people no doubt added to the extraordinary sense of occasion but the drama and violence of the day arose from the advance media manipulation of the fight in the public mind and the desires and fears it aroused which spread far beyond the confines of the boxing ring.

This detailed analysis of a single event permits a 'reading' of the specific performance within its social and technological context. The War had brought an unprecedented mutual exchange between the Allies. The French, in particular, were suddenly more sensitive to American life and culture and for the first time able to follow what happened across the Atlantic almost as it took place. France had been saved not just by her own resilience and British support, but at a crucial moment by the infusion of new blood and money from America. But this brought its own problems. Gratitude and fascination went hand in hand with resentment and disgust for American attitudes and American ignorance of, and contempt for, the finer points of European culture, including the established traditions of 'the noble art'. At the same time the ending of the war brought the eight hour day in France and the surge in interest in sports of all kinds that was to be a feature of Europe in the 1920s. The Carpentier–Dempsey fight seemed to sum up the complexity, the mutual attraction and repulsion of the two worlds, drawn together more closely than before both by the First World War and the media revolution that brought not only news reel pictures but almost instantaneous live communication. In this way, a single fight was overburdened with meaning. Carpentier and Dempsey were turned respectively into cultural symbols of French refinement on the one hand, even in its cruder and more violent cultural manifestations, and on the other hand, of New World brash commercialism, competitiveness and ferocity.

NOTES

1. For an account of the fight itself see *Le Miroir des Sports*, 7 July 1921, pp.1–9 and 14 July 1921 pp.17–25.
2. It was the first fight to net receipts over a million dollars. Tex Rickard made $300,000 profit.
3. Jack Dempsey, 'the Lion from Utah', was born on 23 June 1895 in Manassa, Colorado. On 4 July 1919, in Toledo, Ohio, he took the title of Heavyweight Champion of the World from Jesse Willard, knocking the Kansas cowboy to the ground seven times, see M. Golesworthy, *The Encyclopedia of Boxing* (London, 1988), pp.77–8. He lost his title to Gene Tunney in Philadelphia on 23 September 1926. On the life of Dempsey see N. Fleischer, *Jack Dempsey, the idol of fistiana* (New York, 1929); J. Dempsey and J. Stears, *Round by Round* (New York, 1940); B. Green, *Jack Dempsey, champion heavyweight boxer* (New York, 1974); O. Roberts, *Jack Dempsey, the Manassa Mauler* (Louisiana University Press, 1979); see also O. Roberts, 'Jack Dempsey: an American hero in the 1920's' , in P.Z. Zingg (ed.), *The Sporting Image in American Sport History* (New York, 1988)
4. Carpentier was born on 12 January 1894 in Liévin, near Lens. His father was an unskilled worker in the coal mines. He became European Middleweight Champion on 29 February 1912 after his victory against Jim Sullivan for a 'record' purse of 25,000 francs. On 1 June 1913 he beat Bombadier Billy Wells for the European Heavyweight title, see S. André and N. Fleischer, *Les rois du ring* (Paris, 1977), p.76. Carpentier met Dempsey after beating Battling Levinsky in four rounds in Jersey City for the title of World Middleweight Champion.
5. The American press insisted on presenting Carpentier as the 'foreigner' who does not even speak English, see 'Georges Carpentier – Gentleman, Athlete and Connoisseur of the "boxe"'

in *The Literary Digest*, 17 January 1920, pp.130–6. The press stressed his elegance which was thought aristocratic and his hobbies which were not considered proletarian; in short, unlike Dempsey he was not representaive of the average American boxing spectator.

6. Around the ring, the crowd cheering for Dempsey ignored debates about nationalism provoked by the American intellectuals, see A. Bennet, 'The Great Prize Fight', in *The Living Age*, 24 January 1920, p.24; and F. Hackett, 'The Carpentier Fight: Bennet vs. Shaw', in *The New Republic*, 14 January 1920, pp.198–200 and 13 July 1921, pp.185–7.

7. *Le Matin*, 4 July 1921; also G. Benamou and F. Terbeen, *Les grandes heures de la boxe* (Paris, 1975), p.36.

8. *The Daily Telegraph*, 4 July 1921.

9. For the first time, *L'Auto* published seven special editions, following a record printing of 630,000 newspapers, see André and Fleischer, p.81.

10. *Le Temps*, 4 July 1921.

11. *Le Gaulois*, 4 July 1921. 'We should remember that six minutes after the fight we knew the outcome ... and that this miracle was made possible by the genius of a French scientist, who, locked away in his laboratory, was unaware of the tumultuous reception.'

12. *Le Temps*, 4 July 1921.

13. This theme is particularly developed in the English press, for example *The Sporting Life*, 4 July 1921.

14. *L'Auto*, 15 February 1920.

15. *L'Auto*, 6 March 1920.

16. Born in 1871, Tex Rickard was the typical American 'self-made man'. He was the first to see the holding of world title bouts as a purely commercial promotion and designed the advertising of the event with this in mind. His partners were the Ringling Brothers, circus-owners, and he leased them Madison Square Garden for their performances in New York. Little by little, sporting events like hockey, ice-skating and boxing replaced the Circus. He took control of Madison Square Garden, where six-day cycling events took place; when he became director of the 'Garden', he gave the organisation of the sporting competitions over to Chapman and Curley. Among other famous matches Rickard promoted Jeffries–Johnson, Carpentier–Dempsey, and Dempsey–Tunney. His spectacular success explains how he became the object of such interest in the United States. When he died in January 1929, his body was transferred from Miami to new York in a bronze coffin and bought for $15,000 by Jack Dempsey, who became a promoter himself. For two days crowds came to Madison Square Garden's chapel to pay their respects, *L'Auto*, 9 January 1929.

17. *L'Auto*, 9 January 1919.

18. *L'Auto*, 7 July 1919.

19. *L'Auto*, 6 December 1919.

20. *L'Auto*, 8 December 1919.

21. *L'Auto*, 16 December 1919.

22. *L'Auto*, 13 January 1920.

23. *The New York Times*, 26 January 1920 and 28 February 1920.

24. *Le Temps*, 1 July 1921.

25. *L'Auto*, 7 February 1920.

26. *L'Auto*, 20 March 1920.

27. *Le Temps*, 1 July 1921.

28. *L'Auto*, 5 June 1921.

29. *L'Auto*, 15 March 1920 . On this prestigious tour, see G. Carpentier, *Mon match avec la vie* (Paris, Flammarion, n.d.), pp.171–3.

30. *L'Auto*, 14 March 1920.

31. A. Prost, *Les anciens combattants et la société française*, 1914–1939 (Paris 1977), vol.3, pp.19–24.

32. *L'Auto*, 17 November 1920.

Epilogue
Heroes for a European Future

J.A. MANGAN and RICHARD HOLT

Historians have occasionally considered 'the intrusion of myth' in their professional search for evidence and relationships, but for the most part it has been a topic lodged in 'the domain of anthropology'. According to the distinguished economic historian D.C. Coleman myth has been largely thought of by historians

> as a phenomenon of pre-literate societies, bracketed with legend, symbol and folk-lore. Not surprisingly the world of the ancient Greeks, with its intertwining of gods and men, has provided the most fertile European soil for historians to become involved in myth or for anthropologists to become interested in history.[1]

However this is not the whole truth:

> In English history, the troubles of the seventeenth century offer notable examples of nourishing myths of ancient freedoms. Pocock, for example, showed how potent were those which told of immemorial laws and ancient customs; and Hill has traced a different example in his account of the Norman Yoke. Historians of social perception and popular culture have also, more recently, been grappling with the role of myth.[2]

Now, surely, it is time that historians of sport also grappled with it.[3]
History contributes to the myth-making process. Perhaps this is one of its chief functions.[4] It is, of course, invariably history with a specific collective purpose and a particular interpretative intent. It is concerned not so much 'with positive reality', but with the power 'to move men to action' by decoding that reality for them in an appropriate way. Bronislaw Malinowski was emphatic on this point some eighty years ago when social anthropologists added their insights on mankind, presciently, to those of historians:

> myth is ... an indispensable ingredient of all cultures. It is ... constantly regenerated; every historical change creates its mythology, which is, however, but indirectly related to historical fact. Myth is a constant by-product of living faith, which is in need of miracles; of

sociological precedent; of moral rule, which requires sanction.[5]

As David Lowenthal has rightly observed, 'myth, the characteristic form of belief of primitive and antique man, is sometimes a significant category for modern man'.[6] Many modern myths are now heavily associated with sport and are social in function and secular in content – and since sport is now a substantial part of cultural existence, its myths, mythical heroes and mythical messages are increasingly central to modern cultures. They are certainly agents of mass cohesion (and fragmentation). 'The social function of myth,' states Ben Halpern confidently, 'is to bind together groups as wholes.'[7] While Georges Sorel asserts that the function of myth is to bring about radical change.[8] Arguably, therefore, it is time for the sustained creation and projection of *European* mythical heroes of sport in the interest of European union – especially since the multi-million pound public relations attempts by Brussels to create a European-wide sense of common identity in the shape of schemes for ecu lotteries, special European birth certificates, stamps depicting the founding fathers of the European movement, and calendars with festive Euro weeks appear to have been 'an expensive flop'. In September 1995, at the British Association for the Advancement of Science Annual Meeting at Newcastle upon Tyne, it was reported that 'the European commission has spent large sums hiring professional advertising agencies to bolster its public image and devise ways of selling the Community to the public – with little success: 'the strongest sense of European identity, perhaps even an embryonic culture, exists [only] among EU officials and personnel', and furthermore, the report concluded, it is likely for some time to come that a Euro-identity will prove illusive in the face of strong historical memories across member states.[9]

Despite some genuinely pro-European feelings in the Benelux Countries and Germany, this point has been clearly demonstrated very recently. In the anticlimatic moments – for Englishmen – of the semi-final of the 1995 Rugby World Cup and the defeat of England by New Zealand (or perhaps more accurately by Jonah Lomu) a London broadsheet editorial ruminated wistfully on the sad and sudden demise of the mythical Rob Andrew, England's rugby hero of the earlier 'Boys' Own Annual' victory over Australia. The editorial further pondered on the curious manifestation of millions of Englishmen who would not have known their clean ball from their re-cycled ball, who had bellowed, when in beer, somewhat uncertainly about sweet chariots, who dispatched defensive morale-boosting faxes to tabloids about Kiwis and sheep, and above all, who had latched onto a clear-eyed, clean-cut, heroic 'boy' of a fly-half – and his lesser team-mates. All this, the leader writer concluded, represented emotional investment in national sporting success which was '*the most significant source of national pride in the modern world*' (emphasis added).[10] Quite a claim. Chauvinism clearly survives in the European Union sustained by those national icons – the mythical heroes of sport. Their representative role waxes rather than wanes – an interesting fact in an age of collectivities, conglomerates and 'Communities'.

Perhaps sports journalists, in a time of apparent globalisation, trust their instincts with justification when they adopt a particularly conservative approach to national identity, recognising that its elements of tribalism are uncomfortably close to the real truth.[11] Perhaps there is an instinctive realisation among the wider public that 'what many [school text] books now lack is a sense of affinity with people in the past' and that 'episodes in ... national history of momentous significance are treated in the same way as lessons on the American West or the religious beliefs of the Aztecs' and 'stirring tales of heroes and heroines' are no longer available.[12] Perhaps, for frustrated nationalists, sports are now popular carriers of tradition warring against traditionless federated or confederated modernity, satisfying the most persistent 'hungers of the human heart' for the security of repetitive ritual,[13] for 'familial' pomp and pageantry *and* for kith and kin heroes who triumph in life and over life. There can be little doubt, however, that now these heroes are frequently to be found in the spiritual sanctuary of the modern worshipper – the stadium.[14] Sports are more than mere games, diversions and pastimes, and are, in fact, 'religions of place'.[15] Sporting arenas are now secular cathedrals in which communality is celebrated, liturgies of union are chanted, common visions are shared in transcendent moments – those times of heroes.[16]

Who, then, will be the historical heroes and heroines to bind a fractured Europe into a holistic Europe in the twenty-first century? Are the Ryder Cup millionaires the archetypes of the secular saints of 'Fortress Europe' in the Millennium of Economic Power-Blocks just around the corner? 'Sir,' wrote a delighted Pro-European Englishman to a rival broadsheet that a little earlier had reflected on sport as the most significant source of national pride in the modern world, 'The European Ryder Cup team have done more in a few days to get the idea of a United European across to the public than all the talk by politicians and businessmen in the last 20 years. For the first time I have been rooting for a European team that has shown it can take on the United States and win. This surely is what is should be all about.' It was about time, he added, that the politicians lifted their eyes from the constitutional wrangles about Europe and reported with enthusiasm about the real and tangible gains that are there for the taking![17]

European unity, of course, cannot be created simply through sport. The costly efforts to place the European logo in prominent positions at the 1992 Olympic Games were not a success. Nor were earlier efforts to count up how many medals member states had won in Olympic competition and speculate on how a European team might have fared. Members of the European Parliament still occasionally put down questions about the possibility of setting up representative teams but there is little response from those in ultimate control: the member states. It could be argued that their timid efforts amount to far too little action in far too unsystematic a manner. Nevertheless, sport is too deeply rooted in national structures to be easily re-planted to further supranational ends. However, there are distinct signs of greater contact between European states through sport. Golf and tennis are less firmly embedded in the nation-state than team games and have in recent years produced figures who could claim to be more European than national, although 'Western' might be a better term for them as part of their lives are spent in North America and the products they endorse are part of the global marketing strategy of multinationals. On the other hand men like Langer and Becker are both German but are also part of a European sporting presence that challenges North American dominance in these sports. The Swedes have recently enjoyed similar success in these events and are now also part of the formal political structure of the European Union. Miguel Indurain, who seems certain to win a sixth Tour de France and establish himself as the most successful cyclist of all time, is firstly a Spaniard but also a symbol of a rejuvenated Europe incorporating the Iberian Peninsula which can resist challenges from North and South America as well as Eastern Europe and Asia.

However, football is the European sport *par excellence* and it is to football that we must look for signs that sport is finally starting to escape from its self-imposed national framework. The growth of satellite television has brought regular talk of a European Super League, financed by a Berlusconi figure, which would run games in tandem with the national competitions. This would undoubtedly place Europe at the centre of the football world of the member states but might do little to foster a benign pan-European consciousness at least in the short or medium term. The ferocious 'local' rivalries within member states would be transposed to the European scene; Ajax and Feynoord, Barcelona and Real Madrid, Celtic and Rangers and so on. Worse still, some very large clubs would inevitably fail to make what would be seen as the top league and would harbour bitter resentments. But then, of course, all this exists at national level and soccer as a spectacle at this level unites as much as it disunites populations. Interestingly the new European Rugby Cup is characterised by the sensible view on the part of all the countries concerned that 'it is better to get on with a European competition, however imperfect' than be without one![18]

Of course, it can be argued that in the new soccer European Champions League we already have a small-scale version of this 'liberating' process sponsored amongst others by Macdonalds as part of a global strategy to give their product a positive, youthful, healthy image. Could the European idea be promoted in the way Coca Cola, for example, have sought to identify themselves with the Olympics? It is conceivable that multinationals will seek to use the European and South American appetite for football to promote more regular and systematic matches between the winners of the European and South American cups. Such a state of affairs would give Europe a common identity *vis-à-vis* another continent also united for the occasion through sport.

The forthcoming Rugby League's European Super League, of course, will be topped off each season with the best two teams in Europe 'playing off' against the best two teams in Australasia – regularised and eventually institutionalised inter-continental sport involving Europe and other continents is virtually up and running! And the catalyst is satellite television.[19]

The European Nations Cup, which extends well beyond the present European Union, is at present more of a source of national hostility than solidarity. Nevertheless European competition has given soccer fans from different nationalities a few great names to remember; the Real Madrid team, for example, of the late 1950s with Di Stefano, Gento and Puskas – an Argentinian, a Spaniard and a Hungarian. These were heroes whose skills reverberated around Europe and a representative European club or multinational side featuring the best players in the Union could act as a focus for a new kind of popular identity. Building a new kind of pan-European structure for representative sport, breaking out of the national stranglehold on the collective identities that gather around sport is an obvious way forward for those concerned at promoting a federal Europe. In the meantime, the recent Bosman judgement of the European Court seems bound to break down quotas of non-national players within clubs and encourage the movement of European and non-European star players. This in turn holds out the possibility of new kinds of European heroes as foreign players are freely adopted as their own by local fans. This, after all, has already happened in ice hockey and basketball, although in these cases the imported players are overwhelmingly North American. And it is happening now in soccer.

However, the extent to which such exchanges have or will break down national stereotypes and prejudice is uncertain as the example of Eric Cantona demonstrates; loved and loathed in equal part, he has certainly raised the profile of French football in Britain. The traditional Anglo-Saxon reckoning of the French as lounge lizards is hardly sustainable but that element of the equation that holds that the French are indisciplined and impetuous – the Latin stereotype – appears to be reinforced. It is not clear that a man so successfully idealised and demonized by different groups has done much to foster mutual understanding.

Nevertheless, we Europeans, as we come closer together at various levels, need to know more about each other – and each other's heroes and heroines. This is the deceptively simple object of these essays. Coppi, to be sure, was well known in France and Borotra charmed Wimbledon but what was Bartali to the British or Jack Hobbs to the rest of Europe? Who, apart from French football fans, know much of Mekloufi's marvellous skills and his strange passage to and from Algeria? And what of the sports heroes of the Irish, the Welsh, the Scots, the Dutch, the Danes and so on?

E. E. Evans-Pritchard, in his thoughtful essay on the relationship between history and social anthropology, maintained that the distinctive characteristics of myth were that it was concerned with the moral significance of situations rather than a succession of events, and was, therefore, often symbolical in form. In this role it was a re-enactment fusing past with present[20] and perhaps, it should be added, future. The archetypal myth was not bound to time or space. It was a bridge across them. Of course, mythological heroes hold in a delicate equilibrium what is universal and what is contingent: .the passing styles and passions of the moment displayed amidst the timeless appeal of exceptional aptitude. Like the players in *Hamlet*, sporting heroes are there 'to hold the mirror up to nature, to show virtue her own feature ... and the very age and body of the time his form and pressure', but more than this, perhaps much more than this, the rituals and ritualists of today's sports have replaced those of yesterday's religions. They are the cement of communities: each Sunday in France and Germany and elsewhere, and increasingly in Britain, 'the sports fan seats himself before his electronic altar as the devout once sat in church ... watching while especially trained performers play out the ceremonies ... rising occasionally from his chair ... to cheer as churchmen once rose from their pews to ... sing hymns', and finally, 'when the ritual is completed, the fan is renewed; it's all right with the world ...'.[21]

The spectacles of the sports arenas are central to contemporary European culture. And 'Life which is devoid of collective myths,' Karl Mannheim once asserted, 'is scarcely bearable.'[22] In a Europe in which on Sundays few now pray to spiritual gods in Heaven, many worship temporal gods on earth as they perform in the new and numerous secular cathedrals. Here are found the rituals that now frequently bond banker and baker – if no longer the candlestick maker. The great unifying quality of sport is that it offers 'a community of involvement which provides a place for everyone, whatever his [or her] age or station, whether ... fan or player'.[23]

To end on a possibly too sanguine, but undoubtedly constructive, note – perhaps Brussels itself should take *more* note of this fact.

NOTES

1. D.C. Coleman, *Myths, History and the Industrial Revolution* (London: The Hambledon Press, 1992), pp.1–2.
2. Ibid., p.2.
3. An early attempt is Donald D. Kyle and Gary D. Stark, *Essays on Sport History and Sport Mythology* (Arlington: Texas A & M University Press, 1990).
4. Quoted in Coleman, *Myth, History and the Industrial Revolution*, p.2.
5. Ibid., p.2.
6. Ibid., p.2.
7. Ben Halpern, '"Myth" and "Ideology" in Modern Usage', *History and Theory*, Vol.1 (1961), p.137.
8. George Sorel (trans. by T.E.Hulme and J.Roth), *Reflections on Violence* (Illinois: Glencoe Press, 1950), p.37.
9. Paper delivered by Dr C. Shore to the BAAS reported in *The Times*, 14 September 1995, p.10.
10. Editorial, *Independent*, 18 June, 1995, p.11.
11. See Neil Blain, Raymond Boyle and Hugh O'Donnell, *Sport and National Identity in the European Media* (Leicester: Leicester University Press, 1993), pp.193–4.
12. Nick Tate, 'Another View: Heroes have their place', *Independent*, 19 September, 1995, p.11.
13. Michael Novak, 'Sacred Space, Sacred Time', in David L. Vanderwerken and Spencer K. Wertz, *Sport: Inside Out* (Fort Worth, Texas: Christian University Press, 1985), p.728.
14. Ibid.
15. Ibid.
16. Ibid.
17. Letter from D. Foster in the *Independent*, 28 September 1995, p.11.
18. Stephen Bale in the *Independent*, 31 October 1995, p.23.
19. Report in the *Independent*, 7 November 1995, p.28.
20. E. E. Evans-Pritchard, *Anthropology and History* (Manchester: Manchester University Press, 1961), p.8.
21. Arnold R. Beisser, *The Madness in Sports* (Bowrie: Charles Press, 1977), p.143.
22. Karl Mannheim, *Ideology and Utopia* (London: Routledge and Kegan Paul, 1949), p.119.
23. Beisser, *The Madness in Sports*, p.145.

Notes on Contributors

Christiane Eisenberg is Professor of History at the University of Hamburg and is completing a comparative historical study of British and German sport in the later nineteenth century, for which she has been awarded a Research Fellowship from the German government.

Jean-Michel Faure is Professor of Sociology at the University of Nantes. He is directing a project on top athletes in Europe and has recently written an article on professional soccer in France in *Actes de la recherche en sciences sociales*.

Siegfried Gehrmann is Professor of History at the University of Essen. He has published extensively on the Ruhr regime, especially on football, and is the author of *Fuseball, Vereine Politik 1900–1940* (1988).

Richard Holt is Research Fellow at the University of Leuven, Belgium, and Visiting Professor at DeMontfort University and the University of Brighton. Among his books are *Sport and Society in Modern France* (1981) and *Sport and the British: A Modern History* (1989).

Roman Horak is Research Fellow at the Institute of Cultural History in Vienna and has published extensively on interwar Viennese history.

Pierre Lanfranchi is Research Professor of History at De Montfort University and has recently written, with A. Wahl, *Les footballeurs professionels* (1995).

J. A. Mangan is Professor of Education, Director of the International Centre for Socialization, Sport and Society, University of Strathclyde, Glasgow, and Annual Visiting Professor, University of California. His recent publications include the edited works *The Cultural Bond: Sport, Empire, Society* (1992), *The Imperial Curriculum: Racial Images and Education in the British Colonial Experience* and *Tribal Identities: Nationalism, Europe, Sport* (1995).

Tony Mason is Reader in Social History at the University of Warwick. He is the author of *Association Football and English Society* (1979) and edited *Sport in Britain* (1989). His most recent book is *Passion of the People? Football in South America* (1995).

Stefano Pivato is Professor of Contemporary History at Urbino University, Italy. He has published widely on secularism, politics and sport, and Italian history, including *Clericalismo et laicisme nella cultura popolare italiana* (1990), *La Bicicletta et il sol dell' avvenire* (1992) and *Les enjeux du sport* (1994).

André Rauch is Professor of Physical Education at the University of Strasbourg. His recent publications include *Boxe, violence du XXe siècle* (1992) and *Les Français en vacances* (1996).

Alfred Wahl is Professor of History at the University of Metz. He is an authority on German history and the history of French football. Among his recent books are *Les Archives du football* (1989) and, with P. Lanfranchi, *Les footballeurs professionels* (1995).

Index